JAILHOUSE
JOURNALS

MIKE MAHY

Printed in the United States of America

ISBN 979-8-89114-139-1 (sc)
ISBN 979-8-89114-140-7 (e)

Library of Congress Control Number: 2024923557

2025.04.24

MainSpring Books
5901 W. Century Blvd
Suite 750
Los Angeles, CA, US, 90045

www.mainspringbooks.com

FOREWORD

Welcome to this book: Jailhouse Journals. This book contains controversial content from a Christian point of view because it contains intimate details of my index offences and also speaks about my sexual identity. Not everyone will agree with the content contained herein and may cause a negative impact emotionally. Reader discretion is advised.

So why did I write these journals if there is going to be controversy stirred? The answer is simple: obedience. God has not only asked me to write these journals for my own therapeutic and spiritual wellness, but also he's asked me to share my story to the public. God is greater than I am, and I surrender to his call for me. If that is the case, then I believe these journal books stand as hope for others who may struggle the way I did because God can work miracles in those lives just as he did in mine.

The Lord used my friend George, a fellow inmate, to encourage me to start writing while I was carrying out my jail sentence in Ford Mountain Correctional Center in Chilliwack, British Columbia, Canada. Writing in these journals was a little slow going at first, but then as I started writing, I noticed that miracles were starting to happen all around the camp as well. I couldn't help but write them down!

After a few months of being at the camp and writing in the journal books, I also started to receive "downloads" from the Holy Spirit. It was really cool to experience this. It seemed like a never-ending supply of inspiration! Journal entries, speeches, and poems — they were things I never wrote in great quantities prior to my time in jail. The inspiration from the Holy Spirit was awe-inspiring; it felt like I was a computer being plugged in, and then all this information would just then flood into my head, which I would write it all down. Sometimes I had a hard time keeping up! All this was helping me experience true love, freedom, joy, and peace for the first time in decades, because prior to this experience all I could feel in my heart was pain, death, and destructive feelings. I was dying on the inside and no one, even my spouse, knew about it.

My time in Ford Mountain Correctional Center had brought a major portion of transformation in my life. The beauty of the camp surroundings, the ability to work five days a week while incarcerated (it is a work camp), the effective programs offered by the staff, the special relationship I formed with the chaplain at the camp, and the amazing relationships I formed with many of the other inmates, all contributed to a significant portion of inner healing and growth personally and spiritually. Because of these journals, and the positive experiences stemming from my time there, will never be forgotten.

I was able to put onto paper my feelings about God and personal experiences with him, feelings about my index offences, and had a chance to have deep reflection of how I have affected others negatively and a chance to express my remorse and admission of my wrongs done to them. I was able to come to terms with my sexual identity while at the same time honoring my life with God out of pure love for him with what the Scriptures declare in truth. I was able to start dealing with my feelings toward the relationships I had with my family, friends, and even clients - feelings ranging from love, regret, remorse, fear of loss, and disappointment, and then to bitterness and anger on the other side of the spectrum. It was amazing how God can take a person deeply engrossed in a cesspool of sin and bring out the best he's got in them.

To those who read these journals, it is my hope you can gain information of what it is like to be in a medium-security correctional center, what this progressive corrections program offers to those who are incarcerated, and can bring an understanding that inmates are human beings too. Yes, we've been convicted of crimes, and we need to repay our debt to society. That is why we are sent there. But there is a better way to rehabilitate someone in the jail system by using spiritual, educational, and relationship-building tools. They help give each inmate a chance at being a better citizen in society once they are released. These programs reduce the incidence of those being released to repeat the crimes that sent them to jail in the first place. Rehabilitation is key to the success of anyone serving a sentence in jail.

The other intent of this book is to share the love of God and the power he has to help change our lives, so we can be the ones receiving the fullness of his call, purpose, and destiny in our lives. God is more than capable to arrange, facilitate, and change people's lives, if we choose to engage with him in spirit and in truth.

Finally, I encourage you, the reader, to be open-minded about what is spoken in here. There are many people, possibly in your circle, who have secrets about addictions and sexual sins, hidden like I had, and are petrified to have them exposed for fear of feeling and being rejected by their families, friends, and peers. We need to set aside our prejudices for the sake of those who desperately need to share their truth of their struggles in their lives and come into a place of healing and restoration. With that, I hope you find this book fascinating, powerful and transformational.

JOURNAL
BOOK 1

Inspirational Writings

Journal Date: November 27, 2017

Entry:

Today I am grateful for the little things:

A day off (after working 11 straight days)
A pair of glasses (after not having them for 3 weeks)
A comb (after not having one for at least a week)
A room to myself (after sharing a cell from October 25 to November 20)
Freedom to pray
Freedom to worship
Lots more exercise
Solid friendships being built with other inmates
My friends who have stuck with me on the outside
A God who loves me unconditionally
A camp where it *doesn't* feel like a prison
Opportunities to learn who I am
Opportunities to learn where I am going wrong and get it fixed
Opportunities to grow and mature as an adult and human being
Support from my support groups
Working in the kitchen doing something I love to do
Being sheltered from the cold
Being given the responsibility to lead Bible study

Thank you, Lord, for all these little things. Help me remember your provision in all of them.

My Story

November 19, 2017

Note: (names in bold are changed to protect the identities of the individuals)

It was another interesting day today. I saw God's hand! I felt led to call **the only lady in my Bible study** and **Devon Smith** today. When I called **the only lady in my Bible study** I confided in her that the door to bookkeeping and taxes were now closed, but I believe I am to return to Victoria to live and work.

She said, "God has told me to align myself with you, and I want to offer a business partnership with you."

The only lady in my Bible study had a cleaning business. Couple this with **my buddy the gardener's** agreement for me to have a 10 percent partnership with his business. So this means I will have three income streams upon my release, and I had this all lined up prior to my sentencing! Praise God!

When I called **Devon Smith** I was amazed by the support I had from him. He is willing to write a letter of support for me, so I can include it in my parole application. Wow!

One more thing about **the only lady in my Bible study** was, she has offered that my storage be moved to her place; she also offered for me to live with her and help me find a place if her house doesn't qualify! She helped me handle **Fred (my former landlord at the time of my sentencing)**, and the breaking of the lease too! She is an amazing person and a gift from God!

What happened since - The only lady in my Bible study kept her word on everything! She sent me a letter of support in January 2018 stating that for my parole, she was going to be my business partner and my community support when I get out. This letter was the only one I would need for my parole application and the only letter given to me in support.

She is now my business partner in the cleaning business; she moved my belongings to her place in February, 2018 and her house is still on the list for me to successfully live when I go from day parole to probation. As for **Devon Smith**, I never got a letter from him, nor did I talk much anymore to him as he had a change of heart.

December 1, 2017

Note: (names in bold are changed to protect the identities of the individuals) (names in black are the real names and used by permission)

Today I called **Corrina** to see how business was going. She said my sister Lisa had e-mailed her to say she was ready to talk to me. As soon as **Corrina** said that, all kinds of different feelings went through me. At first, I felt agitated and afraid, not knowing what to say to her if I did call her. So I told **Corrina** what was going through my mind – resentment, anger, bitterness, fear, sadness. I told **Corrina** that I didn't realize how dysfunctional my family was until now and that I wouldn't know how to talk to her, how to respond, what she would say, among others. **Corrina** suggested I take it slowly and maybe speak to my counselor about it before I call. I thought that was a good idea. If I call, I am scared that I will feel more isolated from my family, and I don't know how I will deal with that.

God grant me the serenity to accept the things I cannot change, the courage for the things I can, and the wisdom to know the difference.

December 2, 2017

Note: (names in bold are changed to protect the identities of the individuals)

The last few days, I realized that my stomach is starting to bulge out. Gotta cut back on eating. Exercise wasn't keeping up!

I had a vivid dream last night. I dreamt about **Charlie**, whom I've known since he was four but was now in his twenties, was talking to me, and he wanted to reestablish a relationship with me, but he didn't tell the rest of his family yet. But **Terry** and **Clara** came to his house and discovered that I was there. **Charlie** didn't know what to do, and I didn't know what to do. I was nervous but, I approached **Terry** and **Clara**, and they expressed conciliatory feelings toward to me. **Terry** held out a fist to give me a fist bump, so I started talking to them. They asked about jail, so I told them what it was like and what I learned there. Then we talked about the length of the jail term and the two years I received. I said the Crown Counsel (Canadian equivalent of a District Attorney) wanted a jail sentence of three to five years (in reality, it was three years, but this was a dream), but my lawyer managed to get me two years instead. I couldn't remember much more except for seeing red serving trays from the kitchen here at Ford Mountain and the place I was at was **Charlie's** house.

Then I woke up.

Lord, I don't know if this is just a dream or this is a picture of the future, but I lay it in your hands. I ask for their forgiveness while I am fighting tears while writing this down. Love you Jesus. Love you **Terry**, **Clara** and **Charlie**. Sorry for what I've done.

December 7, 2017

Note: (names in bold are changed to protect the identities of the individuals) (names in black are the real names and used by permission)

Two days ago, I went and saw **Sheila**, my counselor, for a session. I was in tears most of the time. I was talking to her about my sister and the rest of my family. I told her I was scared of being rejected by them, especially my sister because she has known since Easter of 2017 of what was happening in my life. **Sheila** asked what I felt, and I told her I felt empty inside because of how I felt, how badly I had failed my family, how I put them in such a bad position and how badly I have fractured our relationship. When the session was over I told **Sheila** I was going to call Lisa immediately.

I was able to get through the first time, and Lisa accepted the call. Amazingly she was alone, on the ferry, so she had no distractions or interruptions while talking to me. The first thing she said was she didn't reject me, but she needed time to sort through things in the aftermath of everything being on the news and then left "holding the bag" in dealing with everyone. She told me how much she loved me and how much I will need her in the family restoration. I told her how sorry I was for everything I caused and done. I was bawling when I told her. She accepted my apology and said we will get through this. We will talk again next week. I was relieved now that the unknown has become known. The rest of my immediate family was very angry at me, and I didn't blame them.

Lord, only you can bring restoration. I trust you in this process. Trust, believe, obey, and don't be afraid.

December 10, 2017

Yesterday was a breakthrough day, but let me go back to last February where God put forth this in motion. Back then I was pacing back and forth in my house, like I typically did when talking to God, and I heard him say to me, "You will tell your story." I knew exactly what he meant by that, and at the time, my internal response was great fear. I was petrified! I wanted to hide my past from everyone, but God had different plans when it came to my story. Of course, since then, everything about my charges were now in the open - TV, newspaper, and social media since October 2017. God ensured his plan, not mine, was going forward.

Back to yesterday, I went to my support-group-for-sex-addiction meeting and actually shared publicly, for the first time, the fact that I was gay and the exact nature of my crimes (no names mentioned though), and that I affected dozens of people because of it. I listed them off in groups: the victims and their families, my own family, my partner and her family, friends, acquaintances, and clients. I told them I lost everything - most of everyone listed here including family, many of my belongings, my business, big debt, etc. - as a result, and now here I was in jail. I couldn't believe everyone's response! There were ten of us there, and they all shared no judgment on me, which I feared the most. Some applauded my courage for sharing and two even hugged me (first real hugs in more than a month)! Also, when I went walking after, God spoke to me and said to me in my heart, "I am so proud of you! You are going to be great!" I cried when I heard that!

Lord, keep me humble, direct my path, guide my ways. I surrender to you and you're my only treasure. Give me strength to share what you want me to so I may bring glory to your great name.

December 15, 2017

Today I learnt something about myself while in class taking the Big Book program this morning. Let me backtrack a bit first. When I first recognized I was a sex addict, it was when I said in my first meeting, "Hi, I'm Mike, and I'm a sex addict." It was then I realized my thinking wasn't right; the visions of those I thought about in my sexual fantasies would want me sexually too was deviant. I was believing a lie, and I was delusional in my thinking patterns. How could I believe this garbage and accept it as real? My instructor today differentiated *deviant* from *addiction*. *Addiction* would be something like "constantly looking at pornography but no other action would be taken." *Deviant* behavior "would take it further – it would be taking action like touching young boys inappropriately, and would be considered predatory in nature."

"Deviant behavior," our instructor said, "would need more than just a twelve-step program and twelve-step support. It would require more – counseling, and specific education to help the offender."

I would be classified under the deviant behavior so I am going to sign up for the criminal addictive thinking course in January. I am already receiving counseling here, and I will also take the sex offender program when it comes available.

Thank you, Lord, for showing the error of my ways and lead me to right thinking, right attitudes, and in your direction. I can't do this by myself. I need your help and the help of those who understand this.

December 17, 2017

Note: (names in bold are changed to protect the identities of the individuals) (names in black are the real names and used by permission)

I went for a walk with Chad last night around the compound. While we were walking, I decided to share how God, in leading me to jail, was a controlled implosion. (This part isn't in order of how I shared with him but these were included in our conversation – I will write as I remember them.) This conversation started with me telling Chad about God allowing me to see family members (aunts and cousins) in visits with my immediate family in February, and then again, in May. I was telling him, now looking back, how my story of my sentencing ended up all over the news, and that it was possible that I was allowed to see these family members, who I rarely see, just one more time, in pleasant settings, with pleasant memories, because just possibly I would never see them again. These family members were my two aunts and three of my cousins, some of whom I hadn't seen in years!

The following is a supplemental comment to this story:

> So what makes this so interesting is two things. First, my commitment to Jesus is higher than anything else in my life. I have him on the throne of my life and he is my only treasure. Second, I will forsake family in favor of the kingdom of God. I am the only Christian in my family and I love them all dearly. I pray for their salvation, and from the news of my sister, the only family member speaking to me right now, everyone is in shock about what I have done and no one wants to or can talk to me right now. I don't blame them. I lied, and I hid, trying to keep it quiet as to try and minimize the damage. Only my sister in my family knew beforehand about the charges, my real reasons for the separation with my partner, and the sentencing. I am a poor Christian testimony to them. I was a hypocrite, a liar, and a deviant in terms of my behavior to them.

Sorry, Lord, for what I have done. Please repair their hearts. Show them the way of love, forgiveness, and of who you are, not for my sake but for their eternal sake.

Now back to my walk and talk with Chad. So as I told him about these peculiar visits with my family, I told him more of how God has led me to this very moment. (To save space in my journal I will only bring out the highlights of what I shared):

1) God systematically shut down activities, relationships with people, and positions of authority prior to my first arrest (The Holy Spirit spoke to me directly about taking these actions). He had me retire from all my sporting activities – indoor soccer, floor hockey (both of these in 2014), and slow-pitch in 2015, which not only had me stop playing but pulled me away from all those people too. God told me to step down as elder in my church at the end of May 2015 as well.

2) He fostered two specific relationships in 2015: **the only lady in my Bible study** and **my buddy the gardener.** This relationship development was given to me prophetically by **the prophetess of our church.** God said, through the prophetess of our church, that he wanted to use them as an example; and of how he wanted to powerfully use them as businesspeople and I was to teach them. These two were now my strategic business partners for when I get out as God has shut the door for me being a bookkeeper and tax preparer. These two people are very special to me. They were more than just business partners; more importantly, they are my brother and sister in Christ and my very close friends.

   Lord, bless their businesses and foster our relationships.
   Build us in your image, in your likeness.

3) I shared God's favor during the time I made my plea to the judge. I gave Chad details of how I got switched from a busy courtroom to a quiet one, then got bumped up from second on the court docket

list to first, not needing to even say a word to the judge. My lawyer did all the talking on my behalf, not one charge was read aloud but spoken as charges 1, 2, 3, and 5 and that I was pleading guilty to all of them. This took a total (at least, it only seemed like) of eighty seconds from the time I stood up to the time I left being before the judge.

This is all I told Chad in our walk but there are many more evidences of God's hand in this – the prophecy revealed during a Bible study with friends; **Corrina** taking over the bookkeeping business immediately after my sentencing and how that unfolded; **the lady of the North Island's** prophecy of putting all my possessions in storage beforehand and her vision of seeing me in jail; my business going from five offices to one in 2014, just to name some more. All these stories only showed that not only was God real, but he truly loved us.

He disciplines those whom he loves, and if you choose to listen, follow, and obey, he will guide you with great favor if he chooses to do so. He is an amazing God and I will serve him all my days. Lord, repair my heart, fix my mind, transform my life, restore your son to how you originally intended. Amen.

December 18, 2017

I felt led to continue telling about God's miracles and provision during this season of events leading up to my arrest and sentencing. I wanted to focus this entry on God's financial provision for my partner before my first arrest.

In July 2015, there was an excess amount of money in my business account and the Lord told me to transfer $6,000 of it into the business savings account. I didn't know why at the time but I transferred it in obedience. He had me just leave it there, so it sat.

In the 2016 tax season, it was particularly good, but there also were some outstanding debts to pay. As of March 15, 2016, we had the following debts (other than our car loan): $2,900 for my personal taxes, $5,900 for corporate taxes, $19,000 on my Mastercard, $2,000 on our LOC; and $12,000 on my partner's Visa, totaling almost $42,000 in debt. With my partner's large tax refund and my having a good run in March during tax season, we were able to pay off my personal and business taxes by March 31. April was even better, setting a "best April" financially so on May 2, I was able to put $19,000 on the Mastercard and pay it off. May was also a solid month, and June was solid too. By June 15, I knew that I was in trouble with the law and started asking God for his mercy and spare me from my sins. Instead, he told me to transfer the $6,000 into the business checking account and have my partner sit with me so she could watch the rest of our debt be paid off: $12,000 on the Visa and $2,000 on the LOC. She was made debt-free by God's hand of financial provision on June 25. On July 21, I was arrested.

Thank you Lord for your financial mercies to my partner and lifting a financial burden off of her. She has been through enough.

December 19, 2017

Note: (names in bold are changed to protect the identities of the individuals)

The Lord allowed me to learn how to expand and manage multiple offices for my company from 2010 to 2014. It was amazing how the team (the four other office members) came available within 18 months. What was more interesting was God's exit plan to shrink it all back to one by November 30, 2014.

In September 2014, my partner and I prayed about a business partner and me to acquire and sell properties in California, to sell the client list from the asset I had available – my business – to a prospect, therefore being financially liquid enough to go into this new land acquisition business. Four days after that prayer, I received an offer in the mail from a large company expressing interest in purchasing the company I owned. I took this as confirmation of God's will and slowly proceeded forward. I shared the idea with a couple of friends and colleagues, and within three weeks, there were four parties interested in buying the business. I finally let the rest of the offices know what was going on, and some of the responses were incredible.

The second Saanich location sent me an e-mail back, saying this was divinely orchestrated by the Holy Spirit because he was intending to shut down his office (which I already knew about) next July of 2015, but because his back was hurting so much that he was relieved to shut down his office earlier. My Nanaimo location also was quite happy about this because he wanted to go and study to become a nurse. For the first Saanich and the Brentwood Bay locations it wasn't so easy. We were able to come to terms about the departure from my company and a seamless exit plan came forth where all parties were satisfied. I was grateful that I did hear God about the shutdown and exit plan he created, but in the end, it was never meant to be for my business partner and I to go to California and acquire/sell properties for a profit. The major company that was originally interested never e-mailed me more than once in reply. The accountant interested said my pricing was too low for him for it to be worth his while. My colleague said it wasn't the right time, and finally, the last party interested gave me an offer. I went to prayer on it and got a check in my spirit; received counsel from the Holy Spirit from my dear friend **the prophetess of our church** saying, "The Holy Spirit has laid a certain price in your heart, so be firm in it." That gave me confidence to say no to the offer.

What happened afterward? The Lord protected the other members of the offices from embarrassment of being affiliated with me as part of God's "controlled implosion" regarding my arrest and sentencing. The Lord used the expansion and exit strategy as teaching tools for **the only lady in my Bible study** and **my buddy the gardener** during the "Business With Purpose" business class, and the Lord helped make my company be more seamlessly transferred to **Corrina** as part of his complete exit strategy upon my sentencing.

Thank you, Lord, for your tender mercy on the other offices, your provision for **Corrina**, and your taking care of me, all at the same time. It shows that you know all things, and you truly take care of all those you love. You even provided for my partner, too, as you spared her from "holding the bag" (as far as the business goes) at the end. Amen.

December 24, 2017

I keep hearing the Lord say to me, "I am so proud of you!" in my head, and every time I heard him say that to me I start crying, and then I start fighting against his love and favor for me.

I am tearing up as I am writing this because I still struggle with God's unconditional love for me. I must write this down, so I can get my feelings about God's love for me out. You see, ever since I became a Christian in March 1990, I have always expressed my love to God, but I never let him love me fully back in my heart. I realize this is very selfish. But I have also been afraid to let him love me back because of how I have seen myself all these years. I have never thought of myself as someone who deserved God's love and therefore never opened my heart to it. While I am here in jail, I am starting to learn something important – I am *allowed* to love myself, and therefore, I can let God love me too!

This is part of the healing process in my soul, a part of the transformation of my thinking in my mind! The greatest gift God ever gave us was his son Jesus, born of the Virgin Mary, who died on the cross for our sins so we can be reconciled back to him. What a gift! And I believe and receive that gift. Every day, I will get stronger, love myself more, and therefore let God love me more too. This will then spill over into my other relationships; it will allow me to give my whole heart in love to Jesus (John 14:15-16).

Thank you Jesus for your unconditional love. Amen.

December 26, 2017

Today, the Lord asked me in my heart to have confidence in talking about my sexuality and sexual preference.

I was married to my partner for twenty-three years. She is the only woman I have ever loved, and to this day, she is still the only woman. I missed her, and I was sorry I wrecked our marriage. She did not deserve to face or experience the consequences of my sin. I hoped and prayed she will forgive me one day, and at least a friendship will be restored. I hid; I lied and kept from her the benefits of the marriage bed because I was a coward in facing my sexuality. She didn't deserve this. Secretly, even though I hated it, actually I despised the fact that I was, and still am, attracted to men. It is here in jail that I have finally reconciled myself to the fact that I prefer men.

However, I am also sold out for Jesus, and he is my only treasure. So how do I reconcile that? The Holy Spirit has given me confidence to accept this fact that I "swing the other way" and he is graceful in giving me this confidence. It doesn't change his viewpoint on the sin of homosexuality, meaning, saying no to lustful thoughts and actions. By the power of the blood of Christ, through the power of the Holy Spirit, I supernaturally receive help to "stay inside God's schoolyard fence," meaning, the parameters of the Word of God, which is the clearly laid-out boundaries of his Word. God is giving me supernatural strength in his love, telling me he loves me so much. His favor upon me is ridiculously insane! I shall live a life of abstinence in response to his love and his favor; staying "inside his schoolyard fence." In it is his favor, protection, love, joy, peace, and strength.

Thank you Lord. Amen.

December 30, 2017

This was the first time in a long time where I need to start being careful, keeping my pride in check because since my second arrest and up to now, I have been on a hard road of confession, repentance, learning to trust God through trials and tribulations, a change of identity from the old Mike to this new Mike, and a transformation through the renewing of my mind by the power of the Holy Spirit. For the last couple of weeks, I bore witness of God's power, seeing what he is doing in the lives of my fellow inmates while watching God move in me, prompting me to obey when he asked me to move, and then when I did obey, it turned out *exactly* as he said it would!

One can get puffed up pretty quickly if pride isn't put in check constantly! It was this pride, this arrogance, haughtiness, and conceit that caused me to sin before, and I started to notice yesterday that some of my old thinking patterns were beginning to creep back in, ones that I now don't like because I have been experiencing victory over them in recent months. I knew God would test our faithfulness to him, but he would never tempt us. This test was in receiving blessings from God.

So this was what I wanted to say, "I want the old Mike dead, kill him Jesus."

I give you permission by the power of your blood. I humble myself before you. I surrender to you and your will. I want to have my heart, my mind, and my life line up with yours, for I declare that you are my only treasure. When you keep flowing in your love, your power, and your blessings, help me be a responsible steward with them, rejoicing in them but never, ever claim glory for myself like I used to do secretly in my heart, and then display false humility on the outside to others, which is disgusting and hypocritical. Help me not to be jealous of how you are reaching others and how you use others so I can rejoice in you and with them, so they can be built up in their faith in you and you alone. Help me *get out of the way* so that your glory may be shown, and that you receive the credit due for it. As Paul has always preached, "I preach Christ and Christ crucified." This is my heart and my heart's desire.

Lord, line up my heart for me so that my fire burns for you and you alone. Through you, I and others are destined for great things and great works you will do through us in these last days. Your final outpouring is coming soon. Prepare your church for it. I and the others here at Ford Mountain are called too, those who are willing listeners, willing doers for Christ. Teach us to move in the power of your spirit in humility, in obedience; learning to trust you completely and not trusting in ourselves. Help us see you as King and King alone – King of our hearts, our lives, our will. In Jesus name I pray, Amen.

December 31, 2017

Today was a bit of a tough task. I made a detailed list of who I need to make amends to. What was so hard about it was who I could and who I couldn't meet face-to-face to apologize for my actions, ask for their forgiveness, and make no excuses for what I did. But I finished the list, which is part of my healing process. Thankfully, some of the people on the list I have already made amends with, and those amends had been successful. I realized they would not all be this easy, and some amends will take longer than others, while I would need to accept the fact that the opportunity may never come.

Thank you, Lord, for showing me a hard path to recovery. Give me strength and wisdom to move according to your way and with your timing. Help me be transparent, accountable and willing to listen to those whom I've affected. Help them recover, too, so that we all may be healed and restored. I don't expect reconciliation from anyone I've hurt, nor forgiveness either; for that, is theirs to give. So, God, grant me the serenity to accept the things I cannot change; courage to change the things I can, and the wisdom to know the difference. Amen.

Ford Mountain

November 15, 2017

Something interesting happened today, but let me backtrack to the first day. On my first day, when I was getting a tour of Ford Mountain and when we got to the kitchen, one of the kitchen workers came out and immediately asked me if I was new here and what experience I had in the kitchen. I gave him my credentials, and he promised to fill out a special request for me to come into the kitchen and work there. Within the hour he filled out that special request for me to work there and asked me to sign it.

I arrived here on November 8. I knew that until the kitchen position opened up I would be working in the wood pile, starting – supposedly, as this is a work camp and you work typically five days a week – the next day. So November 9 came – no work; November 10 – no work, November 11 – 13 (long weekend), and November 14 – no work! No woodpile yet. *Hmmm....*

Now today there was finally work, and this morning, off to the woodpile I went! The Holy Spirit urged me to work hard today so I was very willing to do so. It was fun! Moved 30' logs that weighed 200 – 400 lbs.; they got chain-sawed into foot-long pieces, then they got wheel-barreled over to where they got split, then wheel-barreled to covered storage areas. After carrying logs, wheel-barrel the cut-then-split logs, I was getting pretty tired. After three hours, we broke for lunch. After lunch we went back to the woodpile (did I mention that it was raining and only 46 F or 8 C?), and not ten minutes later I was pulled off to go see Mr. M, a guard in charge of the kitchen. When I saw him, he told me to go see the chef in the kitchen, and that I was in the kitchen tomorrow. Wow! Praise God! I wasn't expecting to go there until December.

I am seeing God's hand of favor on me. Thank you Lord! You are good.

November 20, 2017

Note: (names in bold are changed to protect the identities of the individuals)

Sayings of the day:

1) Authority is to be carried out diligently and responsibly;
2) Saying "yes" to everything may not always facilitate the best outcomes, but it will put you on an interesting ride.

Today, **Chris**, my cell mate, moved out of the room. This was the first time having a bottom bunk since I have been in jail. I went to Wilkinson jail (Victoria) for twelve days, North Fraser (Port Coquitlam) for overnight, Fraser (Maple Ridge) for overnight, and now Ford Mountain. I was also staying in a room by myself for the first time too, which was an answer to prayer.

Thank you Lord for answering small requests, even in here. Now I have liberty to read the Word and prayer with very little hindrance. I can now increase my one-on-one fellowship with you Lord.

November 22, 2017

Note: (names in bold are changed to protect the identities of the individuals) (names in black are the real names and used by permission)

Interesting evening. I felt the Lord lead me to go to the NA (Narcotics Anonymous) meeting tonight. I wasn't going to go, but I obeyed. Before I talk more about tonight I must tell you that a week earlier they announced over the PA system about a Bible study. But when I showed up with my Bible in hand it was the NA meeting instead. Even though I had no addiction to any type of drugs, the leader asked me to stay, so I did. Going this week wouldn't be hard since I've already gone there once. On my way to the building one of the other inmates, **Marty**, was walking there too. We sat together through the NA meeting. Once the meeting was over and we were heading back to get our medication (insulin for me) by the guards, I felt led to invite **Marty** to Bible study. He said sure and he wanted to bring George, my mentor for my support group for sex addiction. They both showed up! **Darcy** (the other Bible study participant) and I prayed the night before for more participants. The Bible study started slow, and I was concerned that they would lose interest. Thankfully the second part of the study increased the interest, and the talk of the church's failures came up. The topic of celibacy and sex was brought up too. Ideas were shared, and now I believed the Lord was taking us on a journey with topics that will interest the inmates.

God help me with your message of hope.

I guess going to that first NA meeting wasn't such a fluke after all.

November 23, 2017

Note: (names in bold are changed to protect the identities of the individuals)

Today I just wanted to be reminded to be grateful for even little things that so often we take for granted. I was without reading glasses for three weeks and if it wasn't for **Charles**, a fellow inmate, to loan me a pair, I would be without them for yet another week.

Thank you, Lord, for your mercies and your provisions are plentiful. You remind us about true riches, which do not rest on earthly things, but in you and you alone. Bless **Charles** and the rest of the inmates, guards, and staff. Show them your love, mercy and your sacrifice you made for us.

November 25, 2017

Note: (names in bold are changed to protect the identities of the individuals) (names in black are the real names and used by permission)

Another interesting night last night. After playing racquetball **Sean**, Chad and I sat down by the benches in the gym, just casually talking when Chad asked what we were up to for the evening. I said that after meds I was leading Bible study and was explaining to them that Bible study was topic-based and the topics were picked by the other inmates. I also said that George wanted to learn more about spirituality and shared that the Lord gave me ten different Scripture passages by his revelation. I knew **Sean** was a spirit-filled believer but I wasn't so sure about Chad. I looked at Chad and asked him if he understood what I was saying, and this led into what felt like an hour and a half talk about God! Chad revealed that he received Christ a little over a year ago but didn't attend church. Chad shared that in his struggle in his faith a couple of weeks ago, he asked God for a sign that he would see an eagle. Well! The next day, a female eagle ended up on our baseball field, standing on the pitcher's mound, and God allowed me to bear witness to this event! It stayed there for at least three minutes, not afraid, even though there were at least six of us standing there nearby, watching this thing of beauty! Chad shared that he was dumbfounded that God answered his prayer and would give him this sign! After he shared I invited him to Bible study and he said yes. I believe he enjoyed it. **Sean** decided to come too and shared boldly the gospel.

Thank you, Lord, for bringing who you want in and answering my and **Darcy's** prayers. Lead your people. Fill the hearts with your spirit of love.

November 28, 2017

Note: (names in bold are changed to protect the identities of the individuals) (names in black are the real names and used by permission)

Another upgrade was given today. Finally I have been transferred into a room where I have a single bunk. I also have my own key to my room. Not a bad jail, huh? Thank you Lord for your tender mercies.

Tonight **Darcy** and I are going up to the Holloway House community room to pray. Bible study is now Monday, Wednesday, and Friday. The move from five days a week to three was confirmed by the chaplain yesterday when I met with him in the morning. He had the exact same thing in mind. Praise God!

Darcy leaves Ford Mountain this Sunday. I pray the Lord finds him suitable housing that meets his court conditions and is also affordable.

I am seeing George being touched by God in our Bible studies. I pray God moves on him and all the other participants. May they know you deeply.

And for **Marty**, touch his spirit and give him hope through your loving kindness. Amen.

December 11, 2017

Every day is getting a little bit better. There is less pain in my heart; every day it grows a little bit brighter. I see greater hope. I look at countless possibilities. Don't feel guilty; I am more sober-minded than ever. Ford Mountain doesn't even feel like jail, but more like a hospital. First, the surrounding beauty of the mountains, the evergreens, the snow caps on the top of the mountains are sights to behold, take in, and meditate on. God has created such a beautiful place! The food is decent, and if one chooses to partake, there are all kinds of activities to do here – volleyball, basketball, racquetball, baseball (when the weather gets nicer), card games, video games, walking and running, reading at a really good library here, church, Bible study and two community rooms to have meetings here – so in all honesty, it is almost impossible to be bored. Most of the guards are great too and are willing to work with you to help get better. There are five meetings a week (two as a whole "Right Living Community" and three just with those who live in your hut), which focus on change and positive outcomes. There is school (high school, trades school/programs, university) and amazing self-help programs taught here – "Big Book", a guide to Alcoholics Anonymous 12-step program, anger management, seeking safety (for PTSD), criminal addictive thinking (CAT), and sex offender program (SOP), just to name some. You have medical staff and psychological counseling available. Finally, there are peer support groups to help us with our addictions.

Thank you, Lord, for your provision, your many blessings here and your presence. Lead me in the way of everlasting. I surrender to your will.

December 23, 2017

Interesting to be my age. I am part of a generation where if computers, electronic devices, and modern comforts were taken away from me (like here in jail), I can go back to writing on paper, research from books, and be resourceful "the old-fashioned way." God has me here in jail, first to be healed, but also I have time to read the Scriptures, and then write down my thoughts on paper, not feeling "lost" without my computer. In talking to the younger inmates, I hear their struggles as being more profound without the their computers and other devices. They seem more "lost" without them.

Thank you, Lord, for your mercy, for raising me up in a generation where one can be comfortable in both the computer world and in the paper and pen world. Both are powerful and effective.

Reading a book called *The Four Agreements*. It speaks to the heart of man, not the heart of God. I won't recommend the book to anyone. I consider it dangerous, new age in content and intent. It is the enemy of truth and love; something I came out of in the late 1980's.

Thank you, Lord, for discerning your truth. Thank you for giving your truth, you are the true giver of life, the one true Lord, in the mighty name of Jesus. Amen

What happened since: I ended up realizing there was a benefit in talking about the agreements themselves, and in taking the neutrality of the agreements to use the basics of the agreements themselves as part of a Christian Bible study. I had the help of a friend put the study together and ran it by the chaplain to ensure it was biblically accurate. I was able to focus on the Scriptures in the New Testament and also in the book of Proverbs as the pure basis and content of the agreements so that Jesus could be glorified instead. The Bible study went four sessions and was led by the person who helped me form the study, and the participation level was very high and very successful.

December 28, 2017

Note: (names in black are the real names and used by permission)

There were more cool stuff happening, watching God move in here. The Lord wanted to show both Eric and Tarsus his glory yesterday. Eric and I planned to meet at 5:15 p.m. to discuss how God is moving in his life and also share yesterday's journal entry, since it was about him. I sensed at the 2:30 p.m. roll call to ask Tarsus to join us, so I did, and he said yes. I told Tarsus to bring his Bible so we could read the Psalms, just as Tarsus suggested we do a few days earlier to help build our faith. At dinner I asked Eric if it was okay for Tarsus to join us, and he okayed that. When it came to 5 p.m., I prayed and asked God to show himself to them, and I would just get out of his way and watch him move.

The Holy Spirit prompted me to go to Tarsus' hut and get him to ensure he'd come. Usually he would forget and would have been in the gym playing racquetball instead. I obeyed the Holy Spirit's leading and went to his hut. Sure enough he was there. We walked up to Holloway House, and Eric arrived just as we arrived. We all sat down, and Eric and I started sharing to Tarsus how God was moving in Eric's life, and at the end of the time of sharing the Lord prompted me to tell Tarsus that this testimonial was also for his benefit and that I believed God wanted to show himself to him too.

Well, we started reading the Psalms, starting with Psalm 1. By the time we got to Palm 11 Eric joined in with us (he left to copy down yesterday's journal entry for himself, so he could read it to his partner) and within a couple of minutes Glenn came into Holloway House, curious to see what was going on. When he found out we were just reading the Psalms out loud I felt led to invite Glenn to join us in reading them, with Eric and Tarsus piping up in support also.

Glenn replied, "Well I'm not religious but thank you. I will be going."

We all replied, "Well we are just reading the Psalms, come and join us!"

He hesitated at the door for a couple more seconds, then decided to come and join us anyways! We didn't make a big deal about it, and we read from Psalm 15 right through to Psalm 28, everyone taking a turn reading one out loud. We all read Psalm 23 together in unison! That was cool. When we finished reading Psalm 28 Eric and Glenn left into their dorm while Tarsus and I headed back to our huts. Tarsus told me he really enjoyed reading the Psalms together, and then I told him how God had used him just now. Had it not been for his idea to read the Psalms in the first place Glenn would have never shown up! The cool thing is Eric, Tarsus, and I all obeyed God together and we each received a blessing through watching God move as a result!

Thank you Lord. You are our living testimony. We put our faith in you! Help us be humble and listen to your voice. Amen.

December 29, 2017

Note: (names in black are the real names and used by permission)

More amazing things happening here at Ford Mountain. Last night, after racquetball, I felt led to talk to Chad in the main community room. The Holy Spirit prompted me to bring this journal book with me to share with Chad the last two days' of entries. So I let Chad read them. The Holy Spirit afterward prompted me to say to him, "Something is happening here in Ford Mountain. God is moving and showing himself not only to me but to others. Now the Lord is having me to tell you that he is going to show himself to you as well very soon."

Chad replied, "You know, Mike, this is exactly what I have been praying for."

I love it when I am led by the Holy Spirit – that confirmation of that leading was brought about. Chad then shared with me his interest in the spirit realm and that we don't fight against people, his rekindled interest in the process of forgiveness, and he shared with me a Christmas miracle with his family all being together Christmas day, more than what he asked God for in prayer!

Oh, Lord, you are a God of abundance. You love your children. Thank you for your miracles. Thank you for answered prayer. Lift up our faith and teach us to fully surrender to your will. Teach us to be humble, and by the supernatural power of the Holy Spirit, guide us to walk in holiness and righteousness. Thank you for the shed blood of Christ on the cross for our sins and the glorious power of your resurrection. Without these two, we have no hope and our faith is futile. Amen.

January 1, 2018

Note: (names in bold are changed to protect the identities of the individuals)

There was yet another divine appointment last night. God is good. After work yesterday in the kitchen I got back to my room, and all I wanted to do is lay down to have a nap. I thought, *No, I need to go for a walk and get some exercise.* So I went down to the gym, even though the snow was more than a foot deep, and it also rained the day before (I also fell on black ice, twice!) and everywhere was icy.

There were two others walking in the gym, but I minded my own business. After about fifteen minutes of walking, **Ehud** came through the door of the exercise room and introduced me to **Joe**, a new arrival at Ford Mountain. Both are Christians and **Ehud** wanted to let **Joe** know that I was the Bible study leader here. At first, we stood around talking for about fifteen minutes, and then we started walking around the gym together, still babbling away. **Ehud** started talking about his homeland, and how he was treated while living there. He is very angry at Islam and those who practice it, and did not trust Muslims at all, for which he had his own reasons. His mother was killed by them and he lost four years of university education for being a political activist in a Muslim-dominated country. He even wants President Trump to attack his homeland.

I felt the Holy Spirit prompt me to ask **Ehud**, "Have you ever forgiven those Muslims for what they did to your Mom and to you at university, and what would that look like?"

Ehud looked at **Joe** and I quite sternly and replied a simple but firm no. Now earlier in our conversation, **Ehud** did share with us that for the past several years living in Canada, he struggled to learn reading, writing, and speaking English. But since he has been here in Ford Mountain, he experienced a major breakthrough in his comprehension! I asked him if that was him, the Holy Spirit, or both him and the Holy Spirit providing that breakthrough.

He gave credit to the Lord for this, and he recognizes that God has helped in this area. So I talked to **Ehud** about how unforgiveness operates in our hearts, how it can be related to being like a jail, where you put yourself in jail, throw away the key, and refuse any nourishment (food and water), and therefore slowly die on the inside.

"In contrast, when you choose to forgive, the person truly being set free is you," I said to him. "This is why God in Jesus Christ died for the forgiveness of our sins, and when we forgive, it is one of the most powerful tools God has given us! Forgiveness is a weapon against the enemy! It is a sign of strength!" I said.

I told **Ehud** while walking to church service, "Now that Jesus, while he was up on the cross, said, 'Father forgive them, for they know not what they do.' Meanwhile, the chief priests, Pharisees, Roman soldiers, and those who got stirred up against Jesus to mock him, spat at him, and cursed him."

Ehud just silently listened to me, and then the subject ended.

Father, as you have been teaching me about the power of forgiveness, how it sets you free from anger, bitterness, rage, anger, resentment and a host of other sins, I ask that you help **Ehud** become an overcomer in you. Show him that forgiveness doesn't mean to trust them, but in letting it completely go, he is now set free in his heart. Show **Ehud** this is your sign of strength, and if it is in your will, you will avenge his enemies and not him. What they desperately need is you Jesus, as their eternal destiny is hanging in the balance. Teach us the power of forgiveness and what that looks like. Show us the power of your mercy and what it would look like if we were merciful too. These acts are true expressions of your love and kindness to us. Help us to be the same, to be Christ-like in every aspect of our lives; that we would be holy and blameless before you, honoring you with our lives, our bodies, our actions, and our attitudes. Show us the way to everlasting joy, peace, and love and experiencing your amazing presence and awesome favor! Amen.

Speeches & Poems

Just finished reading and doing the FMCC (Ford Mountain Correctional Center) Right Living Community (RLC) orientation handbook. What an eye-opener! These people know what they are doing. They truly want to help, and I want the help. In the workbook I wrote a poem about it:

Realizing I Need Help

All the pain in my heart, the sorrow, the shame;
It is a realization that I need help.

The choices, the consequences, causing more pain;
It is a realization that I need help.

Delusion, visions of grandeur – those thoughts never end;
It is a realization that I need help.

Lying and hiding, my thoughts never abiding;
It is a realization that I need help.

Coming clean, saying the truth – this is the beginning;
It is a realization that I need help.

Staying the course, my actions now winning;
It is because I realized I needed help.

December 22, 2017

God's Gift

Thank you, Lord, for the abundance. Thank you, Lord, for hope. You are all that is in me, and truly this is no joke. You bring me new beginnings – a light that seems so new, even though it's always been there, I discover that you are you.

My life is changing – new life each day. My thoughts are singing,
My heart's at play!

"God is so real," I declare today. I won't back down.
I'll say what I say

Rejoice with me, who listen to my story.
I shout with glee, "Jesus is my glory!"

I bow to him. My heart's surrender, saying, "No more to sin,"
So I become tender.

Thank you for salvation. Thank you, Lord, for life,
You are all that is in me – no deceit, no malice, no strife.

You bring me great, great joy, beyond one's imagination,
So full you fill our lives, your great gift of salvation.

JOURNAL
BOOK 2

Inspirational Writings

It is so important to listen before speaking, be patient in your thoughts before opening your mouth, because the Lord gave us two ears and one mouth, and to use it in its proportion. This is part of a humble walk before God, pleasing our master in heaven first. Even when the Lord raises you up as leader, remember this: More will be required of you by God, as he will ask you to become servant of all (Luke 12:48; Mark 9:35).

Servant leadership is, in my opinion, the most effective form of leadership, where you lead by example, motivate others through positive direction, affirming their value no matter what position they are in. Encourage those underneath you to do well in everything they do, even to the smallest detail, and that God, who is watching, will reward you richly, even when no one else notices (Colossians 3:22-24; Ephesians 6:5-8). When you choose to completely surrender to God, you will discover your life purpose and will be completely filled with his love and favor, being able to withstand the attacks of the enemy and the evil will of men. By the Holy Spirit, you will be granted wisdom, power, and love (Matthew 10:30; 11:28-30).

Lord, give us your strength, your power and your wisdom, for we are completely dependent on you. By your mercy show us the error of our ways so that we may repent of our sins and humbly walk before you. Glorify us in what we do for your great name. Amen.

January 5, 2018

Always do your best, work hard, laugh out loud. Make friends, bless your enemies, hold tight to your convictions. Don't let anyone else influence you otherwise to what you know is true. Let your heart be touched, let your eyes soak in the beauty that is around you, whatever that may be. Allow God to soak into your heart and allow him to transform your life. Enjoy your journey with him as he leads you to the precipices of life.

There may be danger around the corner, but God will lead you through the straight and narrow path, even when there are twists and turns, bumps and bruises, maybe even broken arms and broken legs. Do not fear, your healing will come, whether it is on the inside of you or out. God is there for you. Listen to his still, small voice, so precious and full of love. He will guide you to the way of truth, holiness and righteousness, all wrapped up in his love. Jesus is the way, the truth, and the life. No one comes before the Father without him. Let us, the believing community, never forget that. Give everything you are and have to him and there will be treasures in heaven. You are immensely loved. Amen.

January 21, 2018

The Lord has taken everything away from me. May the name of the Lord be praised! He has taken away my family, so that I may grow to trust him and him only. He has preserved my relationship with my sister alone, so I may have some sanity. He has taken away my friends, so that I may realize where my dependency must fall. He has preserved a few, a precious few, so that I can ever be so grateful for their friendship. He has taken away any financial power and has placed me deep in debt, and this on purpose so that I put my trust in his provision and not my own. I will believe in his financial restoration, so that I will be guided by his direction, and his direction only. He wants me to teach others to do the same. He has taken away his business from me, the one I loved to steward so that I won't love it any more, and that I would put my heart toward Jesus, and Jesus only.

My heart is for Christ. My life is for Christ. My soul is for Christ. My strength, knowledge and wisdom is hidden in Christ. In him, I can do all things, according to his will and purpose. I do not fear, now, his rod of correction, for this is out of his love. Little did I know how this would change my life, my heart, my attitude, and my thinking, for his glory and my benefit! I have joy, not fear. I feel loved, not despised. He is preparing me to do great works for only his great name! Amen.

January 22, 2018

The Lord has given me everything to me. May the name of the Lord be praised! He has given me hope, where dreams exist, where dreams are fulfilled. He is love, the kingdom of heaven overflows with it. From heaven's treasure chest is truth, power, and healing. He heals the soul, makes the mind whole, and restores one's sanity. He gives his gifts in great abundance. He never holds back to those who wish to partake, those who want to willingly come into alignment with his ways, who delight in his precepts, and rejoice in his counsel.

Today, I put on tranquil music, and for the first time in decades I feel what it is like to be in a tranquil place for longer than just a few minutes, where a safe place exists in both my mind and my soul, where God's perfect love permeates my whole being. I don't remember ever letting God in this deep into my soul before! And I feel safe! I feel safe! Tears are welling up in joy as I write this down. Transformation is happening! The "cancer" in my soul is dying a slow death, but dying nevertheless. I am now going to lay claim to God's love, for I now perceive nothing more valuable. He is my rock, he is my salvation. Now I see him as the lover of my soul. I am starting to feel free. I'm being set free. The bondage has to go; it's not allowed to hang around anymore. So long self. (A song title from MercyMe)

February 14, 2018

Being Valentine's Day I thought I would write about God's love. What is God's love? First it is divine; it is God chasing us in an intimate, personal relationship with us. John 3:16 says, "For God so loved the world that he gave his one and only Son, so that whoever believes in him shall not perish, but have everlasting life." He goes after everybody – the rich, the poor, the old, the young, the sick, the healthy, the educated, the illiterate, no matter what sins we've committed. He loves the unlovely, as Scripture says in Romans 5:8, "While we were still sinners Christ died for us."

Where do we see the hand of God's love? Well, through his favorite instrument – people, for example, when people provide shelter for the homeless, food for the hungry, clothing for those in need of them. It can also be through disaster relief, medicine and education provided for at no cost to those who couldn't afford it. Or, helping governments not capable for providing for their citizens in times of an earthquake, tsunami, hurricane or tornado. People may see the human spirit in this, which their efforts are so commendable, but I see a greater power at work – the Creator of love, the Creator of empathy, the Creator of compassion.

When we love our spouse, children or significant other today, let us also remember Jesus, who loves us as sinners so much that he gave his life for us. There is no greater act of love than one laying his life down for his children.

MY STORY

January 3, 2018

When you need to deal with adversity, negative people, negative opinions, and negative comments or actions, you need to take the high road in response. I haven't so much as taken two steps in the other person's shoes, let alone a mile, and I don't know what is going on in the other person's head or life. When we choose to react positively to a situation that results from a negative action, comment, gesture, or attitude (like how I am using my journal to process something that just happened a few short minutes ago), I am the one making a positive choice, taking the high road. Actions, comments, gestures, or attitudes displayed negatively from others do not constitute a representation of who you are, unless you are the one that has caused it. It is then you need to take a good look at yourself and ask, "What have I done?"

Anyways, my response to the other person in this particular situation, even though I was angry, was, "Let us both take a good look at what you've claimed together and see where I went wrong." It's best not to assume, and I will take responsibility for my actions before I will blame others.

Lord, thank you for testing my pride and teaching me to be humble, as I asked for this morning. Show me your way through adversity, both big and small. In Jesus name, amen!

January 6, 2018

We are in this amazing partnership with God. I just asked God for those in the Bible study class who have personal testimonies of how Jesus had moved them, touched them, or did something amazing in their lives. But then I prayed, "But even if they don't share any testimonies, you are still sovereign and you will still show yourself in our Bible study." This brought me to tears because I realized something very important; we can ask God for anything. But if you deep down allow God have full control and, as part of your partnership with him, surrender your will and prayers to him in absolute humility, he may not only do what you ask of him, but he will do something *better*, even if it might look messy on the outside of it.

I have a saying that I love so much: "Not everything is as it seems." I didn't make it up but read something close to it in a story years ago involving two angels. All I know and believe is that God is sovereign, he is love and I can fully trust him. He has entrusted the task of leading Bible study to me and now I surrender it back to him.

Lord, I pray that you show up to these Bible studies. Show yourself no matter how *messy* the conversation gets, and help me be an amazing steward of your Word, a fantastic custodian of the relationships built here, and a brilliant caretaker for your glory so that you are magnified! Pour out your Spirit, love, peace, joy, fellowship, and the message of hope – salvation by the blood of Christ, amen!

Note: The story is actually called "Things Aren't Always What They Seem" – author unknown

January 8, 2018

I am enjoying my first full day off from working in the kitchen in three weeks. A day of rest is nice. Reading the book *The Jesus I Never Knew* by Philip Yancey, I have a hard time putting it down. The book is game-changing thinking for me; it gives a look at Jesus through a lens that isn't sanitized by our society, our North American Christian culture. God wants us to know he is real, that he really came to earth, had real feelings, experienced real hardships and trials just like we do, and that even his life on earth was messy, just like so many of our lives are. Sometimes and especially in the past few years, I feel like my life have been compared to that of a dog's breakfast; or at least that's what it looks like. But when I look closely, very closely, I see God's hand woven in and through it. He has been guiding me through the toughest time of my life, and in it I have become more and more like Christ.

Five days before my sentencing the Holy Spirit spoke to me while praying. In this time of prayer he gave me four distinct words: 1) *trust me*; 2) *believe*; 3) *obey*; 4) *don't be afraid*. Since that time God has put me through the refiner's fire and has been pruning his branch, all to make me holy, pure, and blameless in my thoughts, and actions, but also to prepare me so I can bear even more fruit for his kingdom. In this I shall surrender to Him. Amen.

January 9, 2018

I talked to my sister today. I told her how much better I am doing, how I have taken ownership of what I did, and the steps I am taking in receiving help for my mental illness. She knows I am seeing a psychologist, and I'm currently signed up or actively participating in four programs: My support group, which I've been involved in since my first week here at Ford Mountain, Big Book, which I am in my fifth week; Criminal Addictive Thinking (CAT), a cognitive behavioral therapy (CBT) platform, which started today, and finally, the Right Life Choices program, which is starting this Sunday. When I told her what I was doing and how I was doing she was crying. I also told her that I came out and said I was gay last night while leading Bible study and she was relieved that I finally admitted it. I told my psychologist too when I was in session with her today.

I am not afraid to talk about it now but I also tell those, especially in my Christian circles, that I love God so much that I *shall* honor him with my body and I *shall* live by his Word and stay "inside his schoolyard fence." This means that unless he chooses to heal me, I will stay abstinent the rest of my life. No compromises.

God give me the strength by your love and power to live by your Word, to honor you with my body. Amen.

January 11, 2018

Appreciation.

What do I appreciate? I appreciate

- what God has done for me,
- for giving me life,
- his salvation,
- hope for the future, and
- the continuous healing for my soul.

I also appreciate my true friends – the ones who have stood beside me through thick and very thin. No matter what I've done they have been there for me, and I shall be there for them.

I appreciate my fellow inmates, many of them, for when they stood by my side when I first came in, didn't judge me when I came out, and support me here day in and day out.

I appreciate working in the kitchen, God gave me this position (thank you!) by way of small miracles. We are spoiled there, food-wise, as compared to the rest of the population, and we seem to be treated better by the guards when we are in the kitchen/dining area.

I appreciate the programs available to us and the teachers that teach them.

Finally, I appreciate my sister, who has stood by my side when no other family member has. I don't blame nor will I judge my family for their choices. That is their decision, and I respect that. But my sister has chosen to see past my poor choices and love me unconditionally anyways. That is a great miracle and it means ever so much to me.

I love you, God. I love you, my friends. I love you, my sister. I love you everyone else, no matter how or what you think of me.

January 15, 2018

I just realized something while pondering on two sports I love to play – tennis and golf. They are predominantly individual sports, but they can also be played in teams. What I realized was the "snobbery" of the games – they can have a "hint" of arrogance in them, and there is a high amount of etiquette to both sports, especially during major tournaments where there are both very large crowds watching and they are televised. Of course, many of the etiquettes such as Quiet please! Hand back the tennis ball if it goes into the crowd, don't touch the golf ball if it goes into the crowd – are common sense. They help benefit the enjoyment of watching some of the best players in the game be able to concentrate and do their best. But the sport itself just seems to have a higher percentage of *arrogant* players than, say, in team sports. It might just be me, what do I know. But I do enjoy the *classy* players – the ones who are genuinely humble, especially the big stars of their respective sports. I want to be like them. God calls us to be humble, and when he raises us up to greatness, we need to be even more humble, with the left hand not knowing what the right hand is doing. This is where we need to be, no matter where we are in our lives, and watch God honor us because we chose to honor him.

January 16, 2018

I am getting excited about teaching the "Business With Purpose" Bible study tonight. I don't know how it's going to go or who will show up, but I'm leaving all that in God's hands. I do pray that whoever shows up benefits from the opportunity of possibly looking at an alternative possibility of starting their own business once they are released. I pray they also receive different thinking, meaning, that if they surrender their business to God and trust that he can do things with it, that they would bear witness to miracles so they can put their faith in him. So now I am going to take the lead and surrender the study to him. I will do my part, say what I am supposed to say, and trust that God will move. On a side note, I just heard in the hallway by one of my hut mates, "I don't know how Mike does it, taking all these courses and still working in the kitchen." Well, even though it can be stressful, God is giving me the grace to do all that I am doing right now. I've learned that even though there is a heavy workload, humility, not panicking, and a good attitude is helping me through this period. God is showing me through all this that I have a long road ahead of me, but with Jesus I will come to a place of new and better thinking, new and better understanding, new and better hope. Each day it just gets better.

Thank you Jesus, you said five days before my sentencing date, "Trust me." Now I see why! I trust you! Amen.

January 17, 2018

The Lord has told me, "Don't be afraid." So what is it that I shouldn't be afraid of? First, I am not to be afraid of being put in jail. It has been made blatantly obvious that he has a way better plan than I do, which I chose to surrender my life to him, which includes letting him control my direction. In this, I've grown to trust his judgment, and I am learning to not lean on my own understanding. Here, I am receiving one blessing after another, healing in areas of my heart I never thought possible, and opportunities to do things, like teach the Word of God and teach business. Next, I am not afraid of the guards. Before I came here, I was so traumatized by my arrest that when I saw a police car, Sheriff's vehicle, or peace officer vehicle I would shudder, thinking I would be taken away. But my relationships with the guards here have helped me realize the human side of them, which has helped heal the trauma. Finally, I am not to be afraid of the inmates. Some of them here have a "jailhouse" mentality, although most don't as we are a medium-security prison. I am not to judge them; I haven't walked so much as two steps in their shoes let alone a mile. I will lift them up and the whole camp in prayer. Bless those who curse you, pray for those who persecute you that I may walk in the way of the kingdom, as Jesus has taught us. Amen.

January 20, 2018

Note: (names in bold are changed to protect the identities of the individuals)

I love hearing the Holy Spirit and his leading of my life. Jesus said, "If you love me you will obey what I command" (John 14:15). That is both believing everything said in the Word of God and hearing God through the leading of the Holy Spirit.

Last Monday, the Holy Spirit told me to fill out my application for parole. I obeyed and made a draft copy of the answers to the questions. It took only about 40 minutes to complete. The Holy Spirit gave me "downloads" of what to include in each question, and the flow was fluid and easy. Two days later, I received a letter in the mail from my friend who was **the only lady in my Bible study** in support of my parole, and it included that she was wanting me in full partnership in her business when I am released, an important component to my release plan. I never expected this letter as she never told me she mailed it. Next, I waited on the Holy Spirit to talk to my case worker, so I waited for the Lord's timing, not mine. On Thursday evening, my case worker was there at meds time so we arranged to meet at 7:00 p.m. on Friday. On Friday and before our meeting, I surrendered our conversation to the Holy Spirit, knowing he has been in charge of this right from the get go. As a result, our conversation was fluid and he is in full support of my early release from jail. He asked me to finish the application today and hand it to him tonight.

This is what happens when you choose to listen to the still, small voice of God. Do exactly as he asks, and obey him completely. I do the easy part, he does the hard part. Thank you, Lord, for opening my ears and heart.

What happened after: See January 28, 2018 entry for what happened after!

January 23, 2018

I was learning about criminal and addictive thinking. It is a very interesting course to help you identify faulty thinking patterns. I am beginning to see that my thought patterns are definitely lining up properly as I am having a hard time answering a lot of the questions due to the fact that they surround the issues of alcohol and drug abuse and general addictive and criminal behavior. As my crimes have to do with a sexual nature, some of the questions I have to answer applied, but so many more do not as I had no addiction to drugs or alcohol. I didn't steal or had a "jailhouse" mentality. Heck, I was put into protective custody and have never seen the doors of the general population of a jail where it can be very nasty.

Here at Ford Mountain, it's more like Club Med than a jail. For some of my answers, I had to go back more than twenty years before I could remember a situation so I could write down an answer. But I must continue. I was learning valuable information every day, which was helping me learn more about myself and who I am in Christ.

Thank you, Lord, for bringing me here, bringing me to my senses, and teaching me new ways of thinking and behaving. I bring all my shortfalls to you and repent of them so that by the blood of Christ and the power of the Holy Spirit, you can heal my soul. Bring me to your way of everlasting that I may partake in the treasures of truth, love, and mercy. In Jesus name, I pray, amen.

January 27, 2018

I've got to learn to stop trying too hard to please God because he kept saying to my heart that he is already pleased with me — so many times already. Right here in Ford Mountain, Jesus has spoken directly to my heart and has said, "I am so proud of you!"

I am tearing up while writing this because I am still in this struggle to accept God's love in its absolute fullness. I know that a major part of my struggle has been because as far as I can remember, I have tried to win my mother's approval, but our toxic relationship has caused such strife, such division, that I've never heard of that fullness of approval, that fullness of acceptance from her. But how could she? My mom is hurting, really bad, and I cast my finger at Satan for deceiving her. Only God can give the love I am truly looking for anyways, so I am going to stop looking in the wrong places. I am going to choose to stop striving to win God's approval when I already have it. I repent of this selfish attitude. In walking in God's approval, I will just seek to choose his ways first, put him first in my heart before all other things, and rest in his love, choosing to fully accept that he already loves me, unconditionally, and that I will love him back with all my heart.

To him be the glory, to him be honor, to him be the power and majesty. I choose to worship Jesus first and foremost, amen.

January 28, 2018

Note: (names in bold are changed to protect the identities of the individuals)

Talked to **the only lady in my Bible study** on the phone last night, and I shared with her how I am learning to trust in hearing God's voice, then acting on it. On January 15, the Holy Spirit said to me, "Fill out your parole application." Believing it was him, I obeyed. The process flowed nicely, and I had a rough draft completed in about forty minutes. Then I waited on him for the next step. Two days later, a letter came in the mail from **the only lady in my Bible study** in support of my parole and a commitment for me to be her business partner. I had no idea that the letter was coming, as I hadn't talked to **the only lady in my Bible study** for a couple of weeks by this time.

I waited on God again but started to look in the camp for my case worker, **Mr. X**, a really nice guard here at Ford Mountain. By the end of that day, the Holy Spirit said to me, "Put in a special request to see **Mr. X**. So I filled out the special request and put it in the box. That night during medication call, **Mr. X** was on shift to watch over the inmates taking their meds, and when I came in he said, "Mahy, I received your special request." And then right there started trying to tell me what I needed to do.

After listening respectfully for a few minutes, I interjected and asked him, "**Mr. X**, if we could please have a formal meeting so I can explain my case to you, it would be appreciated. I would like to explain my release plan in more detail, in person." There were two other guards present during this discussion, so he consented and told me to bring my application Thursday night, January 18, at seven. The next night, I came to the *bubble* – that is the term used for the front end of the admin building at Ford Mountain – and sure enough, who was right at the window? **Mr. X**! He acknowledged me right away and gestured that he'll be a minute or so. A few minutes later, he came to the door and invited me into an interview room. When we sat down, I started speaking immediately, respectfully asking him to hear the background and basis of my application. When I finished telling him about the crimes I committed, that I owned up to them to my lawyer immediately and that I never changed my mind during course of the bail, plea, and sentencing. The Holy Spirit ensured I never changed my mind out of fear. Every time I "checked in" with the Lord he always told me to plead guilty, uncontested. And as a result of being here in jail, I have been getting the help I needed by taking the programs offered here and support groups, all voluntary, and that the help has been so immense that I want to continue any program and support groups on the outside, whether or not parole is granted. I handed him my application and he read it.

After reading my draft, he then responded, "Mahy, I see two Mahys here – the Mahy who is the professional and the Mahy who has made a mistake. I see that you have owned up to your mistakes and since I have gotten to know you, I see that you want to get help. I will fully support you in your parole application. Take what you've written here and put it into the application. Bring it back to me tomorrow night, and I will review it again."

He gave me two extra blank sheets of paper to fill out the overflow of the application. I did exactly as he asked. The next night, I didn't come to the bubble exactly at seven, but I felt the Holy Spirit nudge me to take it down around 7:10 p.m. Sure enough, **Mr. X** was right at the window, again no waiting (waiting is usually what happens). He stuck his hand through the pass drawer, like one you would see at a twenty-four hour gas station, and asked me to give him the final copy of the application. He told me he would give it back at medication time, which was an hour later.

When I got in the medication lineup, **Mr. X** called me down to the window. He said, "Your application is excellent! I will pass it to one of the guards giving medication and you will receive it back there. Go see **Ms. Grandview** on Monday morning and hand it in. So I waited the weekend. Monday morning came and after eight-thirty roll call, I went back to my hut, seeking the Lord when I should go back to the office with my application. Within a few minutes of being in my room the Holy Spirit told me to go. I obeyed, grabbed my application, and stood there, first in line at the office. It only takes a minute to walk across the compound and more often than not, especially on Mondays, people are in front of you waiting to see someone. So guess who opened the door? **Ms. Grandview!** What were the chances of that? She motioned me forward and asked me who I was looking for. This was my first direct interaction with her since I've been here in the camp. She usually works just in the office and the only time anyone sees her is just during morning roll call.

I said, "Actually it's you I'm looking for." She smiled. I went forward and handed my parole application to her and said, "I want to hand in my parole application."

She replied, "Are you happy with what you've put in your application?"

I responded, "I had two meetings with my case worker, **Mr. X**, and he said it was excellent!"

She said, "Then I shall process it."

That was January 22. By the following Thursday, **Mr. X** came back to me privately while walking in the compound and let me know that **Ms. Grandview** faxed off my application the very day I gave it to her, and now we will wait for their response.

Thank you, Lord, for as I listen and obey your voice, it is you that opens the doors. I choose to stay surrendered to you, and I trust your judgment regarding my life more and more. You are showing me your path for my life. Help me be humble in spirit and action. Show me your ways. I will follow you and only you. Amen.

January 29, 2018

God, in his infinite love and compassion for us as his people, is always looking for ways to give us "upgrades" in our lives. The Scripture is true, "If you, though you are evil, know how to give good gifts to your children, how much more will your Father in heaven give good gifts to those that love him." (Matthew 7:11 NIV) Ever since I've been here, I have received one good gift after another in plentiful abundance. Some have been material; some have been spiritual. Just now, I just received a larger screen TV without even asking for it. I was content with what I already had. The greater "upgrade" I've received is that I don't lust or covet after bigger and better material possessions anymore. In my repentance of that sin, God has not only healed me, but has replaced it with a greater sense of appreciation and stewardship of material things when he entrusts them to me. The Scripture is true. "For everyone to whom much is given, from him much will be required, and to whom much has been entrusted (committed), of him they will ask the more." (Luke 12:48 NIV) Whether we live on an abundant continent like North America materially speaking, or whether we live on a continent like Africa where faith, family, and love come in great abundance, God will look to "upgrade" his children. In all circumstances, we must yield to the leading of the Holy Spirit in full surrender, giving ourselves over completely to God.

February 3, 2018

Note: (names in black are the real names and used by permission)

It is very interesting how sometimes a planned event can quickly get derailed by unforeseen circumstances. What I want to share in this case was that scrapping our planned meeting for the sake of a brother in need was more than appropriate.

Two nights ago, we were scheduled to have our next installment of "Business With Purpose" Bible study. While I was walking up to Holloway House with Chad, a new inmate was following up behind us about forty feet behind. He is the only Latino that I know of in the camp, and although he spoke pretty good English, his language skills were still a work in progress.

I stopped and turned around and said, "Hey Milton, how are you doing?"

His head dropped, and his shoulders cowered down. "Okay," he replied.

I responded, "Are you alright?" I started walking toward him.

He said shyly, "I guess." and then started crying.

I said to him, "Come here." and wrapped my arms around him and held him long enough for him to say, "I miss my children." And he just kept crying. Right there, I knew in my spirit that I needed to be prepared, as a leader, to be flexible and go with what was most important at this study because Milton was heading to the study too. Chad, Milton, and I walked slowly the rest of the way and I introduced Milton to Chad. I told Milton that Chad had children too, and in a transitional comment, I said, "Chad understands what you are going through." and motioned for Chad to take over the conversation so Milton could be encouraged.

We got to Holloway House, and I went inside, leaving those two to finish talking alone at the entranceway. When I saw George in the room (he is the camp leader here at Ford Mountain), I motioned him close to me and whispered in his ear, "Milton is in tears, he misses his children."

He acknowledged it now that he was aware of why Chad and Milton were still outside (he was mildly teasing Chad for not coming inside). Chad and Milton finally came in and then after settling in, I still was watching Milton and seeking the Holy Spirit as to what he wanted to do. Everyone (seven of us) were all still gabbing, but I could still see tears in Milton's eyes when George piped up, "Mike you said that in business Bible study, we need to watch the time (or something to that effect)."

I responded to George, "I'm threatening to cancel business Bible study tonight because I believe there is a more important issue here." (Again, something like that). I told the group that Milton was having a rough night and asked everyone, through a show of hands, if we could suspend study and just share for Milton's sake. It was unanimous and I could see Milton start lightening up almost immediately. At one point, I asked the fathers I knew in the room how many children they had and how old they were. Each dad was actually sitting immediately adjacent to him (Milton) who had young children themselves! Was that a fluke?

I think not. I was seeing God's hand on this night, as each father (Eric, Evan & Chad) shared their stories of how they miss their children too, but that this situation is temporary, and they will see them again soon.

Evan, who has some of the biggest challenges to seeing his daughter again, read out from his journal book a letter he wrote to himself of the recognition of what he's done, the challenges he faces, but also the hope he has because he understands that with the right choices his life and life opportunities can change. Even the youngest study members of our group (two others who have no children) had something encouraging to say to Milton. Needless to say, Milton was greatly encouraged. He didn't feel alone and was deeply grateful for all of us. Glenn and Eric both hugged Milton too.

Thank you, Holy Spirit, for guiding this study; for by listening to your leading, you allowed all of us to partner with you in love. This is how we surrender to you, and I know that you, through the power of your Spirit, work through every one of us, whether or not we recognize it. This was a special moment, and I choose to give you the praise and glory. You are teaching us love in action, for we were made in your image and therefore designed to work in your image. Help us grow to be more like you every day. Amen.

February 12, 2018

Today is a day of confession, a confession of secret sins still lingering in my heart. They are covered by the blood of the Lamb, and without that plus the supernatural help of the Holy Spirit, we are helpless to stop the raging madness in our hearts. I confess hatred, hatred to myself for what I've done so I repent of it. Jesus is my covering. So in my heart, I must accept the sacrifice he made for me. Next, I confess my pride, and I repent of this sin so that my heart may open up to the healing power of the Holy Spirit instead of trying to do it all on my own, in my own strength. Next, I confess my anger and judgment, because both together it is bringing me to cite blame, pointing my finger at others for my problems. This is delusional. I confess that I am solely responsible for my actions and may I be forgiven by anyone and everyone whom I had caused harm. I, too, forgive anyone and everyone for any harm they have caused me. Next, I confess my sexual lust, for without the help of the Holy Spirit, my heart will always be in darkness. This sin stems more often than not from loneliness, which is a lie. God is always with me. I open my heart to this truth in repentance. I bring myself low in humility and worship.

O Lord, you are my light and my salvation. You delight in me, and I gladly give my heart and my life to you in complete surrender. You are my joy and my peace. Only you lift me up. Receive my confession, O Lord. My sin has been thrown deep into the ocean floor, never to be remembered by you ever again. Amen.

February 15, 2018

I pray for all those whose minds are stuck in the world, stuck in the devil's lair. In the last couple of days, I have heard about things that I just don't think about, talk about, or joke about. I choose, even here in jail, to surround my life, my conversation, and my thoughts to things that are pure; things that are holy; things that are noble; things that are praiseworthy. I choose to ignore the coarse joking, the foul language, and the worldly talk. I choose, in love and compassion to others who don't know Christ, or who are weak in their faith, to see past how they talk so to engage with them. I coexist with my fellow inmates peaceably, as Christ desires. I desire to live the way of Christ, and I know through the power of the Holy Spirit I receive supernatural help. To live is Christ. While I live here, that is all I want to do. Christ is my treasure. I love him so much. I love Christ deeper and deeper every day as I receive this amazing healing in my life. My heart doesn't hurt as much. My hope grows brighter daily. My walk with Christ is that much closer; my thoughts much clearer. I want to be humble; it's awesome to be this way before our mighty God as it is the very thing that gives me total peace in my heart. I want nothing else. I will do exactly as I'm told so that I never lose that peace! I have found my greatest treasure – the love of God dwelling deep in my heart; and deeper it goes day by day.

February 16, 2018

I was given a good reminder of how pride can creep into us, especially when things are going well and life is pretty good. It was in my Big Book class this morning, a twelve-step overview of Alcoholics Anonymous, and other related anonymous support groups available here in Ford Mountain. These support groups help us "check in" and they are amazing in providing accountability too.

Someone shared a personal story during today's class and it caused me to take a good look at myself. And I saw that pride was creeping in.

I am blessed with many abilities and could comprehend many things, but my pride and awareness of these capabilities could cloud my judgment. It was best to step back and allow God guide my day and just choose to always yield to the Holy Spirit.

I recognize that he is smarter and more capable than I could ever be; therefore, I have confidence to put my full trust of my life into his hands. This also brings me the greatest joy.

Thank you, Lord, for keeping me in check. I confess my pride to you and turn away from it. I yield to you for you are my light and my salvation. No one is equal to you. Grant me peace in my heart as I give my all to you in worship. I love to surrender everything to you. You are my God, you are my life. In Jesus' name, amen.

FORD MOUNTAIN

January 7, 2018

I just looked at the front of this book and it reads, *Thinking Leads 2 Change*. I do a lot of thinking here at Ford Mountain because my life has been put on pause – deliberately and by design by God. Even though I am serving a sentence for my crimes, this correctional facility is unique from all the others in British Columbia – a beautiful, mountainous setting, much freedom to walk about the facility, many programs to help you get better if you choose to take them, and you also work here to help keep you busy. So I feel like I am more on a sabbatical than serving a sentence. Part of this thinking is that I journal almost daily; something I never did before. Putting my thoughts on paper has helped me process so many things because I am not bottling up my thoughts anymore. I am letting them out. Release the hounds! God is using this place the help me heal but he is also using it to help me grow in my faith and relationship with him.

So yesterday, I was looking at my *faith*. While looking at it I started comparing it to the Roman centurion (see Matthew 8:5-13) and started thinking, *I don't have that kind of faith! I know I should, so why don't I?* I surmise that when it comes to faith, I overthink.

Overthinking things can stop you from taking action in the faith department. In fact, faith is supposed to be so simple that a child naturally possesses it! And Christ said himself that even if you have faith like a mustard seed you can move mountains! So now I am putting my thoughts down, writing them on paper. I want this kind of faith. I see it as an amazing treasure from God. I want as many treasures from God as he is willing to give me, and now I am not ashamed to ask. I will come to God with childlike faith and ask him for more faith, a higher level of faith, and I desire to see this faith manifest itself from the heavenlies right into the earthly realm. This is so that I may declare to those reading that this is the Christ, our Savior of the world, as one showing himself as the true and living God. I bear witness to miracles given by the Holy Spirit as a result of my faith (and theirs), so that those who want a personal, life changing, dynamic relationship with him can get it!

Lord, heal my soul, as I confess my sin and forgive those who have wounded me. Help me walk in the ways of holiness and righteousness because by your blood, you have made my spirit whole and pure. Restore my soul, and allow me to partake in doing great things for your great name so that my faith may grow and grow and grow. In Jesus' name I pray, amen.

January 10, 2018

I am so encouraged to constantly think in terms of abundance, hope, confidence, joy, and love. Every day, I grow in confidence and walk in peace; transformation in my life, at least it seems, is accelerating. I am finding I am becoming more patient and more empathetic with others, looking at the bright side of things without losing its reality. I am not only bearing witness to changes in my life but in others as well, especially those I spend quite a bit of time with. God is moving here at Ford Mountain! I am excited to be a part of it. God works wherever you are, no matter your circumstance, if you let him in.

I pray for the hearts of those here in Ford Mountain, my fellow inmates, guards, staff, and teachers. I ask that you bless them. Show yourself to them so that they may receive you as their Lord and Savior and then grow in you. Teach them your ways, O Lord, and pour out your Spirit on them so that through this you may be glorified. Glorify yourself, and show your glory! Amen.

January 13, 2018

It was a cool morning today! The Lord inspired me to co-write the first six lessons of the business Bible study, aimed at both the believer and the seeker. It was just so easy to write. The flow was amazing, and I'm not sure if it was the Holy Spirit downloading the info with such incredible flow or angels, delivering the info to me in person. Either way, it was far too easy to say I did it by myself. In fact, I mushed up one of the exercises, so I decided to rewrite it but couldn't finish the rewrite because I had to work in the kitchen. I was sharing with one of my co-workers and in our discussion I discovered that I was missing a couple of components of the lesson! I told him that God just used him to help me out too!

It just goes to show that God is the God of details when you allow him to control each situation you are in and are humble enough to surrender, hear his voice, and know when he is using others to bring glory to his great name!

Bring glory to your great name, O Lord. Bring glory to your great name! Show me your ways that I may walk in the path of righteousness for your name's sake. Your name is glorious, Lord Jesus, and I worship you. Raise your servant up that I may see your power, riches, and glory. Amen.

January 25, 2018

Note: (names in black are the real names and used by permission)

Last night I learned a lot about public speaking from my new mentor, Chad. Chad was a gifted public speaker and was attending the Bible studies. Last night he addressed some key components of which improvement can be made:

1) I need to work on limiting the time of which a person dominates during an interactive discussion. Chad suggested to limit it to no more than five minutes – I let one go for more than twenty minutes. He said the rest of the group ended up getting disconnected and lost interest in the discussion because they didn't feel included anymore. Chad gave me awesome solutions to steer the conversation back to include everyone without alienating the person "hi-jacking" the discussion.

2) Next, Chad mentioned that, while pacing was good as a facilitator, I paced too wide and far, which in a group of eight or nine people I should narrow my pacing to no more than three to four feet on either side of center.

3) Lastly, Chad mentioned that I use hand gestures far too much and they end up being a distraction to what is being said. He said hand gestures are great to emphasize certain point, but not every point. I can't wait to try out my new skillsets and put them to good use!

Thank you, Lord, for Chad. Thank you for making us all feel valuable, even here in jail! Amen.

February 4, 2018

Someone Has to Believe In Us

Last Friday we had our Right Living Community (RLC) meeting, and I was asked to do the closing positive message. I was also told that we had guests coming in from the Kamloops Regional Correctional Center (KRCC) because they were interested in seeing how this unique medium-security model worked. The meeting was the best we've had since I've been here; both the guards and inmates put their best foot forward collectively to make it happen.

But why such a collaboration? Why does it work so well? Is it just because of the beauty and openness of the facility, nestled inside a beautiful mountain range? That certainly helps! Is it because of the relative comfort and privacy of the facilities of which the inmates have semi-autonomy? Well that helps too. Is it all the programs available, whether it is staff- or inmate-run, to help us with mental, spiritual, and emotional well-being, putting important life skills in our toolkits, or have classes to better train us for better education? This is a bonus. Is it that we can learn different trades and apply those skillsets in a work environment, which also helps our days go by faster? I certainly appreciate that. It's more than all this. Someone had to believe in us inmates, and like a successful corporation, that vision, that belief, had to start from the top.

We see it in how the RLC model was developed and implemented, tested, and approved. The visionaries of this model get credit for that. Next, it was government support to allow such a model to exist in their system. Then it was the warden, who oversees the implementation and training for all the staff to ensure the model runs smoothly. Then it was the guards, who we see on a daily basis, who are trained in this model and are asked to buy into it, and carry it out, twenty-four hours a day, seven days a week. And we saw them – the guards, the instructors, the medical staff, and our spiritual mentors – all play a key role in providing a positive impact to help see our lives, us inmates, change. And so many of us here in Ford Mountain were changing for the better, and that was because someone had believed in us. Many of us have on the outside friends and family to support us, and possibly on the inside, plus our faith to help keep us strong. But when we see, day in and day out, someone believing in us, it increases our chances of success when we get released back into the community.

To the guards and to the staff, thank you for believing in us, even though it isn't perfect and sometimes messy (what's a little spice in life anyways?) But overall, without your important contribution, this model just becomes that – a model. It is you that helps bring forth change. Thank you.

February 10, 2018

So I have reason to believe the enemy is trying to cast doubt that the info written up from this morning is not of God (referencing to the teaching on spiritual warfare). I am about to meet two young Christians (meaning, their walks are less than five years but both are in their thirties) to teach them the basics of spiritual warfare. I have said this before in my journal writing, but I have heard very recently again – this time from our chaplain – something is happening here in Ford Mountain. This is God's show so I am surrendering this to him. I pray he gives me discernment to see if these two are ready for this, and if I am ready for this too. I believe we need to take this slowly. Taking territory for Christ is a partnership. We need to hear God's direction, and then we need to take action once we receive it. I pray we hear God's still, small voice. I pray we receive it. I pray we receive courage, faith, and strength in this. I pray for us to grow as a result of God's lessons being taught through this. I pray we grow in humility as we openly confess our sins. I pray we grow in surrender as we make room for Jesus to be King of our hearts; that we may look to heaven for our treasures and not be fooled or distracted by the ones on earth. Build our faith; open our spiritual ears – in Jesus' mighty name. Amen.

February 13, 2018

Note: (names in black are the real names and used by permission)

"Bible Study Doesn't Belong to Us, It Belongs to God"

Yesterday I was led by the Holy Spirit to ask Glenn to lead Bible study for last night's session, even though he was not a Christian. Outside the Ford Mountain facility, I would probably never dream of asking a non-Christian to lead, for many reasons, let alone scripturally it just doesn't line up. But this wasn't the outside, this wasn't a traditional jail, and this wasn't a traditional Bible study. God had been known to make exceptions, and this was one of them. I clearly heard the Holy Spirit's leading, so I humbly obeyed. I wrote down the Scriptures for the study and the subject title so Glenn would have something to teach. Now, Glenn has attended both the regular and business Bible studies for weeks and reads his Bible every day. He asked questions, lots of them, sometimes very hard questions. God has given me the honor to speak life into him and he has received two prophecies both of which have been fulfilled in the form of dreams. It's clear God is after him. When I asked Glenn to lead the study he said yes without hesitation. Now, when it came time for the study we had a full class (seats ten).

Glenn opened up in prayer as best as he knew and led the study as best as he knew. I was amazed how fluid the study went and the high level of participation and engagement with the class. I enjoyed it immensely. I was glad I yielded to the Lord's leading. Something was happening to Glenn. God knew best how to lead him. I got out of God's way. That was obedience. Amen.

Speeches & Poems

January 30, 2018

"Full Surrender"

I can trust my loving God
For he is with me. He is always with me

His love for me is abounding
It never fails. It never fails

He is the shepherd of his sheep
And guides my soul, guides my soul

He will lead me on his path
And guide my destiny, guide my destiny

Goodness and joy shall follow my days
For he is with me. He is with me

I will never let go of you, Lord Jesus,
For you are my light, my salvation.

January 31, 2018

I was asked to do the closing positive message this morning in our hut meeting. After a quick prayer to the Lord (I didn't have much time to get something written down), this came to mind:

Accepting change means:

- go with the flow,
- learn new things,
- know what to keep, and
- know what to let go.

The only thing consistent in life – is change.

Thank you, Lord, for your inspiration, for giving me words of wisdom to share with others. I pray for my hut, that they may know you personally, see their own salvation. This is the greatest gift you have given the world. In Jesus' name, amen.

February 1, 2018

Yesterday, I went and saw a parole officer for my first interview. Like in the PSR (pre-sentence report), I had to disclose the dirty details of my crimes as part of the process. When it came to my faith and my sexuality, however, the same issue surrounding these two arose, just like in the PSR! Basically speaking, it came to this: how could I believe what it says in the Word of God when you've identified yourself as gay? I responded to him that this is a politicizing of the issue and that 2 Timothy 3:16 is clear that all Scripture is God-breathed, etc. etc.

I believe what the Word says about homosexuality, he didn't agree with me. So there is a perceptual lack of reconciliation between people in the secular world and the Word of God, and it seems that they struggle more with my sexual identity and faith as it pertains to the accuracy of God's Word. What they are missing is the relationship I have with my loving God and that as I "plug in" to him, he gives me the power to: walk in his ways, never feel alone, always feel loved, and he gives me strength by his Spirit to obey. They don't get that part. On the other hand, I foresee issues with the church regarding my sexual identity too. I will be judged. There will be strong words for my position. I am not afraid though. I have a job to share my story, as God has called me to do in obedience. He will give me the strength and courage to give a message of hope to those who have an identity like I do. I will share with them God's love, God's mercy, but also how to fully surrender to God's will so they can "plug in" to the Holy Spirit just like I do and still have the desire, will, and strength in love to fully obey God's Word. I will teach them to fully honor him with their bodies as living sacrifices, all with the supernatural help of God! Furthermore, I will see healings in this area too! I can't wait to bear witness to that. In the meantime, I wrote a poem to share my current struggle in the arena of "political football" between so many people in both the secular world and in the church. I pray this poem gives others strength too while they deal with the same issue:

Stuck In the Middle

I'm stuck in the middle of a message God wants me to say,
To only follow his Word even though I'm gay.

I'm asking God to help me express these words today,
To show all that he loves me, he loves me anyway.

The Word is clear, the Word is fine, I agree it's all from God,
I do not bend, I do not bend, I honor him with my bod.

In abstinence, the choice I make, he gives me strength to succeed,
Not in dogma, nor it in politics, or sways me not to take heed.

I will follow his ways; I love his law – it's eternal and does not change,
The world doesn't agree, church sticks to its guns, both see me as strange.

My identity in Christ, my faith in God – they're as solid as can be,
My hope in him, his love for me – this is what's set me free.

No more games. I'll tell the truth; my life has come anew,
But not because of other's opinions, it's all because of you!

February 5, 2018

When you have set good goals and have achieved them, you have done well. To perpetuate your good goals this is called a process, you have done even better. When your good processes has become a good habit, you have done your best. So, it is worth it to try your best in life.

Mike Mahy – written on the chalkboard of "B" Hut in Ford Mountain, by the inspiration of the Holy Spirit

I could hear God's voice, in part, because I choose to surrender my life to him completely. Jesus came to me, after asking me to go to Calgary for four days (May 19-22, 2015) and stay with friends. It was my last night there. He came up behind me, while I was lying on my side, stopped and said, "I want all of you." His voice was soft but strong, firm but gentle. He was challenging me to be the best I could be because he knew what was inside me. But then again, he was the one who designed me! He has designed us all, and we can be everything we can be, if we so choose to surrender, voluntarily, to our Creator. We can trust his omniscience, his omnipresence, his omnipotence, and his holiness, for these are the true characteristics of our God, all wrapped in his most amazing attribute – love! There was no comparison to our mighty God, who brought me out of the pit, cleaned me up, and has set me on a straight path, by his supernatural power, to lead me to a glorious purpose and destiny, all because I said yes to him to fully surrender of my life to him. I said yes because I could. I have the most beautiful gift in the world – a free will. You do too. What would it look like if we all lived according to Philippians 3:7-11? Read it to find out what it says! To live in Christ is to have a brand new life. "Taste and see that the Lord is good." (Psalm 34:8) All this because you can.

Because You Can

You can choose because you can.
You can live a full life because you can.
You can receive God's love because you can.
Walk in full purpose and destiny because you can.
You can overcome obstacles because you can.
See obstacles as opportunities because you can.
You can trust God's power because you can.
You can trust God's provision because you can.
You can trust God's strength because you can.
You can see God's glory because you can.

JOURNAL
BOOK 3

Inspirational Writings

February 26, 2018

God is using this time in my life to do many things – correct me, execute justice for what I did wrong, refine me, provide change in my life, protect me, and build my faith and trust in him as a result. I am amazed since 2013 of how my faith has grown in God. The biggest thing I've noticed is how much more I have trusted in who he is – his omniscience, his omnipotence, his omnipresence, his holiness.

I have the privilege of seeing Jesus sitting on his throne through my spiritual eyes. I don't see him with great detail; but I see him sitting on a big throne, with his arms resting flat on the arm rests and his fingers cupping around the front of the arm rest, pointing straight down. He is dressed in blazing white, a white gown, and a purple sash wrapping across his body from his right shoulder to his left waist. He has a large crown on his head, but I don't see it clearly. I can say it is made of pure gold with jewels – rubies – inset into them. There may be different jewels – onyx, jasmine, amethyst, sapphire, and emerald – they may be in there, but I personally can't really see them. Beside him is his staff – a big, long golden staff with what looks like a crown on top, laden with diamonds. Even his throne is made of pure gold, an amazing sight.

I see this when I come into deep worship and adoration, basking in his presence. For some reason, he keeps showering me with gold coins, too many to count, falling through the ceiling, and they are coming from heaven. These are all very cool spiritual blessings I get from God. But what I've loved the most lately is the peace in my heart he's given me; and when the Holy Spirit speaks something to me and I obey that still, small voice, it actually is anointed and turns out exactly as he said, whether it is a word for someone, a directive, or a command for me to follow through. What I've been learning is to hear the shepherd's voice – know that that this voice is his – not mine, not the enemy's – and then respond in obedience. This is what pleases him most. This can't be done without repentance, surrender, obedience, walking in the truth, and holding steadfastly in walking in truth, in forgiveness, in love. What amazes me most is how he's healing this "cancer" he told me that's in my soul. It's still there, but it's slowly being healed. I am starting to see differences in how I walk with God and believe – knowing what is walking in faith but not operating in witchcraft, a controlling nature; staying in peace; trusting God's moving of things; and choosing not to worry about them. Again this is a form of control.

When worry creeps in, I just remember the four very directives God gave me five days before my sentencing; *trust me, believe, obey, don't be afraid!* I know who is in charge, and it's not me. I am getting closer, day by day, to where God wants me to be as he said to me when Jesus came in person on the wee hours of the morning of May 22, 2015: "I want all of you."

I'll never forget that trip to Calgary. In response and through a series of events, prayers, transformation, and repentance, I finally humbled myself on June 7, 2017 and said to Jesus, "I'm done. I give all of myself to you." This was when I was living on Glen Lake Rd in Langford.

Lord, I continue to give my whole self to you in full surrender. I choose to walk with you. You are my provider, my giver of life. I am completely dependent on you. Show me how to grow deeper in you, showing love, mercy, grace, patience, kindness, self-control, and abiding in your truth, loving your precepts, loving your ordinances, delighting in your law. Show me your ways, O Lord, and that I will not lean on my own understanding, but learning through the supernatural power of the Holy Spirit. In Jesus' name, amen.

God Is Good

God is good. God is gracious,
God is love. God is bodacious.

He gives freely. He gave his life,
To save us all from misery and strife.

He's my confidence. He's my counsel,
And without this, I'll drown myself.

Through all the noise the world will bring,
I'll tune it out, to hear him saying,

"I love you son, my daughter too,
I'll raise you up, and see you through.,

You are my joy, my delight, my pride,
I'll give you strength to stay in stride!"

This your calling, your purpose too.
Your destiny awaits. I will make you new.

March 1, 2018

Here are a couple of sayings I felt inspired by the Holy Spirit. The first one was a closing positive message from this morning's hut meeting. The second was in a thought response to what is written on our hut chalkboard:

This morning's closing positive message: Hard Work

I love this saying: *effort = results*

But also, what you put into something, you will get out of it, whether it is a job, running a business, creating a literary work, or music or art, or even fostering a relationship with family, friends, or your spouse. Hard work – it isn't easy, but it's worth it.

Now as I was walking by the blank chalkboard, I visualized all the comments written on it. The chalkboard is sometimes like a spiritual battle zone. As soon as someone writes something positive on the chalkboard, it doesn't take long for the saying to be altered to make it funny, ridicule it, or make it outright negative. Others just post negative comments below the positive one. This got me thinking:

If you feed negativity, you will breed negativity.
If you feed positivity, you will breed positivity.
Which one will you feed and breed?

Thank you, Lord Jesus, for your inspiration. Being fed your love, peace, and joy and teaching me patience, repentance, surrender – and all that through suffering – they make me grow. I now see positive in so many more things because it is not the circumstances that govern my life; it is you who does. Amen.

March 2, 2018

What Does It Take to Be A Leader?

It takes submission to be a leader – one who serves God, serves his/her fellow man/woman, leads as one who serves.

It takes surrender to be a leader – letting go of all your preconceived thoughts, turning all your resources, talents, intellect, and connections to almighty God, who will empower you by the Holy Spirit, to lead you, to guide you, to inform you of what to say.

It takes humility to be a leader – to consider others before yourself, to put others' needs before yourself, without ignoring your needs which are directly fed to you by the reading of the Word, prayer and fellowship, and by personal care.

It takes patience to be a leader – to know the right time to do things, to work with those diligently who may pose challenges to you, to make good decisions not in haste or out of compulsion, but after careful thought and counsel.

It takes confidence to be a leader – confidence in God, who will help you lead the way; confidence in the calling you have received; confidence in the purpose you've been given; confidence in the talents, abilities, and intellect you've been given; confidence in the giftings that God's given you.

It takes obedience to be a leader – to obey God's Word as it is written, to obey God's leading and direction, to obey your instincts when you know they are good and true, to obey the leading of the Holy Spirit as you hear his voice.

It takes trust to be a leader – trust in God, in his character and essence; to trust your God-given abilities and use them for good purposes; to trust others who you know can do the job with diligence and allow them to carry out their duties respectfully and with honor.

It takes courage to be a leader – to listen and move forward when God says, "Don't be afraid." He is your strength – believe in that strength.

March 4, 2018

If people attack your character and abilities, falsely accuse you of something and finger point, I mean literally finger point, forgive them. It is not a reflection of who you are or how God sees you. Again, forgive them, bless them, pray for them – that is what Jesus taught his disciples, that is what Jesus is teaching us. It is an opportunity to grow in character and also realize how Jesus suffered on earth too. His character was attacked. His abilities were attacked. He was falsely accused, and I wonder how many fingers were pointed at him.

I have noticed that strong, mature Christians handle awkward and sometimes downright nasty situations with patience, tact, and a forgiving heart. They have this part of their walk with God refined and are now in tune with the Holy Spirit. God is showing that he is refining me in this area too, not to take things personally. Don't assume anything, if you don't have all the details at hand. Forgive quickly. Let God have the controls in each situation, meaning, don't take charge of it. Remember who you are in Christ and react only to how the Holy Spirit is directing you.

Did someone hurt your feelings? Give those to God and let him help you walk through it. In each situation, each accusation, each personal attack, God can use it for his glory. Put your trust in God and in God alone. People falter. People fail. People make mistakes. Even the ones who are closest to you. Jesus uses us anyways, and we are to walk and do as Jesus did. I will. I choose to walk as Jesus did. My only prayer is that each *opportunity* for character growth comes, that I will respond in a better manner each time, flow in forgiveness without fail, and in this, see myself more and more like Jesus.

Dear Lord, thank you for the opportunity for me to become more and more like you. You suffered in your ministry. You suffered and died on the cross for us, even though you didn't have to. Show me how to live and walk like you, in suffering, in power of the Holy Spirit, in love, in mercy, in truth, in forgiveness. My sins are wiped away; they are deep in the ocean floor. My past doesn't define me. Who I was is not who I am today, which will change even again tomorrow. Help me live in you right now, for this is where you are as your name is *I Am*. Amen.

March 9, 2018

Every day, I desire to grow more and more dependent on you. It doesn't matter if anyone notices or if anyone else cares. All who cares is you. Psalm 119 is being driven into my soul – oh, how I love our precepts, your statutes, your law, for I delight in them! All I want to see is Jesus, sitting on his throne, full of glory and majesty. I worship you, oh my King, my Savior. There is none like you. You sing into my mind, and it pours down into my soul. You light my life up; you give me hope. When I am here with you, I just don't want to leave. Your presence infiltrates my whole being. You mend broken hearts, repair broken lives, and renew our minds. You lift up the downtrodden in their time of need. You bring us joy. You give us purpose. There is no one you will exclude from your kingdom who wholeheartedly and willingly come to you. No not one. You are worthy of our worship, and there is nothing that we see hasn't been created by you. There isn't anything that escapes your notice. We are valued by you. You freely forgive those who ask for it.

Show us how to do the same so that we can be like you. Disciple us, O Lord, and show us the way of truth and the path of righteousness. Teach us not to be double-minded or jump ahead of you. Show us how to be patient, to be kind, slow to anger, and quick to forgive. Show us how to love in its fullness and walk in royalty as sons and daughters of the living God. We are your children. We are your holy nation. We are your peculiar people who will show forth the praises of him, who has called us out of darkness into your marvelous light. You are the light of the world, the true vine, the resurrection and life, the bread of life, the way, the truth, and the life, the gatekeeper, the good shepherd, and all your sheep whom you protect. You are the Alpha and Omega, the First and the Last, the Beginning and the End. And finally, your name is *I Am*, and I worship you, Lord Jesus. Amen.

March 12, 2018

> *"Having material wealth doesn't make one more special*
> *in God's sight; it just makes one more privileged."*
>
> - Mike Mahy

We as believers always have the privilege of walking in God's blessings. The kingdom of heaven is always open to us. We can come to the Father through Christ at any time we want. This is our joy and our privilege. When we see from Christ's perspective of who we are in him, a mountain of abundance comes flowing down on us. Blessings, as I see it now, come in so many different forms. They are not just favor for your home life, a big bank account, and perfect health. I now see the abundance of blessings in our trials, in our afflictions, in our challenges of life. Sufferings bring forth perseverance; perseverance brings forth character; and character, hope. And hope doesn't disappoint us (see Romans 5:3-5).

These are true treasures from heaven, and God wants his children to grow strong and be mature. All too often, we in North America "rescue" those suffering from calamities, trials, and tribulations. This is God's refiner's fire that we are deliberately snuffing out so that the sufferer doesn't get hurt. We are not called to do God's job for him, but we are to come alongside someone who is suffering. If we were wise partners of God in his kingdom, we would choose to step back and ask the Lord what would be best to assist someone through a trial without interfering with God's plan for his child to grow stronger in him. We need to be careful not to make executive decisions for someone else in God's name without consulting the Almighty first, then once you've received orders from heaven, if any at all, to carry out those exactly as directed – no more, no less. There are times when God says, "Let them fall, and let me deal with them alone."

Our greatest responsibility, as well as a treasure, is trusting God's omniscience, trusting God's omnipotence, his omnipresence, and holiness. We, through trials, learn to trust God more. In the end we will love him more too. We need to learn to let go of control and let God do what God does best – be God. It's our opportunity to stop "helping" him and interfering with his plan in growing the faith of someone who is suffering, going through trials, or receiving correction!

March 16, 2018

"Who We Are"

We are chosen.
"We are a chosen generation, a royal priesthood, a holy nation, a peculiar people who will show forth the praises of Him who has called us out of darkness into His marvelous light" (1 Peter 2:9).

We are blessed.
"The Lord bless you out of Zion, and may you see the good of Jerusalem all the days of your life" (Psalm 128:5).

We will prophesy, see visions and dream dreams.
"And it shall come to pass in the last days, says God. That I will pour out my Spirit on all flesh; your sons and your daughters shall prophesy. Your young men shall see visions. Your old men shall dream dreams" (Acts 2:17 & Joel 2:28).

We are not condemned.
"There is therefore now no condemnation to those who are in Christ Jesus, who do not walk according to the flesh, but according to the Spirit" (Romans 8:1).

We have a covenant with God.
"Gather my saints together to me. Those who have made a covenant with me by sacrifice" (Psalm 50:5).

We are predestined to know him.
"For whom He foreknew, he also predestined to be conformed to the image of His Son, that he might be the firstborn among many brethren" (Romans 8:29).

We will do amazing things for God.
"But as it is written: eye has not seen, nor ear heard, nor have entered into the heart of man the things which God has prepared for those who love him" (1 Corinthians 2:9, Isaiah 64:4).

We will not be forgotten.
"They shall ask the way to Zion, with their faces toward it, saying, 'Come let us join ourselves to the Lord in a perpetual covenant that will not be forgotten'" (Jeremiah 50:5).

We have received mercy.
"The voice of joy and the voice of gladness, the voice of the bridegroom and the voice of the bride, the voice of those who will say: 'Praise the Lord of Hosts, for the Lord is good, for his mercy endures forever.' – and of those who will bring the sacrifice of praise into the House of the Lord. For I will cause the captives of the land to return as at the first, says the Lord" (Jeremiah 33:11).

March 17, 2018

When your core beliefs finally line up with your biblical values. When the head knowledge finally sinks down into your heart, then you will know and understand the love and truth of God, and from that you will be at complete peace with God and yourself.

- Mike Mahy

March 18, 2018

What Is There to Fear?

"I have overcome the world," Jesus said. When we choose to believe in who he is, we then should fully believe what he has said. We should hang on every word that was recorded in the gospels, book of Acts, and Revelation. There is no name under heaven given of which every knee shall bow and every tongue confess that Jesus Christ is Lord – maker of heaven and earth. He is the Alpha and the Omega, the First and the Last, the Beginning and the End. There is no equal.

He is the sinless Lamb of God, who gave his life for ours, so that we can come into right relationship with him. We who believed and received Jesus as our personal Lord and Savior, God the Father through Jesus Christ call us his children. We are adopted sons and daughters of God. We have a personal, loving, intimate, powerful, restorative, healing relationship with the Creator of the universe. And nothing can stop him from loving us this way. When we choose to fully immerse ourselves into this love, this healing power, fully yielding in complete surrender to the person of the Holy Spirit, you will experience no equal in terms of peace, joy, wholeness, kindness, and love. It will knock you onto your back. It will drop you like a fly, and you will love it.

Being "slain in the Spirit" is a privilege. You won't be afraid. You will want to thirst for more. But you must give everything up in our lives for this. It's free to receive, but it will cost you everything. You must let go of your sins. You must let go of your sinful lifestyle. You must let go of your sinful thinking. You must give over your possessions, thoughts, talents, relationships, and abilities to him. You then become a steward of them – a custodian, a caretaker. When you can accept this price, you will come into such a deep and amazing relationship with the God of heaven and Earth. You will discover the fullness of who you are in him – one who is so deeply loved and valued by God. You will learn to walk in the fullness of your purpose and destiny. In this, your joy will be complete. You will not be afraid. "If God is for us, who can be against us" (Romans 8:31b)?

Your calling will be unstoppable. The anointing of the Holy Spirit will flow in you and through you. You will possess power to forgive, love, teach, admonish, correct, walk in truth, stay in truth, and never let go of the one who has redeemed you. Amen.

March 21, 2018

Now faith is to be sure of what we hope for and certain of what we do not see (Hebrews 11:1 NIV84). When we grow to know Christ personally, we get to know the person of Christ. He reveals himself through the person of the Holy Spirit. You will learn to hear his voice and respond to it. Christian prophets and prophetesses know this and walk in it; but it is available to all of us who are willing to listen, learn, yield, and grow. To maximize this unique relationship, we choose to live the following way: completely surrender your life to Christ and give everything you have – talents, abilities, time, relationships, possessions – to him; live and walk in humility; walk a blameless and holy life; choose mercy over sacrifice; love your enemies and pray for them; dedicate time exclusively to Christ in prayer, meditation, and the reading of the Word; walk in truth; walk in forgiveness; allow yourself to feel and be loved by God; learn to love yourself as well as your neighbor; know that you walk in the freedom of Christ and know you are not condemned by God; and all this wrapped up in receiving Christ as your personal Lord and Savior, knowing he died for our sins and rose again the third day.

In this walk, we bask in the anointing of the Holy Spirit, and we learn what it is to seek his kingdom first. You will want to put Jesus on the throne of everything in your life, and it will become a joy to do so. You will learn to hear God's still, small voice, even from the noise of a hurricane. You will learn to not be afraid, for you will trust God's omnipotence. You will learn to trust God's judgment better than your own, for you will trust God's omniscience. You will feel so loved, for you will learn to be in God's omnipresence. You will learn to walk, think, act, and talk in holiness, for you will learn to see God's holiness. This is the essence and attributes of God, and he pours out his presence liberally on those who love him and choose to walk in his ways. We become like Christ and emulate everything he did. This is our privilege to bask in the abundance of the kingdom. You will know your purpose, and you will let Christ guide your destiny. You will have unspeakable joy despite trials, tribulations, and suffering. Then we will understand the price he paid for us. Amen.

March 26, 2018

I'm not looking for a solution, I just want to be heard

How often do we *vent* only just wanting to be heard? Not trying to provide a solution, give a pat answer, a word of wisdom, or a tidbit of insight, just to be heard, and acknowledgment of being heard would be icing on the cake. So often we just need to vent, get something off our chest, something off of our mind. Quite often we hear but don't listen, watching someone's mouth move but not perceiving what is coming out of them. Nowadays when someone comes to me and starts venting, when an appropriate time comes along I ask, "Are you looking for a solution or just want to be heard?" Quite often, I get thanked for asking, so the conversation becomes far more fluid and engaging, even though I know it will be mostly a one-sided conversation. We just need to learn to be sensitive to other's needs, and in developing good communication skills listening, empathizing, and responding appropriately fosters good will, better relationships, and trust.

Conversely, we need to take time to stop and listen to God. Listen to what he has to say about us, the direction he wants to lead us, and sometimes he just wants to be heard. Our response to just hearing him? Worship. Adoration. Surrender. Love. And being loved right back infinitely. When we hear his still, small voice, we come into alignment with the King and Creator of the universe. We will know joy. We will receive healing for our wounded souls. We will become transformed. Our minds will be clean and new.

It takes time to be still and know that he is God. Practice it every day. Read and meditate on his Word. Stop and spend intimate time with God. Take time out from your hectic schedule, crazy responsibilities, and set your priorities straight by putting God before everything else in your life – family, health, spouse, children, career, calling, leisure, responsibilities. Put Jesus on the throne first before everything; and seek his kingdom first (Matthew 6:33). Then you will have strength through the Holy Spirit to make it through each day.

March 27, 2018

I really enjoyed last night's Bible study. The two Scripture passages that stood out to me were Matthew 6:1-4 and Matthew 6:5-8. The first one talked about doing your *charitable acts* in secret, so that only God knows what you are doing. The second one talks about praying in your prayer closet and again where only God sees what and how you are praying. For if you do either of these publicly, you have received your reward. What I have learned about God and the kingdom of God is that it's nothing like any kingdom on earth. The living and thinking in the kingdom of heaven is upside-down from the living and thinking on earth. Put others before yourself. Pray for your enemies. If your enemy is hungry, feed him/her. Love those who don't love you. Give until it hurts, and after it hurts so bad, keep giving anyways. Help those who can never repay you. If you loan money to someone, treat it as a gift to be given away never expecting it back.

These are the thoughts, actions, and attitudes of the kingdom. Jesus did. He fed four thousand and five thousand. He healed ten lepers, and only one came back to thank him and praise God. He healed the sick, made the blind see, the deaf hear, and raised the dead. The world still persecuted him, jeered him, hated him, and eventually killed him. He still acted kindly back, forgivingly, even when he was on the cross, "Father, forgive them, for they know not what they do" (Luke 23:34a).

When we grow to know Jesus, we will know how much he loves us, and in receiving and accepting this love, learn to grow and love ourselves in him and then love others the same as a result. We will grow into a spiritual maturity never thought possible. We will become Christ-like, full imitators of Christ, wanting nothing else but Jesus and walking in the abundance of the principles of the kingdom, being heirs of God and co-heirs of Christ, knowing God and being known by him intimately. That is what our hearts truly yearn for – the infiltration of the love of God in our souls, soaking forever in the Holy Spirit, and knowing that no matter what happens in this world – triumphs and trials, victories and tribulations, tests and temptations – all these will help us grow in character and spirit, maturing us and leading us to grow closer to him who knows us intimately. Amen.

April 2, 2018

> *For they all saw him and were troubled. But immediately he talked with*
> *them and said to them, "Be of good cheer! It is I, do not be afraid."*
> — Mark 6:50 (NKJV)

I can't even imagine how the disciples felt when they saw Jesus walking on the water. Peter, at least, had enough courage to step out and walk on the water with him. There are times in our lives when God asks us to have the courage to "walk on water." For me, this means to have the courage to be obedient in telling my story about my past, my sickness, and what God is doing with me to bring about healing and restoration. Some things in our lives just don't get healed instantly, but there are times when God isolates you, puts you through a refiner's fire, molds you more into his image, so that he is even more pleased with you and desires you to carry out your purpose and destiny that he has designed you for.

On June 7, 2017 I said to Jesus, "I'm done. I now completely surrender to you."

Today, I still choose that route voluntarily. I now choose to obey whatever he asks of me, whether I like it or not. Yesterday, I was a little mad at God for having me write down on paper the exact nature of my wrongs (step 5 of 12 steps). When I realized what the Lord was leading me to write, fear entered my heart. I guess this fear would be like when Peter saw the waves while walking on the water with Jesus and took his eyes off of him and started sinking. This fear I had caused me to take my eyes off Jesus, and I started worrying about the judgment, the criticism I would receive from those who hear the message. So today, I guess Jesus has caught me from sinking in fear and has put me back into the boat. One of his directives he gave me before I was sentenced was, "Don't be afraid." This means I trust that he knows exactly what he is doing and he has the power to back it up. I mean, he walked on water; he calmed the storm; he took my sin; he defeated Satan.

Fear comes from the evil one, and my good buddy reminded me yesterday when we went for a walk and I confided in him about my anger with God to not let the enemy in but pray and make him go away. With that said, I say to the Lord, "Thank you for your patience. I praise your name. I trust your decision. Thank you for allowing me to process this, and if my anger was in sin, I repent." And now I say to Satan, "You have no authority," and as my friend has said, "in the name of Jesus I command you to the back of the bus. You don't have the wheel." And now I say, "Jesus, take the wheel." I am still yours in complete surrender.

April 3, 2018

Read Jonah Chapter 1

When you choose to follow Jesus wholeheartedly there is no turning back.

Jonah ran from God, and God steered him back. The disciples deserted Jesus and every one of them was steered back (except Judas). I better take note. However, in these cases, Jonah was used to steer a whole city to repentance, and the city of Nineveh was now recognized as one who would rise up on judgment day and judge, rather than being judged, all because of one man's obedience. It doesn't matter that he was angry with God the whole time and even had a pity party about it later. The disciples were steered back together, and on the day of Pentecost, their lives changed forever, and so did the world's. Starting with these eleven originals, plus a few hundred more, the world today has more than one billion believers to Christ.

If God ever calls you to do something, even if it is unpopular, causes you to be judged, makes you part of the "fringe" of society, and the world looks at you as eccentric, a loser, an outcast, or just plain weird, remember this: you do it for Jesus and the kingdom of God first (see Matthew 6:33). If the treasure in your heart is to fit in with society; seek after being accepted first; chase after money, possessions, fame, relationships, recognition, position, or power; these things will distract you. No, it will lead you away from God's purpose for your life. If the treasure in your heart is to seek the kingdom first, put Jesus on the throne of your life first, choose to give your life completely over to him first – then you will discover the true treasures of life in abundance – treasures of joy, peace, kindness, holiness, self-control, power in the Holy Spirit, visions, revelations, love, moving in the gift of the Spirit, knowing what you are called to, walking obediently, and discovering your purpose in life.

As you show the Lord your trustworthiness in small things, he will entrust you with more. Just know his voice and know to trust him, even if what he is asking you to do is hard, uncertain, awkward, or unusual. He will make you not be afraid to do what he asks because your *marching orders* come from heaven, not man. As God grows you, transforms you, renews you, and sets you apart for his service, he will always give you the tools you need to carry out the assignments he has called you to do. Some tools are spiritual like faith, and some will be physical, like money or provision. No matter, God will provide and provide abundantly to see to it that his kingdom moves forward, and there is no stopping it. Amen.

April 4, 2018

God is merciful. I will praise him for his mercies. He does not punish his children as they should deserve, even though he rebukes and corrects them. He lavishes his love on us; his tender mercies flow in us. He is patient, slow to anger, quick to forgive, bestowing favor in his tender mercy. I will praise him for his mercies. I cannot stop praising him for his tender mercies. He is glorious; he is majestic, bestowing love, honor, and favor to a thousand generations to those who love him and walk in his ways. He is my deliverer, my rock, my salvation. In him will I put my trust. I will lift his name on high and worship him who was slain for our sin. I confess my sins to my almighty God and repent. I choose to think as you think, so by your Holy Spirit teach me how to think. I want to act the way you act, so heal my soul so I can act like you. I want to worship you with a deep worship, always remembering what you have done for me.

You are healing my heart; it feels cleaner every day. You are renewing my mind, always looking and thinking to find ways to bless your name – your great and mighty name! Teach me, O Lord, in your ways of holiness and righteousness. Teach me to overcome the world as you have overcome the world. Thank you for resting your anointing on me. I surrender and yield this day to you that you be magnified in my thoughts, deeds, and actions. Bring glory to your name, Lord Jesus. Amen.

MY STORY

February 17, 2018

Entry: (names in black are the real names and used by permission)

Tears Heal

I am sitting here praying for specific people in our camp. As I started praying for Eric, I started tearing up, because last night, as a support group leader-in-training, I had to support another group leader's decision to not let Eric chair one of the twelve-step groups here in our camp. The Lord gave me the strength to yield to Eric's vulnerability of the moment because he just started tearing up. Eric so desperately wants to show people (and God too) in the camp that he is a changed man, and this leadership position would be a tangible way of proving himself that he was changed. The thing is that, at this moment, he had some obstacles to face before this responsibility could be entrusted to him. The Lord also gave me the wisdom to articulate to Eric where those obstacles are and would he be interested in someone coming alongside him to help him through it. He thought about it for a few seconds and said, "Yes that would help."

The Lord then reminded me to remind Eric that he is a leader, but he wants to heal the pain, sorrow, hurt, and sin in his heart first so he can be the leader that God has designed him to be. When Eric teared up, I just hugged him and held him long enough to let him know he is dearly loved, and with God's supernatural help he will get to the destination he has been called to – just that the road to recovery is going to be rough.

Here at Ford Mountain we have people who are broken, and some very broken, who need Christ's love so desperately. We are called to bear one another's burdens, just as Christ has bore ours. Bible study, twelve-step groups, and yes, sometimes even our church services can be gong shows at times, with the level of immaturity running at high levels at times. The Lord has shown me to set the bar real low for the participants, showing great patience and grace to those who behave less than respectful. There is a line drawn, of course, when people's or the group's boundaries are crossed. Name calling, demeaning, divisiveness, taking over the study, and hijacking by talking too long – those things are held in check. But as Christians, especially us mature Christians, we need to lead, teach, and guide those who are genuinely interested in the Bible a chance to hear God's message and let God do his part; otherwise, we will just chase them away. "A smoldering wick he will not snuff out, a bruised weed he will not break" (Isaiah 42:3). We need to be like Jesus so we can co-partner with him to help build his church.

Lord, show us your way and not our preconceived ideas when it comes to sharing your Word to those who don't know you. Speak to their hearts, so much so, that their tears lead to repentance and salvation. Amen.

February 19, 2018

A few days ago, I was confronted yet again of bitter, resentful feelings toward my mom, stemming back decades. Growing up, I was a very needy child, I didn't have the best social skills. Actually I was a social misfit, a compulsive liar, because when I behaved badly I was petrified to get punished for what I did wrong, so I habitually lied, which only made things worse. You think I would eventually learn to tell the truth, but I never learned that lesson. I rarely told the truth growing up. I would exaggerate stories too, just so I would get noticed. I kept doing this right into adulthood. I also kept my deep, dark secrets about my sexual identity and sexual deviancy from everyone, including my partner, again being petrified of being found out just like I did in my childhood. The part that bothered me is that the very person I should have been able to come to but could never trust was my mom. My fear of her constant judgment of me, her venomous comments, her constantly calling me a liar, our toxic relationship – it has caused me to be never open to her, and this has spilled into my other relationships, including my marriage. My mom rarely ever affirmed me, and when she did it was short-lived. All you ever want to hear from your parents is, "Well done. We're proud of you." But what if that never comes? This is what I am doing about it:

1) My parents are fallible, not perfect just as I am. I choose to forgive them for their shortfalls, their actions *and* inactions (such as lack of support). For me, forgiveness for both my mom and my dad is a continuous process, as I discover new situations that stir up angry, bitter, resentful feelings toward them. Depending on the situation one is in, forgiveness may be a one-time shot or it could be a continuous process;

2) God is the lover of my soul, and the one who truly wants to say, "Well done." God's perfect love should have been the prize I should have pursued. You can personally feel and experience God's love, God's peace and although intimate human relationships are important for our overall well-being, a personal, intimate relationship with

Jesus is what will truly give us security, true well-being, and hope for our lives;

3) I choose to let go of the past, for with it comes a jail sentence. I am letting go of the future, with its unknown path yet to be written. I choose to be in the present, where God is; for his name is *I Am*.

February 25, 2018

I was reading John chapter 4 here in my worship and meditation time when the thought crossed my mind – something more needs to be done about sex addiction. I am convinced that it is the Holy Spirit prompting me to write this down. Sex addiction is a destructive sin. From it people become adulterers, fornicators, pedophiles, porn addicts, and/or nymphomaniacs. They focus on the lusts of sexual pleasure and sexual release and all too often get caught up in their own fantasy world where reality just doesn't exist. Some end up becoming sex offenders and break the law. We see on TV and the Internet that this is becoming an epidemic. Teachers, police, politicians, famous people – the list goes on – are being exposed for their crimes involving sexual sin. I am one of those people.

Is there hope for us? Yes there is.

Is there hope for the victims of sexual crimes? Again, yes there is.

For those who have committed the crimes need to make a choice – a choice to confess what they've done, repent of what they've done, and seek ways to remedy their sinful behavior. One can start by joining a support group that specifically addresses and helps such addictions. One may need to get counseling. One may even have to turn themselves in. By hiding sexual sin, denying it is there, and lying to yourself, your loved ones and others that don't have this problem will only allow the problem to fester and possibly grow until you can't manage it anymore. This addictive behavior affects you mentally, psychologically, spiritually, and physically. It not only affects you, but it affects people around you. When you see your life sexually starting to unravel and spin out of control, humble yourself and get help. I did, albeit late, and it is transforming my life. Support with and from others who struggle like you will, and can, become your best resource and catalyst for recovery so you can live a life of balance and regain a healthy sex life instead of one that is mutated. God can help you with this, and he is the key to your recovery. Just ask the thousands of people who are well on their way to recovery who know this important part and are practicing their spiritual renewal with God. We can't do this by ourselves. Give God a chance and he'll do wonders with your life.

For those who have been victimized by the sexual addiction of another, I pray you find it in your heart to forgive us what we've done, for the power of forgiveness sets you free, not the victimizer. God can supernaturally help you too. Remember, forgiveness does not equal trust; they are not the same. You can forgive someone and still not trust them. That is understandable.

As reconciliation in a broken-down relationship is always a possibility, it isn't always reality. I know I have altered the lives of those I have committed sexual sin against, and I am deeply sorry for what I've done. Their lives may never be the same again. I do pray that if they choose to forgive me, that their lives will go into the process of healing, and with that they, with God's help, be slowly restored to where they were originally intended to be in their lives, their purpose and destiny. That, in reality, is the best I can ask for, and leave the rest in God's hands.

To my ex-partner, her family and my family, I ask for your forgiveness too. I have caused embarrassment, anger, rage, and disgust as a result of my choices; and this has led you to not talking to me. I am deeply sorry for how my choices have affected your lives. I don't know of any other way at this time how to express my remorse for what I've done.

To my friends, especially those who have stood by my side during this dark period of my life, I ask for your forgiveness. I have been less than a friend to you by hiding this dark side of me from you. But then again, I hid it from everyone. I am deeply sorry that your association with me has embarrassed you and angered you.

To my church family, I am deeply sorry for my poor Christian witness. I should have sought help when those opportunities presented themselves, but I didn't. I was too prideful and too arrogant to notice I needed help. Pride, arrogance, fear of being found out, shame and guilt – all these stopped me from admitting that I needed help. I humbly ask for your forgiveness.

I have, by my poor choices, affected so many people – former clients, colleagues, acquaintances, business contacts, and the list goes on. I am on the path of correction, and I thank God for this. I can now move forward, day by day, knowing I am getting the help I need. Whoever is reading this, I hope that you get the help you need too – whether you are the victim, or the victimizer.

February 28, 2018

I am working on a section of my life that is drudging up a lot of feelings of despair, confusion, anger, and resentment. I am looking at the history and the general subject of sexuality with a couple of close friends and the chaplain here at Ford Mountain.

Growing up, I knew very little about sexuality because I don't remember my parents teaching me the subject; very little was taught in school too, and although I had sexual desires that I didn't understand starting around age eleven, I just wasn't interested in engaging sexually, at least, not out in the open. I remember looking at my classmates when we would have to go to the showers after gym class and it would arouse me, but I had no one to talk about it. I just didn't feel safe to talk to anyone about my sexuality, or my sexual preference. I wasn't even a Christian growing up (I didn't come to Christ until I was twenty-three). In fact, there was a period in my mid-teens to my early twenties where I didn't believe in God at all, yet deep down inside I felt there was something wrong with who I was attracted to. I just decided to bury my feelings, hide them from everyone, and trust no one, if the subject ever came up. Only when people I knew during my teen years and early twenties would I sneak off and "get it on" with them, never fostering any attachment to them emotionally. I only did it because I loved the sexual act, not them. I saw them as my means of release and temporary affection. Once I was finished with my sexual release, I felt better and had no attraction to them. But there were times as I got older that I started stepping "out of bounds," wanting deep down to recapture my youth as it were and started touching young boys for this release of affection. This is warped and comes from a depraved mind. This is what has put me in jail, deservedly.

Now I need to learn to accept where my sexual preference is currently – be abstinent because I love God so much that I will honor him with his Word, honor my body as part of that love for his Word, get supernatural help from the Holy Spirit to keep me pure, and work through the pain, brokenness, sin, and wounds with God as he heals my soul and restores my life. I believe in miraculous healings, and this is one area I desire a healing, but if God says no, then I will humbly walk in his grace a walk holy through abstinence as long as I am living to serve him and serve him only. I just want the pain in my heart gone.

God, heal my broken heart. This is all I really want, in Jesus' name I pray, amen.

March 3, 2018

> *"Most assuredly, I say to you, he who does not enter the sheepfold by the door, but climbs up some other way, the same is a thief and a robber. But he who enters by the door is the shepherd of the sheep. To him the doorkeeper opens, and the sheep hear his voice; and he calls his own sheep by name and leads them out. And when he brings out his own sheep, he goes before them; and the sheep follow him, for they know his voice. Yet they will by no means follow a stranger, but will flee from him, for they do not know the voice of strangers."*
>
> *- John 10:1-5 (NKJV)*

I am so excited about my divine appointments here in Ford Mountain. There have been so many. But the Lord is directing me, as we speak, not to write any specifics down so I will be obedient to his leading.

God is moving here. I am seeing changes in people whom I have been in direct contact with. Many are afraid of their changes, and their actions and attitudes are reflected in that. On the other hand, others like myself are embracing the changes, and their actions and attitudes reflect that. Hence, their growth and mine are steering in the right direction.

I am still struggling with my sexual identity, but I am growing to accept it. I will be honest; I don't like this sexual confusion. However, I choose not to sin by engaging in homosexual acts, desires, or thoughts. My heart's desire is always leaning to want to please the Lord, and I know he is pleased with me because as I am writing this I have his peace, his joy, his love. My thoughts being written are flowing from pen to paper – my personal sign of God's hand flowing in me and through me. I am growing in being loved and accepted by God, and he has asked me to share my story about my sexual life. Somehow, some way, he wants to use my story for his glory.

When he spoke to me about this in February 2017, I was petrified. He created a series of events where my fear of sharing this story went to, "Now I have nothing to lose in sharing it." So today, I choose to share, but to share in humility, share in repentance, share in surrender, and share with no fear. Fear is the enemy's tool, not God's. I am not interested in going into the enemy's lair unless God directs me to do so. And if he does, I know I will go into dark places in confidence because he is right there with me.

Just like Daniel, just like Moses, just like David, just like Jeremiah, just like Paul, and just like Peter – they had no fear of standing up to kings, warriors, governors, or their own countrymen because they knew in their hearts who God was, and is. They were convinced beyond measure that God would give them the strength, spirit, and courage to carry out the assignments they were entrusted. They were loved and hated, respected and disrespected, honored and dishonored, held in high esteem and despised beyond measure. This is the road to God's glory, for we know this life is temporary, and what we do for God here will be measured in heaven when we finally meet him face-to-face.

How will you carry out your walk? In fear? In hiding? In shame? Or with no fear? With confidence? Trusting God in every move he leads you?

March 8, 2018

Transformation – that is what the Lord is bringing here in my life. This morning, I asked the Lord to help keep me humble while things are going well so that I can have Jesus always as my only treasure in my life. The Lord then reminded me that he will provide those situations in my life to keep me from being conceited. My heart's desire is to be mature and grow confidently in the Lord. He keeps reminding me of his four directives he spoke to me in person five days before my sentencing – *trust me, believe, obey,* and *don't be afraid*. Staying centered on Christ keeps me balanced, helps me be focused, gives me a solid direction, and gives me a hope and a dream. I am changing a little bit more every day. I am slower in my decision-making process to allow for the Holy Spirit guide me and direct me. I am slowly learning to let things flow, although sometimes I still force issues.

God, show me more of your perfect timing and perfect patience. I am learning to do nothing or take no action when seeking for a certain direction on something, and in turn, nothing is shown to me. This takes a lot of practice, a lot of patience, a good amount of faith, and a high amount of trust in God's leading.

I was noticing this morning that I was in danger of taking over control of the responsibilities I have been entrusted here. So in response to that realization, I gladly, in my heart, relinquished control so that the flow of the Holy Spirit is a maximum in my life, and in relinquishing control, I am bringing glory to his great name.

Thank you, Lord, for bringing me reminders, as you speak to me internally and also show externally through circumstance the value of being in continual surrender to you. Help me keep a holy, contrite, and humble spirit so that my thoughts, attitudes, and actions reflect your character and being. Help me be more like you every day. And as I started this writing I will end it the same way. Thank you for your transforming power. In Jesus' name I pray, amen.

March 20, 2018

I can't live in the past, but when I look at the harm I've caused as a result of the sexual abuse I have caused others, it still haunts me. It is a reminder never to go down that path ever again and to run away if temptation ever presents itself. I have caused harm to innocent victims; their lives will never be the same. I hope and pray that one day they will forgive me for what I have done to them, but the act of forgiveness is not for my sake but for their own. The act of forgiveness to release their own hearts from bondage; from anger; from bitterness; from confusion; from rage; from depression; from reclusiveness; from isolation; from hatred; from sadness; from distrust of others; and from vices of co-dependency, alcohol, sex, drugs, over-eating, gambling, or any other addiction that has trapped them. That through forgiveness they may learn to love again, especially in themselves, believe in their God-given abilities, trust those who are worthy of being trusted, to believe in God in a way never thought possible.

I pray in the process of forgiveness, there is a complete healing of their mind, will, and emotions (their soul), that they be made whole again, that their lives will be completely restored. I pray that the very things they have been robbed of will be handed back to them, that their future will not be bleak but bright – brighter than ever before. I pray that they can put their faith back in humanity and in God.

Forgiveness restores those things. I may never see the victims I have caused harm ever again, and I certainly don't expect them to trust me either. But, if an opportunity comes forth to express how sorry I am for robbing their innocence, their faith, their trust, their very lives, I will do so with humility and a contrite heart, without expecting anything back in return. I leave this in the hands of the living God, maker of heaven and earth. So this is my confession and my prayer. I am sorry for what I've done and repent. I now turn away from that life, that thinking, the sin altogether. Only time will show how sorry I really am. Thank you, Jesus, for giving me strength and courage to put this confession, repentance, and prayer to paper. Amen.

March 23, 2018

It's important to be on our guard, especially when fatigue sets in. Yesterday, I was so tired. My thoughts were going everywhere, so I just chose to lay down and nap in between shifts in the kitchen. But even after work, I felt so mentally drained, emotionally spent, and physically tired that I laid down and passed out, oblivious to everything going around the hut. I knew it was the best defense – to rest. And that I did. I still had a good night's sleep, and today, I felt safe to open up to God confidently, confess my sin, open my heart, surrender my day, and let him be King in my life. Although that is always my desire, yesterday, I didn't feel that. Feelings don't always mean they are my choices. I just felt that yesterday my heart felt a little hard too, kind of like when one "circles the wagons." I wanted to not give the enemy any room to tempt me yesterday – to anger, to judgment, to sexual sin – so hiding was my best option. God was right there with me, protecting me in my vulnerability. Thank you, Jesus, for guarding me, guarding my heart, guarding my mind, guarding my actions.

Today, I feel blessed; today, I feel confident; today, I feel loved. It's good to be back. I need to be careful to not try and do too much. I want to stay in God's presence, and feel that presence always. It's worth more than the finest gold, the purest silver, the best rubies. I love God's treasure chest – a chest full of love, grace, mercy, and truth. They're the best treasures anyone can get. Nothing compares to those treasures. Treasures of the world make you happy for a little while, but then you get bored of them, and next thing you know, you want something else. Not so with the treasures from heaven. You keep going back to the same treasures time after time, and you can never get enough of it. When you seek God's treasures, you will find them. God flings open the doors so wide they just flood through your soul. And all you have to do is ask with a humble and contrite heart, full of child-like expectation that Daddy (Abba) is going to do, something extra special for you. And he does! He lays on the extra special so thick you don't have room enough for it.

Lay it on thick for me Daddy! Lay it on thick! I want your best in abundance because you love me! I love you back Daddy! Not for what you've done, but for who you are through your glorious Son, Jesus Christ, our Lord and Savior in whom we worship and adore. Amen.

March 24, 2018

Note: (names in bold are changed to protect the identities of the individuals)

> *"I acknowledge that I have been part of the problem.*
> *I take full responsibility for that.*
> *Help me, Lord, be part of the solution."*
>
> *- Mike Mahy*

I was really encouraged by yesterday's events. It started by getting the rest I needed, so I could focus on surrendering my life to God, surrendering the day.

It's amazing when one chooses to "dial back" activities just to rest, so then in the end, you will be able to do more for Jesus. God is bringing the word *rest* to me in a way I've never discovered. I am a doer; we live in a society of doers, so much so that our worship to God, our intimate prayer time, reading of the Word, physical rest, emotional rest and mental rest suffer.

Because I chose to rest, I could help my buddy and brother in Christ with his homework. I had the energy to keep a promise to an inmate in my hut to go with him to a meeting I would otherwise not attend, and God honored that. In that meeting's end, I was led by the Holy Spirit to invite yet another inmate to Bible study, which was right after. He came! He is looking, no searching for a definition of who God is, and because I obeyed in rest, I was able to hear God's leading properly. The antenna was up, and I heard a clear signal. My brother in Christ **Gerald Foster** gave me a word one day prophetically that I will never forget. He said, "Mike, God is giving me a word for you; less is more."

I have yielded to that prophetic utterance ever since – less talking, more listening; less action taken on my own accord and my own strength and allow more of God moving on my behalf by stepping out of his way; less "helping" God by guessing what he wants me to do or say and more of trusting his omniscience and omnipotence; less talking and more praying; less "just me" time and more time spent in fellowship with him. Because I have chosen to yield to this, it has become a key part of my transformation into walking in the likeness of Christ. It has shown me to learn patience, to listen intently, to hear others more clearly, and have less of an agenda that is my own. It has brought me into walking in a greater measure of obedience to Christ. Less is more.

Thank you, Jesus, for showing me your way. Thank you for showing me your power as I choose to yield to you. Thank you for your glorious presence. You are my hope. You love me. And because I am choosing to yield, to slow down, I now feel loved. I feel less compelled to do things for your name, thinking that doing is what pleases you. You have broken this – a people-pleasing spirit – and broken my thinking that works alone justifies my salvation. It doesn't. Faith without works is dead, but I am justified by faith and not by works. I learnt this because I chose to rest when I needed to. Amen.

March 25, 2018

Note: (names in black are the real names and used by permission)

I discovered yesterday morning that I am very good at burying my anger, and I have found it amazing how God is getting me to take a course on anger management without actually signing up for it. I have been helping my friend Milton with his course because he is Guatemalan and needs a little bit of help with his English in the anger management course. So here I was describing terminology and helping him along in this course, but little did I know God was using it to teach me too! Next thing I knew, anger was rising up in my heart over unresolved issues I had been hanging on to for months. These anger issues stem from feeling abandoned, and the abandonment issue goes back decades to my adoption.

I was adopted at ten days old, so of course, I didn't remember being adopted. But I have found out that through medical science that separation anxiety can be experienced by an infant through pregnancy. My biological mother gave me up, which is considered by many a great sacrifice (and I am grateful too because I am alive), but I didn't know how she felt about me during her pregnancy with me, and I didn't know how I was nurtured between the time I was born to the time I was in my adopted mom's arms. All my adopted mom told me is that when I was brought home, I did nothing but scream, not cry, but scream for days. She also said there was a time before my first birthday that I was screaming again. She tried to pick me up and hold me and all I did was push her away. So I don't know in my emotional development if it has been compromised or not, but the evidence seems to lean toward compromise.

Am I angry about this? I don't know.

I'm a sixties baby, a time where drug experimentation was popular, especially in the universities. My biological mother fits in that age category. I have a copy of my adoption papers, so I know my biological mom's name, her date of birth and where she lived at the time. I even know my biological name.

What I don't know is, did she love me? Did she care for herself during her pregnancy? Did she hold me once I was born? Is my emotional capacity compromised because of the failure to act responsibly to any of these? If she failed to act, I must forgive her. What I do know is through the process, of which God will guide me, it will bring me to wholeness. This can either be instant or a process. I will let God choose for he knows what's best for me. All I know is that in this grace and mercy, in his infinite wisdom, in his awesome power, he will make me whole. He will help me deal with my buried anger, and he will show me where and how I need to forgive and just let go. He is the one I trust. Amen.

March 28, 2018

This is a hospital, not a jail. Well, at least, it doesn't feel like a jail. God has deliberately put my life on the outside on hold so that he could expedite my inner healing, my mind being re-programmed, my soul being lifted up, my self-esteem being raised, my faith in Jesus growing in leaps and bounds. I need education, counseling, mentorship, empowerment, and affirmation to help me get through this dark period of my life; and this is exactly what I received here at Ford Mountain. I've said this before and I will say it again: five days before my sentencing, the Lord spoke to me directly. He said, "Trust me." And so I shall, like a small child trusting his papa and mama. I've never experienced childlike faith before now. I have always expressed myself to God, "I love you, but this is a close as you get." And then I would visualize myself straight-arming out Jesus, so he wouldn't get any closer to my broken heart. I am beginning to wonder how I had any faith at all, but God knows the end from the beginning.

All I remember as a baby Christian was God coming to me one day in my apartment in Sidney while sitting at my kitchen table and saying to me, "My covenant is with you!" It was an exclamatory proclamation. I could feel his excitement about declaring that to me, I have never forgotten that feeling of excitement he had for me. That was 1990. I didn't quite know what a covenant relationship was at the time but I did understand when he spoke to me it was something very special, very deep, and very personal.

Today, all I want to do is have Jesus on the throne of my life, and this would have never come to fruition had he not allowed me to get arrested, convicted, sentenced, and then eventually sent here to Ford Mountain. What a journey; and it's only the beginning. I am looking forward to serving Christ in the capacity he's called me while I am still in here and when I get released back into the community. All I know now, and all I want to know is that I am his, and I choose to serve him only all the rest of the days of my life while I'm alive. He is, again, on the throne of my life, and I choose to fully surrender to his will. Amen.

March 31, 2018

> *Everyone who is of the truth hears my voice.*
>
> - John 18:37

It is interesting to live for and hear God's still, small voice. The reason for that is because there have been times when hearing his voice, he leads you to the most unexpected places. He will have us associate or communicate with the most unexpected people, and asks you to perform some of the most unexpected tasks. I am going to use a simple example. This weekend there is a racquetball tournament. I asked my most obvious choices for partners to play (as they are my regular playing partners since last November when I got here), and they both declined to play; so I thought that I would choose not to play in the tournament either. A day or two later, the Holy Spirit spoke to my heart and led me to ask another hut-mate to be my playing partner instead. I was like, "Umm, okay. Whatever you want, Lord, is what I want." So I asked him.

He is a year older than me and isn't a bad racquetball player; in fact, he is pretty good and would only be better if he practiced. The reason I wouldn't have chosen him of my own accord is because of the type of person he is. He's loud, sometimes obnoxious, speaks out of turn, has a know-it-all kind of demeanor, and my hut-mates sometimes go after him because of his lack of consideration for others. Every time I invite him anywhere (twelve-step, Bible study, racquetball, etc.), he just "gloms" on to me, as if I was his long-lost best friend. One would rate his social skills as below average. Yet God asked me to have him as my playing partner. He's a recent convert to Christ, and he's a very broken man. That's who Jesus associated with, and because I have chosen to surrender my life to him, he's asking me to do exactly the same, and so I shall. He's only asking me to associate with him; therefore, I need to listen to his voice so that Jesus can speak to him so he can be healed, reborn, restored. That's God's job, not mine. But he will ask me to do uncomfortable things, humbling things, and wherever that leads me, whoever he draws me to, I must listen. I know in the future I will have privilege beyond measure, but I also know God will cause me to not stop associating with those as Jesus did when he was on earth. The King of kings and Lord of lords associated with the sick, the outcasts, the "fringe" of society. If that is what he asks me to do, I shall obey, just as Jesus did. I am grateful for the privilege. Amen.

April 1, 2018

> *Jesus said to him, "Thomas, because you have seen me, you have*
> *believed. Blessed are those who have not seen yet have believed."*
> - John 20:29 – (NKJV)

It takes faith to change. You have to believe that change is possible. When you come to this place of faith, you witness the power of spiritual experience. I am a born-again Christian, a believer in Christ. I have a personal, intimate, loving relationship with him. I don't have to "earn" favor with him by my religious acts or by good works; I have favor with him only because of his free gift. My faith and works come forth only because I want to serve him. I am compelled to do good works as a result of that love. Part of my service to Christ is to give back to the very thing that Christ gave me as an incredible gift – my twelve-step group.

This group is where I confessed, "Hi, I'm Mike, and I'm a sex addict." When I said those words out loud, I finally realized what I was and needed help. I kept going to the weekly meetings. I felt the Lord prod me to share with the group the exact nature of my wrongs. I was petrified! I mean, who wants to hear that you've been a pedophile? Touching young boys? I asked two of the members and they said, "If you have the courage to speak, we will support you." I did it that next week to ten other men in the room. I was in tears, so afraid to tell my story for fear of being judged. This only took courage; it took faith to do it. No one got up and left the room. In fact, three people after the meeting hugged me and thanked me for sharing. My confidence skyrocketed because for the first time, I got this huge sin off my chest, a public confession to people I hardly know, yet they were people who could empathize with my life choices – poor life choices based on a physical allergy and a mental obsession. It helped me complete my twelve-step workbook. That was last early December 2017.

Today, I have shared my story publicly again with a new group, will do so again in a week or two with a third new group, and finally, wrote part of it down here in my journal, where journaling is part of my healing and twelve-step process. I am now serving by chairing our weekly meetings here in Ford Mountain, and I desire to seek out and attend meetings when I get out – ones that are specifically designed for sex addicts.

God said, "Trust me." It took faith for me to trust him. God wanted me to plead guilty right from the first arrest, and so did my partner. I agreed with both of them. I lost my marriage, my business, almost all my friends, and almost all my family because of this dark secret, which is now out in the wide open. My sentencing got plastered all over the local media and Internet. But what have I gained? Self-respect, love, not being afraid to share, learning to be accountable, walking in truth, freedom in my heart. All these from the God that I know intimately, personally, lovingly, and to those people who understand the nature of my disease, my addiction.

I still have a long way to go, and as long as I live on earth, I won't be able to say, "I'm cured;" or "I've arrived." That will be arrogant and conceited. I will need to go to those twelve-step rooms for the rest of my life and be in fellowship with those who struggle in ways like I do. For the rest of my life, I will also need to make amends to those who I haven't had the chance to do so; and some of them, because of how I have affected them, I will never be able to see face-to-face ever again. That's just reality. All I could ever hope from them is that one day they choose to forgive what I've done, and this not for my sake but their own. This way, their hearts can be freed from the prison of what I've done to them, so that they can start their lives again with new hope and a new direction. Forgiveness is a one-way street; you choose to forgive with or without the other person acknowledging it. Reconciliation is a minimum two-way street, where it takes two or more parties to forgive and work to restore what was lost. And with reconciliation, it takes an act of good faith by all parties involved for it to work properly.

Thank you, Lord, for giving me a new measure of faith to obey your still, small voice and asking me to write this down on paper. Thank you for giving me strength to put in the details of this horrible story, the disgusting facts of what I've done. I'm sorry of how I sinned against you, the victims, their families, my and my partner's families, my partner, my friends, even the community. I am sorry for what I've done. I ask for your forgiveness. I now, with God's help, choose to walk and live in the ways of my new thinking, and stay in fellowship with those who understand my disease, so they can encourage me, hold me accountable, and teach me to grow into the person I was originally designed to be. In this there is hope. Thank you, Jesus, for being there for me, as today I'm writing this is Easter Sunday, the day of your resurrection. He is risen! He is risen indeed!

FORD MOUNTAIN

February 24, 2018

Note: (names in black are the real names and used by permission)

Last night was a very interesting evening. Chad, George, and I went to the community room just to have a chat about the message in the RLC meeting that afternoon. Instead, we ended up talking about what things might look like when we are all released from prison.

George shared that he was getting anxious and wanted to leave, so he could start his new life on the outside. But as he was talking, he started sharing about his spiritual awakening, how he has been drawn closer to God while he's been here at Ford Mountain.

It was here I sensed the Holy Spirit wanted me to zero in on George and finally open the door regarding the hard questions about salvation and eternal life. In obedience to this leading, I asked George, "What does it mean to be born again?"

George is Roman Catholic, and his upbringing in the Roman Catholic church has been very traditional. When we broached this subject, I made him aware that the five major tenets of our faith – virgin birth, death, resurrection, ascension, and return – are what ties us all together in our faith, and we should celebrate that. However, this subject of being born again is in the Scriptures, and because we only operate from the Scriptures I opened up a Bible that was available in the Community Room and read three passages to him: John 3:1-8, Romans 10:9, and Revelation 3:20. I said to George that it is clear from Scripture that you must be born again. And this this is an invitation that Jesus gives us so we can be written into the Book of Life. He said that he has done his confession and believes in

Jesus and his resurrection, and he has welcomed Jesus into his heart, but as he was speaking the Holy Spirit kept nudging me to press the issue, so I continued to obey. I then asked Chad to offer his personal testimony, so George could hear "another voice" on the subject.

Poor George – he was stuck in the religious aspects of our faith as it has been taught for centuries – believe in Jesus, be a good person, try hard. They were all external aspects of our faith but missing this vital transformational, internal piece which will help George spiritually explode – inviting Jesus into his heart. George expressed such hurt toward what I was sharing, so much so that he said that his spiritual journey in the last six months has been a farce and now he thinks he's now not good enough for heaven, so why continue?

I assured him with peace in my heart that this is a crossroads, and God is trying to blow up walls in him so he can come to a saving knowledge of him, and that this is still part of his spiritual journey. I also thanked him for being my mentor because of his love, integrity, and friendship still meant so much to me. He then pulled out the book *The Purpose Driven Life* by Rick Warren and said he is going to read a chapter a day – forty chapters for his last forty-six days here at Ford Mountain. We finished the talk with a hug, and he knew that what we discussed was an invitation from God, and he now had an opportunity to explore what it is to be born again as part of his spiritual journey. I believed Rick Warren's book would have an impact and confirmation about our talk.

Thank you, Lord, for your saving message. Thank you that you chase after us, instead of us having to chase you. You loved us first, and now you're chasing George. I pray for his salvation because you showed me, and I had the opportunity to tell George directly, and also I got to prophesy to him that he will be a force to be reckoned with as a result of this salvation. I believe what you said, and I pray the blessing of this prophecy over him. In Jesus' name, amen.

February 27, 2018

I am seeing a battle going on with some of the inmates here at Ford Mountain. Interestingly, it's the very inmates I've noticed that God is targeting. The enemy is trying to distract them, discourage them, and trying to lead them away from seeing God work in their lives. I am also seeing God using the very same people through their trials – sickness, family issues they can't control, risk of deportation – to refine their hearts, to use it to put their trust in him, and for those who don't know him yet, using these situations as leverage to bring them into the kingdom. God has me interceding for them, lifting them continually up in prayer. Only in certain situations do I feel led to ask God to shield them, but mostly, I am asking God to use these situations for his glory to draw them closer to him. God used that in my life in 1989, and in 1990, I came to know Christ personally through a series of events, with having a preacher close his Bible at an evening service, change his evening message to a message of salvation. I found out a year later that that message was just for me and that he yielded to the leading of the Holy Spirit.

Being a Christian isn't easy, especially if you are one who chooses to completely surrender to him, even here in a comfortable place called North America, where our religious freedoms are still guarded and protected.

I lift up those who are currently struggling in their personal situations. I pray God will guide their actions, thoughts, hearts, and attitudes as they go through whatever trial they are facing; that no matter what is happening, God is still sovereign and that they can put their trust in him, and that they can draw near to him. As God puts them through their personal period of refinement, that they would discover a newness and be refreshingly aware of God's omnipotence, his omniscience, his omnipresence, and his holiness. All this wrapped up in holy love. Where they are falling short, I pray they repent and allow God to repair their hearts. Where they need to forgive, that forgiveness flows freely. Where there are blind spots, that God illuminates them so correction can come forth. This applies to me too. God is good, God is gracious. Nothing escapes his notice.

Thank you, Jesus, for dying on the cross for my sin that I may have life eternal, starting now. Amen.

March 5, 2018

The Lord has shown me sin that he wanted to address as a result of personal attacks by others – as it pertains to my personal integrity. All too often, we hold to our personal integrity and don't let it go. We know from the book of Job that God was pleased with him, and still, he allowed Satan to take everything away from him, including his health. But when his friends came, they made assumptions about his current state of affairs and pointed the finger at him wrongly without investigating the situation fully. Job kept denying that he did anything wrong, and over the course of their discussion, Job dug his heels in quite deeply, holding on to his personal integrity. It became the focal point of defense for him against his friends. Then God interjected and basically rebuked Job for his thinking about what he allowed to happen to him. After Job's listening to God, as he is sovereign and will allow whatever circumstances to our lives to bring glory to his name, Job repented as a result. So now that I've written this, my actions, my being, and my personal integrity being attacked by others pale in comparison to an almighty God, maker of heaven and earth. I confessed the sin of holding my pride and my integrity to two brothers in the Lord last night, and I continued in repentance and humility as I write this down now. I let go of what others say about me, and I turn my heart back to where it should be – in Christ.

Thank you for your loving kindness, Lord. Thank you for your favor. I know you delight in me, and that is all I desire. Help me grow fully into you – who you are – that I may walk in the fullness of your mercy and love and provision. I surrender my heart to you that I may be yours forever. You are using this situation to help me grow and become a mature Christian. I worship you because of your opportunities to bring us into the fullness of who you are, as you lead us to walk in the fullness of our purpose and destiny – our calling. Bring out the best in us, O Lord, and use your refiner's fire to purify us more and more into your likeness that we may obey your Word, your leading, and your voice. In Jesus' name, amen.

March 7, 2018

Help me keep looking at you as my only treasure; that I would not take my eyes off you, resort to my own devices, so that I may know your will and follow in your way. Help me stay focused on you, lift my heart, touch my soul that I may see your beauty in your kingship. You are my rock, my salvation, my refuge in times of trouble. I worship you, O Lord, my Savior, my King.

Last night we finished the final section of the business Bible study. I pray for each participant that as they move forward in their business ideas, that you, O Lord, guide them in their endeavors. I pray that they learn to relinquish control to you and that you may both lead them to glorious things and you may be glorified in them. Grant them pure business hearts and clean business minds that they both live for you impeccably and operate their businesses to the highest ethical standards. Thank you for the privilege to teach them, and now I release them into your care. I let go of them in my heart.

Open my heart to learn Spanish. I am struggling with this. I find it hard to learn. It isn't easy, and I don't find flow. I need to learn it slowly. Help me master new words. Help me think in Spanish so that I am not translating it in my head all the time. Show me your glory in this. I have reason to believe you want me to learn. Help me maintain a positive attitude as I learn.

March 10, 2018

Note: (names in bold are changed to protect the identities of the individuals) (names in black are the real names and used by permission)

Well! I sensed the leading of the Lord twice yesterday! Just before lunch **Gavin** asked me if there was a Bible study for last night, and I told him, "No there wasn't." I felt a *nudge* from the Holy Spirit so I responded back, "Would you like a Bible study tonight?" He said yes! So I went to Milton and asked him, "If we put together an impromptu Bible study, would you come?" He nodded his head.

Then I asked **Owen** and he responded, "Sure why not? I'm not doing anything else tonight."

So the ball got rolling on this, and next thing you know there were ten who showed up for it! Wow! Far cry from the day from when it was just **Darcy** and I alone. That night in late November, we laid this study before the Lord and just gave it to him for it is his study anyways, not ours; we are just his stewards of it.

Thank you, Jesus, for growing your study; it is still yours. I make myself available to you for it. I recommit my stewardship for it and lay the rest in your hands, for it is yours and I am your steward, your available vessel.

Now, to dovetail into that stewardship, the second part of this story is who the Lord chose to lead, not me but Glenn – one who is starving for truth and searching for it. He was not a Christian yet, who could behave immaturely and can still be worldly. Again, right after I got that *nudge* from **Gavin**, I was now talking within thirty minutes of that *nudge*, I felt another *nudge* from the Holy Spirit to ask Glenn to lead the evening's study. He said he would think about it.

By 2:30 p.m. roll call, I went over to him and he said yes, he will come and yes, he wanted to lead. I gave him the Scriptures, and it was set to go for the night's study. When it came time for the study, it was a bit of a gong show – he was farting; there was foul language, very worldly applications to biblical principles, but interestingly enough they started talking about "healthy" subjects, like caring for the homeless, helping the needy, feeding the poor, one druggie helping a homeless person with their child, also homeless. A conversation that probably would have never existed had I led a clean and sanitized study, applying a perfect exegesis of Scripture, as if I was teaching to a sanitized North American, everyday middle-class group. This has woken me up to our twenty-first century reality.

The people of the world understand the problems of the world, and our church *mentality* needs to change with it. I mean, we are just not prepared to deal with the Glenns of this world – un-discipled, undisciplined, sometimes arrogant, rough around the edges, and has "been around the block a few times" when it comes to walking and living a sinful lifestyle. As Christians, we need to look past their *appearances* and ask the Holy Spirit what he sees in someone and at that with great humility!

"Not everything is as it seems."

We need to stop and listen to the Holy Spirit first and ask him what he is doing, especially if I am trying to stop something that God is trying to lead a breakthrough in someone else's heart. If the Lord is asking me, as a leader, to have an immature non-Christian lead his study for one night, who am I to judge? Jesus said to Peter, "What is that to you? Just follow me." Personally, I don't advise anyone to do what God has asked of me yesterday at all, especially if you make a decision independent from the leading of the Holy Spirit, but there will be times when God may ask us into carrying out unusual tasks for unusual circumstances. And with the upcoming final outpouring of the Holy Spirit, the church here in Canada and the United States better wake up and get ready, for we will be receiving into our church bodies the Glenns of this world – immature, addicts, dysfunctional, offensive, even down right dirty (I mean in terms of personal hygiene). God will call us to care for these people, for they will come en masse into our nice, little middle-class churches. They will upset the apple cart. They will stretch the love, faith, and discipleship of each church body that gets hit by this final wave. And it's going to hit hard. Think of a fifty-foot tidal wave coming ashore! That is what this final outpouring is going to be like! Wake up church! Get prepared! God is calling us all to receive every walk of life coming through your church doors! Put on the armor of God, and also arm yourselves with these – love, mercy, grace, and truth. You must also do these with great diligence. Be extremely patient with those who are struggling, operate in the anointing – the fullness of the power of the Holy Spirit – hear their ideas for they have something to offer too. We just need to have a discerning and listening ear. And we must do this in the fullness of surrender to Jesus, letting him have full control of each situation, walking in great humility and complete love for one another. This is our time in history. This is our calling; this is our duty. They will hear the truth in love, and it will set the prisoners free. Just as what God has done for us. We need to be prepared. We need to be ready. Lord Jesus, show us your way, not our own. We surrender to you. Amen.

March 14, 2018

Answered Prayer

We started a new prayer group yesterday afternoon. Five of us were present, all fairly strong believers. We knew it was time to corporately come before the Lord, solemnly, reverently, no gong show permitted. Time for grace was there, as we all need it; but we chose to present ourselves humbly before our God, confessing our sin, pride, arrogance, and selfishness. It was time to pray for ourselves, asking God for protection, a listening ear, and giving of ourselves completely over to him. Prayers flowed, repentance flowed, tears flowed. Next we prayed for the camp – the inmates, the guards, the support staff, and all the programs. We asked God to show us individuals to pray for. He gave us two, so we prayed over them. Then we prayed for our loved ones, and one by one, everyone in our group took a turn praying for the ones closest to their hearts! Then we prayed for other needs in our communities and left it all before the Lord. The presence of God got only stronger as we prayed. It was so amazing we lost track of time! More than an hour passed by, and next thing we knew they were announcing medication time! We walked away blessed. Later in the evening, in med line, one of the inmates, a chair of one of our support groups said he just chaired one of the best meetings he'd seen ever. He said people were opening up, and many who were sharing were in tears! He wasn't supposed to share that outside of group, but he just felt compelled to tell me anyways. Before that, I was walking in the field and I noticed two inmates walking together who hadn't spoken to each other in weeks! I asked one of them this morning what happened, and he said the other inmate just walked up to him and started talking to him like nothing between them had ever happened! Water under the bridge! At coffee today, I pulled our whole prayer group, plus one other who needed to hear this, and I shared these two stories of what God has done and how he has moved. This encouraged them so much that we are now adding a second prayer gathering on Saturdays as well. We prayed and gave it all that God spoke to our hearts back to him, then we watched him move. Surrender, obedience, trust, belief – this were what God was teaching us. Amen.

April 5, 2018

Note: (names in bold are changed to protect the identities of the individuals) (names in black are the real names and used by permission)

You are merciful, so merciful and kind. There are about to be changes in my relationships here in Ford Mountain. Chad is getting out today. George is getting out on Monday. My friends, my teachers, my mentors, my racquetball partners – God has used them mightily to help me get where I am now in my rehabilitation.

George got me in to see **Sheila** when I didn't even have clearance from the health nurse. That was divine intervention. George introduced me to my twelve-step support group the first week I was here (I believe that was November 11), and now I sat and served as the chair of our group.

Chad has mentored me for weeks to help develop my presentation skills. Chad started a presentation class as a result, and for the last four weeks, has given back by teaching myself and five others these skills every Thursday. Tonight was the last class, of which I had the honor and privilege to teach because Chad got his parole unexpectedly yesterday morning. He is leaving this morning. So tonight was the last class, and God had officially closed the Bible study for Business here in Ford Mountain. Yesterday, I asked Chad half-jokingly, "So, who do you think sprung you? God? Or the enemy?" He said both! I laughed. Well, I suspect it was the enemy who got Chad out of here because (God) was using him to raise Josephs right here in jail! Skills for doing God's bidding were coming from Chad, and the participants were receiving it so well! I can't wait until Chad and I reunite on the outside! I want to see how God is going to forge our relationship for the kingdom. George too. But that friendship is just a friendship, and I value him so much. So that's my message for today, and my third journal book is complete. Time to start another.

Thank you, Jesus, for this journey. I surrender my life, my calling, my relationships to you. Build them as you may by the power of the Holy Spirit. Amen.

SPEECHES & POEMS

February 18, 2018

Note: (names in black are the real names and used by permission)

Choices and Consequences

I was asked by my good friend George, the RLC leader of the camp, to write and give the closing positive message last Friday. The only thing was he asked me at 9:45 p.m. Thursday to do it!

He said, "Mike! Can you bail me out and give the closing positive message?"

I said, "Sure."

Right there I knew I would need help from the Lord.

I come to God daily when it comes to writing in this journal, and I ask him what he wants written. When I ask, the flow of writing is so smooth. It's stupidly easy, and quite often I sense "downloads" from the Holy Spirit when it comes to inspiration, like right now, I'm writing and I am getting *messages from heaven* to put to this paper. I love it! Here is the speech the Lord helped me write:

RLC (Right Living Community) Meeting – Feb 16, 2018

Choices and Consequences

When I was asked to deliver the closing positive message, I thought to look at the definitions of the words *choice* and *consequence* in the context of this week's challenge. The word *choice* means "the act of picking between two or more possibilities." The word *consequence* means "something produced by a cause or following from a condition." Choices can be good, or they could be poor. The consequences of those choices can either be positive or negative, depending on the decisions made. Like a pebble that hits the center of a still, quiet pond, the initial splash eventually ripples out, causing the pond to be disturbed further and further out, until the ripples are seen no more. It is the same for the consequences of a person's choices, which could end up being far reaching as well, good or bad.

Now let me personalize this: It is entirely up to you:

+ how you choose to think,
+ how you choose to act, and
+ how you choose to react.

The greatest choice anyone could make is a choice to do the right thing, whether it is personal, relational, financial, spiritual, and so on. The choice to have good values and hold those values in high esteem; the choice to make the effort to better ourselves and watch the positive consequences slowly fall into place as a result.

The negative consequences of my poor choices have brought me here to Ford Mountain. The good choices I make here will bring forth the positive consequences when I leave.

Here is my word of encouragement for you: make good choices and then reap the reward of positive consequences. Thank you.

Thank you, Lord, for providing me a secular speech, but now it's time to include you. Teach us how to feed our souls with your love, your goodness, your wholeness so that we can be nourished. Help us feed on your Word – the choicest of food – so we can feast on it and learn to *choose* to be holy, walk holy, to overflowing. I choose to surrender completely to you; I choose to allow you to have all my heart, all my soul, all my mind and all my strength. I choose to depend on you for my countenance, my strength, my walk so that you will guide me to fullest of my purpose and destiny that you designed me to be. You have declared to me to do great things for your great name, just as you have called all believers, and I humbly accept this position. I choose to be taught to be your steward of resources, a caretaker of your gifts, and a custodian of the calling you're giving me. You've entrusted this into my care, and with your supernatural help, through the power of the Holy Spirit, I will be diligent with those talents, gifts, and resources. Help me be focused on you, and you alone, so I won't be distracted by the lies, deceits, and temptations of the enemy, for you have made him powerless by your death and resurrection. Help me to be wise — wise as a serpent but gentle as a dove. Allow me to bring glory to your great name and your great name alone, Lord Jesus. Amen.

February 23, 2018

Entry: (names in bold are changed to protect the identities of the individuals) (names in black are the real names and used by permission)

Changing Behaviors

It was an interesting morning. **Keith,** one of the RLC (Right Living Community) leaders here at Ford Mountain came to me during breakfast while I was handing out the breakfast condiments to the inmates and asked if I would do the closing positive message after the twelve-thirty roll call RLC meeting. I looked at him, a little stunned, thinking, *At least, George gave me the night before to have something written.* But I said yes to **Keith,** knowing and having absolute confidence that I could come to Daddy for a download through the Holy Spirit. I had that confidence in trusting God's omniscience and that I have access to the kingdom of heaven. God just wanted to give us good things to his children and today I asked for a good gift – a message – and received it in its fullness. The cool part about today was God helped me devise a clever analogy to address the subject of changing behaviors. So here is what the Lord gave me to address the inmates, guards and support staff of Ford Mountain:

RLC (Right Living Community) Meeting – Feb 23, 2018

Changing Behaviors

This week's theme is on changing behaviors. To many, this may seem like a daunting task, because when one looks at it, it looks steep and one doesn't know where it's going to lead. So to assist us all with looking at changing our behavior, I thought I would liken it to creating an amazing recipe. And like any great recipe, we need to prioritize our ingredients in order to maximize results. First, we need a little bit of education, to study our recipe and find out what we need to pull out. Next, we need a little bit of humility, in order to make sure we read our ingredients clearly and concisely. This is followed by a little bit of effort so that what we've learned is now being put together smoothly and properly. Finally, it's all about execution, and with this it will help us bring together a mouth-watering, life-changing product. And that final product is you – a whole new you.

When I was arrested, it was a wake-up call for my life – a life that included changing my behavior. With God's help and when I made the choice to do so, I applied these four ingredients: education, humility, effort, and execution; and with these, it helped change my identity, my attitude, and my life. I like who I am now, and I have no desire to go back to the way I was, even though, like all of us, are still works in progress. If there is hope for me, there is hope for you too. My prayer is that if you haven't already done so, take the first step toward changing your behavior and see where your amazing journey of change is going to take you. Thank you.

I see that with a little more time, an opportunity to work out some of the *kinks* in the message could have been ironed out, but with essentially only three hours to get it done (I had to go back to work for 11:00 a.m. right through to the meeting) it wasn't too bad.

Thank you, Lord, for giving me this idea and helping me write. I couldn't have done this without you. I am grateful for the privilege of being able to hear your voice, and being able to receive direction by you. To you I give honor and glory. Amen.

March 13, 2018

> *"When you are in a place where you don't know where to start, start with an idea and work your way from there. The beauty about ideas; they are always free, and you can change them around as needed."*
>
> - Mike Mahy,
> closing positive message
> for our hut meeting this morning

I just love getting "downloads" from heaven! This morning I realized I had the closing positive message and I still hadn't written anything down! So I chose to come to Daddy and asked for an idea with the subject matter – release planning – kept in mind. The words flowed from the head to the hand to the pen to the paper so easily there was no doubt it came from heaven.

It is such a blessing to walk in the power of the Holy Spirit. I now depend on him for my daily direction so that I don't miss out on his leading. Surrender is the key. Keeping his law written into your heart and allowing the Holy Spirit to remind you of it continually. Allow his love to permeate your being! God makes me whole! God is causing me to blossom!

March 19, 2018

I got up this morning, and while shaving I remembered that I had accepted the task of giving the closing positive message for this morning's RLC meeting. I was pretty certain it was the Lord who brought it to my attention.

He loves bringing glory to himself in situations like this and I love bringing glory to his great name, so I asked God, "Help!"

When I got back to my room to start cleaning it before work (I start at 6:00 a.m. and now it's 5:20 a.m.), I "plugged into heaven" and started seeking the Holy Spirit for downloads on the subject of healthy living. I love how the Lord just started flooding my thoughts with different info that he would like to see in this message. He let it be toned down spiritually and scripturally for me to deliver to them, but then in turn I get to write here in my journal the glory of his helping me write this and give him all the credit for its origin. God did know how to use each situation for his glory, and he has positioned me strategically to carry out his purpose for me in this season, therefore, I choose to yield to his leading. Here is the message for the RLC meeting today:

RLC (Right Living Community) Meeting – Mar 19, 2018

Healthy Living

Life is full of choices, and those choices impact our lives. In this week's theme of healthy living, let us look at choices that will positively influence our spiritual, emotional, physical, and mental well-being.

First, we are spirit-beings, and we need to feed ourselves spiritually. Through prayer and meditation, we can feed our spiritual selves. I personally read the Bible daily as part of that feeding of the soul.

Next, we look at our emotional well-being. Laughter, exercise, having a good positive outlook on life – all choices – contribute to good emotional health.

Then we look at our physical health. Good food choices, and yes, you can make those here at Ford Mountain, and exercise help maintain good physical health. At one time I was almost 220 lbs., and soon after, I was diagnosed with diabetes. I had to take three different pills and insulin to keep my blood sugars stable. Since I have lost all that weight my medication has been cut by more than half, and I am feeling so much better physically.

Finally, to address our mental well-being: become a life-long learner. The day we stop learning is the day we stop growing.

We have all these opportunities here at Ford Mountain. What we have offered here to us is the total package. Take advantage of the healthy living choices made available to you and witness the changes you will see in your life. Thank you.

Bring glory to your name in this camp, O Lord, bring glory to your name. Show yourself to those who need you most desperately. In Jesus' name, amen.

Life Is Too Short

Even though we have eternity, our life here is very short,
So splash in the puddles, look at the trees, smell flowers of every sort.

We live our lives. God has a way, our destinies very sure,
To live our purpose, our attitude, thoughts, and lives be pure.

Live for God, love your neighbor, enjoy all God's given us,
The fullness of joy, the abundance of life, in him we will trust.

When trials of life, suffering too, despair may come our way,
In this we grow, persevere, and patience comes in play.

All these things, God in Christ, experienced here on earth,
To show us all that he does care, your value and your worth.

March 29, 2018

Note: (names in black are the real names and used by permission)

I am participating in business presenting class where you learn to publicly speak. It is led by an accomplished saxophone player and professional presenter. This class is a blast! So much fun! I had to write an executive summary to read to tonight's class (it's held every Thursday up at Holloway House) so here it is:

> Horizon Consulting, founded by Mike Mahy, is an upstart enterprise focused on building strategic business partnerships. Two such partnerships exist in Victoria, while one is being developed in Greater Kamloops and one in Surrey. These partnerships work off the strengths of each person's abilities. The key roles I will play are: administration, finance, government relationships, and operational streamlining. Each partner will work together in marketing and promotions, customer care and quality control. My partners will handle all other aspects of each business operation.
>
> Due to the nature of my role in these partnerships and because of modern communication technology I will be able to fulfill my duties from one location – Victoria. There will be times, however, when I will be required to be present on site, of which travel and meeting arrangements will be scheduled ahead of time. Finally, the last common theme these partnerships will have is a complete commitment and surrender of each business to Christ so that each business enterprise will dually serve as a Christian ministry for God's kingdom.
>
> Thank you, Lord, for these partnerships. I give them into your hands for they are yours. I pray for our partners so that they will become one in heart and mind in these endeavors. I pray your blessing on each and guide us through each day as we seek your face and look to bring glory to your great name. Amen.

What happened since: Only one of those partnerships came to fruition, and it is now coming to a close as well (as of September 5, 2019). God is the one who directs my path, guides my life, and allows me to interact with those in the season I'm called. It is now time for a new season, a new beginning, and a new direction.

JOURNAL
BOOK 4

INSPIRATIONAL WRITINGS

April 8, 2018

> *For everyone to whom much is given, from him much will be required;*
> *and to whom much has been committed, of him they will ask the more.*
> - Luke 12:48

What is *surrender? Surrender* is "the giving up of my right of my will to God in favor of his." It means that I choose to surrender my thinking in favor of his thinking. It means that I choose to surrender the direction of my life in favor of the direction he has for me. It means that I trust him more than I trust my own abilities, intellect and talents.

Does this mean I just become a robot? Absolutely not. What it does mean is that I recognize that God is smarter than I am, more capable than I am, do things better than I can, and can suggest things to me that I would otherwise never have thought of. I am more interested in tapping into heaven's treasure chest than trying to do it all by myself. God has made me his partner, and when he gives me a directive in regards to how I am to walk in holiness, walk in purpose, walk in destiny, walk in humility, walk in relationships to others, walk in surrender, yielding to the Holy Spirit rather than acting on my own will alone; I am much better off. I am content to be a steward, caretaker and custodian of the wealth of talent, intellect, ability, and direction God has given me. If God has called me to produce great physical wealth for the kingdom of heaven and then teach others to do the same, then absolute surrender is the primary requirement, not secondary. And I trust in his timing for all things, not mine. He then seamlessly moves.

God will grant us to wisely steward what he has entrusted us, like I said before, we are not robots. But to choose to give our lives over completely to him is what he asks of us anyways, so why not obey? In that, he will test us, refine, correct us, and prepare us for ministry. It takes repentance, forgiveness, and a turning of our will over to him voluntarily. This is a great responsibility.

Now, who is up for this task? If it's you, he will demand everything from you, then reward you according to his will and purpose. You will know a new life in the kingdom of God (John 12:24-26).

April 14, 2018

Future and a Hope

For I know the thoughts that I think toward you, says the Lord,
thoughts of peace and not of evil, to give you a future and a hope.
- Jeremiah 29:11 (NKJV)

It was an extravagant promise given by God to the Israelites before they went into captivity. They were about to get corrected. They were being sent away as a result of their sin, but God was letting them know he hadn't forgotten them.

I received from a sermon by a former pastor of mine in Victoria, BC, Canada that it's in God's nature to want to bless. At the time of receiving that teaching, to me it was revolutionary, a game-changing comment! "If God wants to bless us," he continued, "then correction and repentance is a natural course toward blessing from the kingdom of heaven's standpoint. If God wants to bless us, then he will bring us to the standard he wants us to be so that he can pour out his blessing on us!" Wow!

So here's the deal: seek God out and look for ways to humble yourself before him, allow his "flashlight" expose those shortfalls, sins, and bad habits so that, in partnership, allow him to bring healing into your soul, rid you of heartache and pain and sorrow in your heart; strengthen your position to forgive, and in doing so, being restored into an amazing, close, loving, strong relationship with Jesus Christ our Savior and God.

The pastor said in that sermon that it was a privilege to repent, and that God was the one who has gave us this privilege so that he can bless us. Invoke that privilege. Take advantage of it! Then watch your life change just as I have seen mine change.

Jesus, thank you for the gift of repentance. It's in your nature to want to forgive and then to bless your children. In this, we have hope and a future. We don't need to be afraid of confessing our sins. We don't need to be afraid of repenting. It's embarrassing, yes; it's humbling, yes. But in it and when we choose to be bold, we receive a thousand times in blessing from you when we choose to come into alignment with you and your standard. Show us the way. In Jesus' name, amen.

Repentance is a gift, not a punishment.

- Mike Mahy

April 15, 2018

We Are Already Rich (2 Corinthians 8:9)

One thing that I have learned while being in jail is learning in greater measure what true treasures from heaven are. As I have stated in previous journal entries, I have lost everything of material value – many of my personal possessions, friendships, family, my business – and with the exception of a few friends and my sister and brother-in-law, they are all gone. Yet I am happy and joyful every day. I wake up every morning with new life and a new hope. God has replaced my sin, my sorrow, my anger, my bitterness, my wrong ways of thinking, false humility, and poor attitude and has replaced them with the true treasure from heaven: love, feeling loved, and finally loving myself, so therefore, wanting to love others properly, respectfully with no strings attached.

A forgiving heart, feeling forgiven by God and finally forgiving myself; a new measure of faith which grows every day; a new confidence in believing in who I am and what I've been called to do; feeling certain about my salvation and my personal intimate relationship with Christ; living a life that is full of abundance and that it will never end because I know who my Daddy is; and having an attitude of wanting to be holy as opposed to trying to be holy in order to gain God's favor because God's favor with us is already there – these are the true riches of heaven.

So why do we pursue things or go after stuff, thinking it's going to make us happy? Why try and get rich through worldly means? It's one thing if God has asked us to; that then becomes part of our purpose and calling. But why do people go after stuff? It doesn't make us happy. Why keep up with the Joneses? It doesn't make us happy. It doesn't make us feel better. It's a deception, a mirage, a smokescreen. It never satisfies. Just read Ecclesiastes because Solomon in his twilight years realized this – a chasing after the wind. It's meaningless, driven by greed, lust, jealousy, and covetousness.

We are already rich – rich with God's love and blessing; and in this we will be content just to be with him, satisfied that we have an amazing eternal position for those who personally know Jesus as their Lord and Savior. When we see Jesus, and have him deep in our hearts, nothing will distract us, for the only thing you will want to pursue is when he says to us, "Well done good and faithful servant," when we finally come face-to-face with him in heaven.

April 16, 2018

We get caught up in doing things – doing things for ourselves, our families, our bosses, churches, even for God, that we lose sight to the little things in life: the beauty of rest, smelling flowers, looking at the beauty of the earth, gazing up at the stars, quietly basking in the love, worship and beauty of God and his creation. We need to learn to slow down.

When we move too fast, sometimes we miss out on opportunities. We sometimes miss the joy, sometimes we even miss our calling for the moment. We get tired, short-tempered, and frazzled.

I am learning to slow down. Slowing down has brought me to writing in my journal almost daily, seeking gems from heaven to write. I love spending time with Jesus, showing my love for him while meditating in the Word and in quiet prayer and then receiving his love back to me. It's a beautiful thing.

I have no desire to go back to the distractions of going at a hectic pace and trying to see how many things I can shove into one day. I confess that I am a workaholic, driven by tasks and completing them successfully. There needs to be time when I just stop. Do nothing. Reflect on my day. Meditate on the Lord. Become quiet and still. It is there I will be able to accomplish more because I am resting on my heavenly Father who is able to do more in me and through me than I can ever imagine. But I now tap into endless possibilities, to the one who is all-powerful, all-knowing, and ever present. When we learn to trust in his divine nature, he will reveal to you the mysteries of heaven and unlock your purpose and destiny that he has designed you for.

Take time out to seek his face and slow down. Wait on him. Be still and know who he is, hear his voice, and only respond when he says, "Go!" To this we say amen and amen.

April 17, 2018

What Is Faith? (Hebrews 11:1)

Faith comes in many different forms, but it requires belief – to believe on faith that God has spoken to you in your head or in your heart, knowing the Spirit's voice; to believe on faith that God has spoken to you in a dream; to believe on faith when someone has given you a prophecy, a word, or a promise and therefore will come to pass; faith in receiving a healing, and even believing in miracles. Most importantly, having faith that God exists. When we pursue faith, it is important to remember it is only a part of God's total package, and I would rather anyone go after heaven's whole package, rather than just the fun parts of it. Here are some other parts of that package: putting Jesus on the throne of everything of your life first, walking in total surrender to God, humbling yourself in all situations, walking in the ways as Jesus gave on the sermon on the Mount, taking the greatest commandment seriously, repenting for your sin, and seeking God's strength to stay away from sin. These parts of that total package will give you the confidence that God is for you and with you. From the position of humility and a contrite heart, you will receive great images of purpose, destiny, and great works for the glory of God and the edification of the church. I want to share two dreams and one prophecy God gave me that still haven't happened yet, but I am still waiting on his promise:

1) God has given me British Columbia and California to do his work in. This was given to me in 1995, and God will reveal to me the purpose. All I know is these two places I will operate in his blessing. I received this in a dream and is in my ministry journal that I kept in the 1990's.

2) I will become an Internet sensation. This came to me in a dream in 2015. God said, "I will make you an Internet sensation!" I replied to him, "I surrender." That was the end of the dream. My conviction (of my sentencing) was all over the Internet but I sense that he has something else in mind for the kingdom.

3) I will make billions. This prophecy has been uttered to me by at least eight people between 2008 and 2016 (in different forms of words given to me). Many of these people who have prophesied this great wealth don't even know each other and are completely unaware of the other's prophecies. Until today I have been too ashamed to even write this down but on faith God is asking me to do this so that there is a record of it.

So there you have it. I am waiting for these to be fulfilled. We are to test them (1 Thessalonians 5:19-22) so now, these are officially now being tested. I trust God, and I believe what he has said. Now we wait on when they come to pass on faith.

April 19, 2018

God is faithful. He keeps his promises. He rewards those who are faithful to him. So what do those rewards for faithfulness look like?

First, his rewards are eternal. They are put into heaven's bank account, and sometimes God draws on that account to bless you on earth, but not always. So do not necessarily seek them here exclusively. We have a tendency to want them here and now, for this is the society and generation we live in. I call it the McDonald's generation – get it now, get it fast, get what you want. That's not our relationship with our amazing God. So, when we are faithful in our actions and to our calling, bank on putting the treasures you create with God into heaven's bank account with your name on it.

Second, what are we faithful to? We are faithful to our undying allegiance to Jesus; standing for his truth, living and walking according to his Word; your body, spirit and soul all being treated as the living temple of God; obedient in your calling; doing the works he's asked you in the manner he laid out when he gave the Sermon on the Mount. Go into your prayer closet unseen where God will reward you for your prayers; don't let your left hand know what your right hand is doing when it comes to charitable deeds; look inconspicuous when fasting; bless your enemies, and pray for them. You get the idea. Read Matthew chapters 5, 6, and 7, then do what it says.

Lastly, don't worry about your life. Entrust yourself into God's hands and allow him to take care of you. Follow Matthew 6:33, and seek first his kingdom. Put his kingdom ahead of your kingdom; put Jesus, throne ahead of your throne. That's faithfulness. Then watch heaven's treasures flow to you – love, joy, peace, kindness, selflessness, self-control. Against these, there is no law and see what God can do for you, whether he allows suffering, trials, and tribulations – all used to clean you up and make you strong in him and your faith; or when he just blesses you with signs and wonders, healings, prophecies, and material blessings. All these will help you on your path to faithfulness in Jesus Christ. Amen.

We are sons and daughters of God
Galatians 4:6-7 & Romans 8:14-17

The Lord gave me Romans 8:16-17 yesterday while I was in church, and then in my reading this morning it was Galatians 4:6-7. They both speak to the exact same message to how God the Father wants us to see him as *Abba* or Daddy. It was so personal! It was so intimate! The God of the universe wants us to have this deep, intimate, personal relationship with him, as one who might experience a healthy relationship with our earthly fathers.

I was adopted at ten days old, so when I read in Romans about being adopted as a son of God, I already understood what it felt like to be *picked* as someone special, taken home, and taken care of. I will forever be grateful to my parents for adopting me, and I will for eternity be grateful for being adopted by God because of the sacrifice his Son, his only begotten Son, who died on the cross for my sins and purchased me with his blood so I could receive the privilege of being adopted through that same blood.

Adoption comes with benefits. We are now eternal residents of heaven. We receive God's unconditional love. Our past is wiped clean, and we have a new beginning. We are co-heirs with Christ for the kingdom. We are sons and daughters of the living God, kings and queens, princes and princesses of the kingdom. We are citizens of heaven. We have access to the kingdom through worship and prayer. We are set free. And the list is endless. Benefits, benefits, benefits.

I choose to walk humbly and in surrender to my God. I have the privilege to worship him, the privilege and opportunity to repent of my sins, the privilege and opportunity to walk the straight and narrow path with the supernatural help of the Holy Spirit. I have access to the one who heals my soul, lifts me up, carries me when at some of the lowest points of my life. This is the life of adoption. This is the life of knowing God as *Abba*. This is becoming more and more real every day in my life. This love relationship is transforming my life. In my adoption, God has given me purpose, and I have hope; my faith has increased too. What a price Christ had to pay because he so desperately wants his children back to him. I'm glad I'm one of them. Amen.

Serve One Another (Galatians 5:13-14)

God grants us opportunities to serve one another in love. In serving one another, we fulfill the second part of the greatest commandment: "Love your neighbor as yourself." But I have a confession to make – I misused this commandment to hide my sins from others, sins that stopped me from loving myself, which in the end hurt me, hurt my testimony for Jesus, hurt my relationships with others, and finally landed me in jail. You see, I have another addiction – being a workaholic. And because God has granted me different abilities, I was able, through works of service, create this huge smokescreen. I tricked others into thinking I was this great guy helping the church through administration, teaching and leading. I helped my community by doing such a good job in helping them protect their businesses from the dreaded taxman. I took care of those who lived with us in our home for free, and helping my mom and dad (when he was still alive) each month by going over for a weekend to visit, take them shopping, and doing some cleaning around their condo unit. I was so good at it! In reality, I didn't love myself, hated my sexual sins, and didn't know how to stop it. I tried through works of service to hide the "cancer" lying deep down in my soul. God has now exposed that and he wants to use my correction – my chastening by him – as a tool of healing for my life so I can finally operate in the commandment "love your neighbor as yourself" properly.

Following this commandment in truth, not in lies, deceit, and cover-ups, but in love – love for myself so that, in turn, I can love others with a wholesome love and not in lust, which is a cheap imitation manufactured by the devil. That garbage the devil makes is full of venom, full of poison, and is a counterfeit to the true love God wants to give us. Lust leads us down to the path of destruction. I know because I've been there, and now God is leading me out of this miry pit of tar, waste, and destruction. I must allow to have God love me, so I can love him back wholeheartedly, which will allow me to love others properly. The showmanship will stop, and true service will start, with pure motives, proper boundaries, and Holy Spirit-led acts of service that will truly glorify God and truly edify the church. These acts of service will be transformational, both for me and others to the glory of the kingdom. The treasures where I have a proper opportunity to lay up in heaven begin now.

April 26, 2018

It's interesting. I try reading Rick Warren's *Purpose Driven Life* and the Lord asks me to stop reading. It's not that it isn't biblically accurate, I made it to page twenty-four, and it was very sound! I was even enjoying the reading very much! I don't read a lot of books personally, except the Bible. I read that daily. I am curious as to the design God has for me is to just focus my time and attention to him more exclusively rather than to the amazing literature, YouTube videos, preachers and popular teachers so that I can grow in the anointing he has given me. Is it possible that I am to learn directly from God more specifically? I don't know the answer, but I know that I don't *follow* any particular teacher, any particular ministry, or read any particular literature like so many of my peers do. I have enjoyed teachings from the likes of Rick Warren, Rick Joyner, and Bill Johnson, to name a few, but the vast majority of my time is just spent in the Word of God and then in prayer, meditation, and fellowship of my peers.

I do know the Holy Spirit is asking me to primarily focus on him. So that is what I will do. I guess it is okay for some of us to read all the contemporary literature they wish while others grow through intimacy in Christ through the person of the Holy Spirit. I must admit that God has used these key anointed men and women of God in my life (Dr. Caroline Leaf and Katie Souza come to mind) and they, at the right times in my life, have been instrumental by God to teach me a new element of God's kingdom whether it is renewal, transformation, forgiveness, repentance, holiness, hope, learning our position in the kingdom of God, and the list goes on. I guess what I am saying is that I am not to be such a bookaholic, such a videoholic, always searching for the latest teaching, chasing after the latest anointing from the latest anointed teacher, becoming a "Holy Spirit chaser." That's not me and I pray that's not you. For all those who have read Rick's *Purpose Driven Life* and have been transformed by it, God bless you, and it was definitely by design that his anointed book was for you. God's purpose for that book for you was fulfilled. In our Christian walk, we need to seek balance between being taught by God and reading literature or watching videos by God's anointed teachers without losing our sense of purpose in God's kingdom. We can end up taking a good thing and use it the wrong way, so in the end, we inadvertently seek to glorify ourselves, the calling, the anointing, rather than glorifying God.

April 27, 2018

Freedom – Part 2 (Mark 10:29-31)

When you leave everything you have for Christ – your life, your family, your possessions, your status in society, key relationships – and face trials, tribulations, or persecutions, you will receive more through Christ than you will ever gain through your own efforts alone.

God is asking us to forsake everything for the kingdom and seek the kingdom first (Matthew 6:33). So what does that look like? It means laying your will, your body, your desires – everything you have – to him and surrendering it all in favor of God's kingdom. In this, you will receive more than you will have ever imagined. In the process towards this, he will put you on a path to "clean you up," put you through lessons of life he wants you to learn, put you on a corrective path, both voluntary and involuntary, in the process of bringing you up to his standard. In all of this he is setting you free – free from bondage, free from sin, freedom to worship in a way never thought before. All upgrades from where you were previously. This is like going through surgery. You anticipate the pain as the result of the procedure, but you expect that, in time, the healing process will make way to a better you.

Jesus is our divine healer, our divine doctor, our divine restorer. Through his blood, we are set on the path to spiritual freedom. When we get to this point of freedom in Christ, it will not matter if we get thrown in jail, tortured, persecuted, mocked, made like fools, condemned, or even killed for our faith in Christ because our freedom is now internal and not dependent on external circumstances. We will experience a freedom like never before. That is the promise of the gospel; that is the promise Christ gives us.

In this, we have been set free.

Thank you, Jesus, for your freedom – freedom to worship whether we are persecuted in places like China or the Middle East or whether we are in comfortable places like Canada or the United States. Teach us to walk in our freedom so that we are holy and righteous before you. Teach us your ways; show us our purpose in life, so that through our testimony, we bring glory to your great name. In Jesus' name, amen.

May 3, 2018

Through adversity, there is opportunity. When you hit difficult times in your life, difficult circumstances thrown at you, difficult spots in relationships, there are opportunities hidden right in them.

Wealthy entrepreneurs know this in the business market. When the DOW plummets, people panic, but true investors look for *waves* in the market before, during, and after a crash or correction and look for opportunities to either buy or sell – whichever is most profitable for them – and take advantage of what everyone else is missing. The same goes for a downturn in the economy; wealthy investors look through the chaos for the right business deal, the right real estate investment, and acquire them for pennies on the dollar, all because they waited patiently for the opportunity when others were panicking or not making the best decisions. It doesn't make them evil; it just makes them wise about market fluctuations and make decisions based on information, not emotion.

We all possess the same opportunity. What I have learnt lately is, when I see circumstances in my life go sideways or when a relationship hits a bump in the road, the first thing I desire to do now is take a look responsibly in my corner and come to God and ask, "What is my part in this? Where or is there a shortfall in my life you wish to address?" Then I wait on the Lord to point it out to me, shine his "flashlight" in my heart, and then seek out the correction through repentance, humility, forgiving or asking for forgiveness, and then restoration. The situation could be trivial; it could be monumental. It doesn't matter. I look for opportunities to grow. I look for opportunities to become the person Christ wants me to be as a child of the kingdom so that I can live and walk in the fullness I am to be in him. So, rather than reacting through blame, judgment, and a critical spirit, which are all outward expressions to others or inward to yourself – all which cause damage – I now choose to react more slowly, thinking through the process, praying and asking for his help and his point of view, then I take God's side on it when I believe I've heard him correctly, which also means it has to line up with his Word in its proper context. These are opportunities, and like the wealthy investor and wealthy entrepreneur, you become wealthy too, from the kingdom's standpoint. Amen.

May 5, 2018

God is Love (1 John 4:8; 1 Corinthians 13:1-8a)

I love teaching the Word of God. One of the ways I love to teach is to *switch* things up a little in the Word, so long as it is not taken out of context so that a better understanding of God's Word is manifested. There are two areas of Scripture where I like to do this. The first area is in Job, chapter 1 where I replace the oxen with tractors, the sheep with Cadillacs and Lincolns, the camels with SUVs, and the house with a mansion to help modernize the story tongue in cheek so that the students I am teaching gain a better picture of what is being taken away from Job. I mean, in terms of material possessions, plus his kids, he is losing everything!

I also like to teach God's love by using 1 Corinthians 13:1-8 by interchanging the word *love* with the word *God*, using 1 John 4:8 as my basis point to allow this change. From the NIV version of the Bible, this is how 1 John 4:8 reads: "Whoever does not love does not know God, because *God is love,*" (italics mine).

So because God is love, and I am using the English word (not the original Greek) as the basis of translation for this teaching purpose, wherever the word *love* is quoted in the 1 Corinthians 13:1-8 passage, I change it out and insert the word *God* in its place, and the word *it* is replaced with *he*. Using the NIV version once more, this is how it would read:

> If I speak in the tongues of men or of angels, but do not have God, I am only a resounding gong or a clanging cymbal. If I have the gift of prophecy and can fathom all mysteries and all knowledge, and if I have a faith that can move mountains, but do not have God, I am nothing. If I give all I possess to the poor and give over my body to hardship that I may boast, but do not have God, I gain nothing.

> God is patient, God is kind. He does not envy, he does not boast, he is not proud. He does not dishonor others, he is not self-seeking, he is not easily angered, he keeps no record of wrongs. God does

not delight in evil but rejoices with the truth. He always protects, always trusts, always hopes, always perseveres.

God never fails.

In the time I've been in jail here at Ford Mountain, I've come to a place to allow God's love to permeate my whole being. Until I was arrested back in July 2016, I never truly let God into my whole life. I never questioned my salvation in Jesus Christ, but as far as allowing him to love me to the fullness that he desired, I would say to Jesus, "I love you," then sticking out my hand as if I am straight-arming an opponent in football as I'm running down the field to gain more yards then saying, "but this is as close as you get." I would not let God love me because of my shame, because of my guilt, because of my unworthiness, and through my selfishness and pride, in my self-pity, I would not let Jesus in. All my faith in Christ was in my head, I would not let his truth, his love, his favor, and his treasures from heaven sink into the deep crevices of my heart, deep, deep into my soul. It took God to exact correction, rebuke, and the chastening of my sins to bring me to a place of deep repentance, deep forgiveness, and through trials and his refiner's fire, set me on a path of restoration, the renewing of my mind, a place where I can walk in holiness and purity.

When I finally allowed God into my heart and let him love me, and receiving his love in its fullness, the result was, I learned to love myself. As I learned to love myself, I learned to love others properly with good boundaries – a love that is pleasing to God because in this love, I choose to come into alignment with his Word. Also, and similarly, I finally allowed God's forgiveness penetrate my heart, and in receiving his forgiveness in its fullness, the result was that I forgave myself, and as I forgave myself, I started to completely forgive others, completely letting go of what they've done to me.

Now I'm walking in the greatest commandment because I let God love me; I let him in finally. Man, can we be stubborn! I am letting go of my pride, letting God *chip away* at my faults and my shortfalls, bringing forth a transformation so that I am truly a new creature in Christ, made new by his blood. This is our hope, and I pray that as you read this, you allow God do the same to you – let him in, let him love you, let him change you – and surrender your life to him. Allow Jesus to be the true God of your life and watch the treasures from heaven fall on you. Amen.

May 7, 2018

The chaplain has said to me quite a few times here in Ford Mountain, "The Holy Spirit can do more for you in a few seconds than what you could do in a lifetime."

So why do we always chase after *good* deeds, *good* causes, and *good* things when God wants so much more for us? Here are some reasons:

+ Often, we just don't know any better. We see things that need to be done in ministry, in callings, at work, even at home, but we only trust our minds, our eyes, and our wills, rather than God's.

+ It's hard to sift through the *white noise* in our communities – we need this; we need that! Then we press into our own efforts to meet those needs because we should stand up for *good* causes, and we do it in the name of God. We wonder after a while, and we get tired and less motivated and less co-ordinated, and next thing we know, the *good* deed fizzles out!

+ We live in a success-driven society. Bring on results! Get things done! They should have been done yesterday! We rarely take time to slow down to hear God's view on what we're doing for our *good* cause, if there is an opinion for him to give at all.

I've come up with inventions, business ideas, and concepts over the years and I thought God was in on all of them. Strangely, none of them came to fruition. I thought it was because I wasn't motivated enough, or not the right timing. I mean, these were all *good* ideas. Finally, one day I asked God about all of them and he said to me, "I wasn't in any of those ideas." Now that's humbling.

I learned, as a result, to hear God's voice, to trust his voice, and not move until he says so. I've also learned to differentiate divine appointments with others and chance meetings.

There is power in divine appointments. As I move along this journey, I will grow in being the person I am called to be rather than the person I think I should be, and this is hard. This is because often we don't know any better. We need to sift through the *white noise* of what others say, and not bow to the pressures of a success-driven society. All the Lord asks, "Be still and know that I am God" (inside Psalm 46:10). Amen.

May 11, 2018

> *And you shall know the truth, and the truth shall make you free.*
> - John 8:32 (NKJV)

I wrote that Scripture passage down, so I could remember where it was. I don't generally make a habit of memorizing Scripture, but because I read the Scriptures daily, I was able to retain a lot of the verses. I loved it while witnessing to someone or sharing in a Bible study, when the Holy Spirit brings forth a Scripture to mind and that would be the exact thing the listener needed to hear.

This is what happens when we receive the privilege of falling under the anointing of the Holy Spirit so that his Word and his works flow through us. We become *available vessels* for Christ, and the truth of his Word is then spoken forth. Does that ever happen to you? All of a sudden, when you are in a conversation with someone, the Scriptures flood your head, and you can't help speak them forth? Or when you are writing in a card to wish them well or bring forth a word of encouragement, then Scripture comes to mind *out of the blue?* That's the power of the Holy Spirit working in you. Truth comes forth, and it brings you joy. It brings encouragement, love, and peace to the receiver because they've read or heard exactly what they needed to read or hear at that very moment. It's divine timing, a blessing from God. This is true even if God is asking you to deliver correction, an admonishment, or an exhortation to someone, especially when you operate in the humility and surrender of the Holy Spirit. The anointing of the Word of God falls on it, so the receiver can receive it in love, even if it is tough love. That is the beauty of God bringing hope, joy, peace, guidance, and understanding into our lives, and it's brought forth in his power. Live and walk in the power of the anointing of God and watch his scriptures come alive in your minds and your hearts. It's there you will know freedom. Amen.

May 12, 2018

A New Identity Thanks to Sin's Death
Romans Chapter 6

I am a new creation. I am being transformed. Every day, I am noticing a difference in my identity to the kingdom of heaven. Sin is dying on the vine. Roots of sin are being pulled out of my heart. This has been a somewhat slow process for me because it has been breaking my pride, my stubbornness, and my selfishness. He has smashed the broken pot, put me back on the potter's wheel, and is re-shaping me into the person he originally intended me to be. He has thrown me into the oven, turned up the heat, taken me back out, painted me, stuck me back in the oven, turned the heat up even higher, pulled me out, let me cool down. In his eyes, I now look shiny and new, beautiful in his sight, a masterpiece from his point of view. Then he will fill this new pot with his water and put me to work because a pot has its uses. So now I let God have this pot and let him use it however he likes, for I am his.

God is giving me a new identity, a new outlook on life, hope for now and for the future. He is my rock and my salvation. In him, I will fear no evil. As a result of this new identity, I am choosing Christ's way over mine, surrendering my life to him in a way never thought possible. As a result, I see things more clearly, not so quick to judge, more quick to forgive, more quick to ask for forgiveness when I make a mistake, see God's love, see God's abundance in everything, and to respond likewise to others, seeing the best in them. I am learning greater wisdom, walking in greater humility every day, being transformed into his likeness, and not resisting this transformation every step of the way like I did before. When God gets a hold of a stubborn child and they receive correction, God knows they will be a force to be reckoned with because he knows they will be sold out for him and him only. That's the beauty of God's grace, of God's love for us.

Let him get a hold of you and change you. In saying this, I promise it will be painful. You will have trials. It will be hard, and it will be amazing, all at the same time. And it will all be worth it because you are worth the changes God wants to make with you, so you can walk in the fullness of Christ, living a life worthy of your calling. Amen.

May 14, 2018

You, O Lord, use the imperfections of life to refine us, and use the imperfections of people – our faults and our character flaws – like sand paper on a piece of wood to help us grow in character, in patience, in perseverance so that we become more like you. You suffered for us, and in our suffering, we are being shaped, being molded. In this, we become more of a blessing to you, more capable when pressed into service, a fragrant offering to God.

Help us learn from our mistakes and our imperfections, and we bring them to the cross. You laid down your life for us, so we could be reconciled back to you. You allowed evil to come into the world because you gave us choice and free will. I have reason to believe that you gave permission so that you wouldn't be the only one possessing that knowledge, and now that we have such knowledge, we will know it like you for eternity. And because of the great price you paid to bring us back to yourself, to those who have received your free gift will be with you forever, and all of us will still possess the knowledge between good and evil.

I choose to forsake evil as you do, but I need your supernatural power to help me. I am dependent on you for everything. Without you, my life is nothing and meaningless. You give me meaning; you give me purpose. I worship you, Lord Jesus.

Lead me to the path of understanding; teach me your ways, as I humble myself before you, in full surrender. You are the giver of life, so we can live life abundantly. Give me strength to walk in my calling, that I may be obedient to you in every way.

You are my hope and my salvation. You are my focal point. I dedicate and give my life to you so that I may know you, the lover of my soul. Amen.

May 16, 2018

True Worship Is Spiritual Experience, Not Religion

But the hour is coming, and now is, when true worshippers will worship the
Father in spirit and truth; for the Father is seeking such to worship him.
God is spirit, and those who worship him must worship in sprit and truth.

- John 4:23-24 (NKJV)

One of the struggles so many people have and so often stops them from coming to Christ is it is viewed negatively in terms of its spirituality. It is seen as a religion rather than as a spiritual experience. It is seen as a bunch of rules that one must follow rather than an amazing journey with a personal, intimate, loving God. God is seen so often as distant, a mean old ogre, unloving, judgmental, and wanting to strike you with lightning the minute you make a mistake. It doesn't help that so many believers walk, talk, and believe as if this is the case. It's because they judge, are critical, and often unforgiving. They quote Scripture conveniently to justify their position, but they are missing the mark to help those come to faith in Jesus, gracefully but truthfully help a new believer, a struggling believer, or even a backslidden believer be lifted up, strengthened, and encouraged to walk and live a blameless and holy life. But we can't do this of our own strength, of our own might, and on our own will. We need the supernatural help of the Holy Spirit to propel us to truth, to holiness, and to righteous living. This is why our spiritual walk, our spiritual experience, our spiritual journey gets skewed, smoke-screened, and clouded because of our poor example as Christians, not showing the love of God in us but listing off do's and don'ts, not showing love, grace and mercy in perfect balance with truth, surrender, confession and repentance and not showing the tenderness of God but our own wrath and judgment instead.

Jesus was the epitome of this balance, and he is asking us to do likewise. When we live for him, we will walk like him, love like him, show truth like him, show mercy like him, and show his supernatural power just as he did, to whichever gifts that has been imparted to us by the Holy Spirit. When we walk in the fullness of our spiritual experience people will see it. They will notice you are different and will want to know why. It is then God will give you words and actions as his *available vessel* to sow and reap a harvest as we all have been called to in the Great Commission. Amen.

May 17, 2018

It is so hard to distinguish between being obedient to the leading by the Holy Spirit in doing God's will and our exercising our own will thinking it is God's will and doing it for his name. Of course, God does use all of our circumstances and our choices to his glory anyways, and in that he knows the end from the beginning. But for those who want to follow Christ and are willing partners in the kingdom to hear, listen, and obey, God desires to teach us to listen to his still, small voice in the wake of opposition, trials, distractions, and temptations. He wants us to learn and hear his voice against the *white noise* of the enemy's and also to our own. This is very, very difficult. So what gets in the way? I desire to share a few ideas, as the variables and circumstances for each person are so wide:

1) Pride gets in the way of hearing God's voice. If we start practicing humility and surrender to Jesus, then it is going to help clear the path to hearing his voice.

2) Fear – God told me to not be afraid before coming to jail. Unhealthy fear can cause us to make rash decisions. It can cloud our judgment, which could lead to poor decisions or not hearing the Lord's or wise counsel from someone else. Rather, we should operate in this kind of fear: "The fear of the Lord is the beginning of wisdom; a good understanding have all those who do his commandments. His praise endures forever." (Psalm 111:10 NKJV).

3) Ignorance – If we don't know what we don't know, we are going to be in trouble. Not knowing, understanding, learning, and then not applying God's Word is a recipe for being led astray. The more we learn God's Word, comprehend it, then apply it to our lives, the Holy Spirit will bring it to our memory (John 14:26). We have God's Word, so let's not make excuses to read and learn from it.

There are many more variables like the operation of the spirit realm, transformation in our souls, renewing in our minds, prayer and meditation, operating in the Spirit, etc. But I, in listening to his still, small voice in leading me to write this down, these were the three we can start working on in our journey to hearing God's voice; and then heeding to it in obedience because of your love for him and willingness to follow him. Amen.

May 20, 2018

I yearn for my heart to be made whole, for the pain to go away. I desire to have the sin in my life gone, the dirty feeling in my heart washed away. I know in my heart the feelings of insecurity and doubt need not be part of my life experience and allowing the knowledge of being loved enter my soul, but some days I am having a hard time expressing the love that overcomes insecurity and doubt. My heart is heavy and in anguish. God, take away the roots of my sin. In the deep crevices of my soul, pull out my iniquity. Eradicate my selfishness and my pride and the evil desires of my heart. I pray that my life, my thoughts, my attitudes, and my desires come into alignment with you; holy, pure, and blameless.

By your blood, you have covered my sins and my iniquities. You are leading me to the path of wholeness. By your deep love, you sent your Son, Jesus, to die on the cross for my sins so that I would have hope, a plan for redemption that you have carried out. Your plan is perfect; by your blood, you are restoring my soul. Because of the resurrection, you defeated sin and death, for sin and death could not have a hold on you. You took from the enemy the keys to death and Hades, you have given us victory. You laid down your life for me so that I can share in your kingdom and your blessings.

Show me the way, O Lord, show me the way. You took my sin and nailed it to the cross. Grant me the strength to believe in your great name, to accept the free gift of salvation in its fullness. Help me receive the fullness of your healing, for your healing power is magnificent. Help me experience the fullness of your magnificence, the fullness of our inner healing. Help me lay down my pride and my arrogance. I raise the white flag in surrender to your lordship. You are Lord and you are God; there is none like you. Nothing compares to you. Help me let go of my fleshly desires that are sinful in nature; give me your strength to help win that war. My heart wants the fragrances of your love, the taste of your goodness, and the touch of your healing power. My whole desire is for you, Lord Jesus, so I ask you to restore my soul and make it whole as I lay down the strongholds and bondage that is keeping me from experiencing the fullness of your love. Help me receive this as I also love myself and forgive myself, so I can be the one you've designed me to be rather than being the one I've been pretending to be. Help me be real, not a counterfeit. In Jesus' name, amen.

My Story

April 7, 2018

I have a lot of people I need to make amends to. I may have written this before, but I feel the need to write it now, just in case I haven't. Some of them I may never be able to, like the victims and their parents. But of those, I may have an opportunity to say sorry to is my partner and my family. I just don't know how they will react if I ever see them again face-to-face, but I can't be afraid. I have to make the effort and do my best. Most importantly, I need to be humble and not be defensive. I need to listen more and speak less. Make no excuses. Just say sorry and hear them out completely. It's more important for them to get things off their chest and for them to say what they need to say. Finally, I need to learn to let go and allow them to re-engage with me if they so wish to. An important reminder to me is they are the ones in control of these conversations, not me. Without this humility, without this letting go of control, the healing process for everyone will be hindered, and the chances of moving forward for all affected by my actions thwarted.

This is what I need to do, and I need God's help to get me through this.

Thank you, Lord, for helping me write this down so that my thoughts are put to paper. Thank you for showing me the way. Grant me courage, humility, and strength to do what needs to be done so that those who have been so affected by my actions and poor choices have a chance to finally speak out. Help me remember the serenity prayer so that I can appropriately respond to each meeting. I leave this all in your hands. In Jesus' name, amen.

April 10, 2018

Note: (names in black are the real names and used by permission)

Entering His Rest (Hebrews 4:11-13)

The Lord has asked me to pull back from some responsibilities here in the camp so that I can rest more in him. In this season, I will have an opportunity for introspection and a closer seeking of the Lord for his will in my life. So last night, I approached Terry, the other Bible study leader, to take over starting next week. This Wednesday will be my last class teaching for a season that is undetermined. I won't even be attending the studies as a student either. I will be letting the chaplain know today so he is aware. I will still lead my support group every Saturday afternoon, but there is someone else waiting in the wings to take over that group too. God is teaching me succession planning; for in my heart, these groups belong to him. They are not mine. I just need to have the discernment to see what God wants, how and where he is leading me without necessarily knowing the why. What I realized last night as a result of events in the afternoon was that I am burning out. It's hard to believe as I'm in jail, but this is not a traditional jail, and one can get pretty busy in here in a hurry if one chooses to do so. I already work six days a week in the kitchen, and I do all these other extra-curricular activities outside of work. Right now, God is just asking me to take the foot off the gas pedal a bit and wait on him. And so I shall obediently and trust that in this time of "rest," I will discover more of his love, more of his wisdom, new revelation, a refreshing of the spirit, a newness of life. Rest promises these things as we seek him diligently in that time of rest. And the cool thing was that God confirmed it today in my reading in Scripture, which was Hebrews 4:11-16. That was encouraging.

Lord, show me your favor during this time of rest. Show me your Spirit. Show me your love. Show me how to receive these things in abundance as you guide me through each day. Teach me to relax and have more fun. Teach me to love life more, and that in all things, I just choose to trust you in rejoicing or in suffering, in rest or in time when you are teaching me hard lessons, in blessings and opportunities, or in trials and tribulations. I now know there is value in all these things, and each has its own weight in value.

You suffered and died for us, and that is of great value to all of us. Teach us to be more like you in every respect and then not to be afraid of it. In Jesus' name, amen.

April 20, 2018

Entry: (names in bold are changed to protect the identities of the individuals) (names in black are the real names and used by permission)

Freedom

It is for freedom that Christ has set us free. Stand firm, then, and do not let yourselves be burdened again by a yoke of slavery.
- Galatians 5:1 (NIV)

Early in the morning before waking up, I had a dream. It was a dream about my two hut-mates and fellow Christian brothers Milton (who has also become a close friend here) and **Andrew** move back to 'A' hut while I was left behind in 'D' hut. We were now separated. I told Milton later in the morning about this dream and then I said to him, "I think God is 'springing' me out of here (meaning, jail)!" Milton looked a little perplexed and I pointed to the outside, "I think I'm leaving here!" He agreed.

Later in the day, around 1:00 p.m., I got called to the office. There was a parole officer waiting for me and gave me good news – I qualified for both day parole and full parole! I signed the papers, got my picture taken, then went back to the hut immediately to show Milton the parole papers and show him that the dream did come from the Lord and this was confirmation of the interpretation. For the next few hours, I was more dazed about what happened but I finally got excited – I'm being set free from jail!

There is another freedom I wish to talk about, a greater freedom. One I learned in greater measure since I've been here in Ford Mountain Correctional Center is freedom in Christ. Freedom to forgive; freedom to repent; freedom to feel loved; freedom to receive forgiveness; freedom to love myself, probably for the first time; freedom to grow and mature spiritually; freedom to be healed of the "cancer" in my soul that God promised he would remove; freedom to worship in a way never thought possible; freedom to receive inspiration from heaven – it's this freedom that no one can take away, save God himself. This freedom was attained through trials, tribulations, suffering, and pain. It was worth every second of it. When one chooses to humble one's self and surrender to the living God, one will witness transformation, wholeness, and restoration. Now that is freedom.

What is Faith – Part 2 (Galatians 2:20)

Faith isn't circumstantial. Faith isn't the result of works. Faith is believing who we are in Christ – the one who died for our sins, and as a result of our faith in Christ, we will not be put to extreme highs and lows in our faith because circumstances in our lives will no longer dictate our *faith* gauge. Like a large ship sailing through a stormy sea, it may rock back and forth, side to side, but the captain still has the command of the ship to steer it to where he or she wants it to go. No stormy seas are going to stop that ship from reaching its destination. So if on faith you receive a word from God about an outcome in your life that he wishes to reveal to you, you can trust in his omniscience that the outcome he revealed will come to pass. He may just not reveal how the journey to that outcome may go. So if you hit trials, tribulations, or bumpy roads on your journey, remember that God is still in control, not circumstances in your life, not other people, not the enemy. If you're praying for more faith, expect God to *turn up the heat* on you so that through the refiner's fire, your faith will be purified and your faith will be made whole. God will be exceedingly glad to give you this amazing treasure of his, but it can come at a cost. In faith, he will bust our stubbornness. In faith, he will break our pride. In faith, he will heal and deliver us from our sins. Then, as a result of this new, restored, purified faith, you, in Christ, will do greater works because he will be able to test you in your new level of faith, and as you show your works of faith in your stewardship, he will then determine whether or not he will entrust you with more responsibilities.

God will try your faith. He will test your faith, and that's because he loves you so much and wants you to partner with him to do great things for his mighty name. The journey to that faith may look bumpy, scary, muddy, and seemingly horrible. But in the end God knows what he is doing and will lead you to the outcome he wants for you – the fulfillment of the purpose and destiny he's designed just for you.

It takes faith to walk in your purpose, it takes faith to believe in God's destiny for you. Don't lose sight of this when life seems hard, when it looks like the cards are stacked against you, when circumstances in your life don't seem to go your way. He is faithful and true and will lead you to a glorious life as you learn to trust him completely in surrender and humility. Amen.

April 22, 2018

I just chaired my last support group meeting last night. It was the biggest group ever to attend. As part of God's plan for me to rest in him before I leave here, I see that God is still so mindful of the details of my life because of his deep love for me, including the provision of two new co-chairs of our support group. God wanted us to be responsible stewards in all that we do, including succession planning. I want to share in reverse order from now to since before my arrest how God has been the one behind all the changes in my life. He showed his love not only to me, but to all of us. So here we go.

God provided two level-headed leaders to replace me in the support group. God provided another Bible study teacher to take over the Bible study here in Ford Mountain. God provided another bookkeeper and tax preparer to take over my company on the day of my sentencing, so much so that all the files were stored in boxes three full months prior to the sentencing date, plus anything else (file cabinets, office materials, etc.) needed for the transition. The Lord also provided for my partner and I to be free of all debts one month prior to my first arrest. It was the first time in our married lives that that had ever happened so she could be debt-free when we separated. God knew what was coming, so he provided one financial provision after another between January 2016 to June 2016, erasing more than $40,000 in debt and taxes during that time span. He also asked me to retire from all the sports I was playing at the time – indoor soccer, floor hockey and slow-pitch baseball (two teams) so that at the time of my arrest I hadn't embarrassed any of my teammates. I retired from them all in 2014 and 2015. He also shrank my company from five offices back down to one in 2014 to ensure that I was working alone, and again, protecting others from gross embarrassment of associating with me once all the news got out publicly of my conviction and sentence. I called this God's *controlled implosion*. God cared enough about me, but equally important, he cared enough about the others around me to create a complete succession plan so that the activities that needed to be kept going (support group, Bible study, the business) he provided replacements – qualified replacements – at the right time. He spared many from embarrassment and saved my partner financially so she could start fresh on her own.

That's a God who loves us, cares for us, and provides for us when we choose to listen and let him have control. Amen.

April 28, 2018

Isaiah 54

The Holy Spirit led me to read Isaiah 54 and had me read it as if he was specifically speaking to me rather than the passage being spoken to the Israelites. The passage really lifted my spirit as I read through it. In my jail-issued Bible, verse 17, the last verse, was highlighted in yellow and it reads:

> "No weapon formed against you shall prosper, and every tongue which rises against you in judgment you shall condemn. This is the heritage of the servants of the Lord, and their righteousness is from me," says the Lord.

I am just going to receive this word from God and believe what he has said to me. I am grateful for how he has corrected me, how he has brought me into alignment with him and his ways, and I receive his correction. I love how Isaiah 54:7-8 reads as it is as if he is speaking to me personally:

> "For a mere moment I have forsaken you, but with great mercies I will gather you. With a little wrath I hid my face from you for a moment; but with everlasting kindness I will have mercy on you," says the Lord, your redeemer.

Walking in this correction, I must now walk in my calling – to help restore those who are lost; to fulfill the mandate of Matthew 25; to share the good news of Jesus Christ; to be the steward, custodian and caretaker of all the responsibilities that he has and will entrust me, both now and in the future. I am to remain humble and contrite for because of my past sins I will be judged, I will be mocked, and I will be ridiculed, but I can't let that deter me from moving forward in the kingdom of God. My focus must be on Jesus and Jesus alone, and in doing so, I will be able to walk in his love, his strength, his mercy, his power, and his Spirit. I can do all things through Jesus Christ our Lord, who walk in the Spirit and not in the flesh.

Lord, grant me the strength to walk in your Spirit, to keep my eyes on you. Show me your way that I may live in the life everlasting, knowing that you are my true treasure and nothing else matters. Amen.

April 30, 2018

I am learning to listen. I am learning to listen to God's still, small voice so that I can hear him clearly through all the noise life brings us. I am learning to listen to my body, which tells me when it's time to heal or time to slow down or time to stop. I am learning to listen to my brothers and sisters in Christ, who have something to teach me, and in doing so, we all get to grow. I am learning to listen to the counsel of others, especially when they are bold enough to gently point out my shortfalls, so in listening to them, I have an opportunity to improve.

I desire to say goodbye to arrogance, say goodbye to conceit, say goodbye to the grand deception that I'm better than others, smarter than others, more able than others. God can take my abilities and my intellect all away from me in a flash or in a blink of an eye. It's a privilege to have what I have and be who he's calling me to be. I just need to put my pride in park, turn off its engine, and get out of that car and walk away from it forever.

We will be tempted to go back, especially when things get tough and trials come, and then in our pride, we get defensive, or worse yet, go on the offensive and in that process hurt our Christian witness, and impede the best possible outcome for both me and others.

Listening allows me to be steered in the right direction, allows me to hear the best counsel, allows me to make the best decisions. It grants me life-giving opportunities. So again, I shall put my pride in park and listen to God's voice, and listen to those around me. In this, I will grow in Christ to be that better person God wants me to be. Amen.

To listen is to learn.

- Mike Mahy

May 1, 2018

I am learning patience. Patience for my brothers. Patience to wait on the Lord and not move until he tells me to. It's like being a soldier in the trenches and not doing anything until the sergeant shouts, "Attack!" or "Fire!" It's knowing what to do and anticipating – waiting – until it's time. So often, we get ahead of God. We receive instruction from him, get excited about it, then run ahead of him thinking, *We've got this!* Then wonder what happened when it doesn't come to fruition or falls apart. So often we like to *help* God out.

Patience is also when we receive a word, a vision, a calling, or a promise from God, and then we don't see the fulfillment of that for days, months, years, or decades. But you know it is from God; you wait patiently until he fulfills it.

This patience is a powerful tool in our heavenly toolkit. With it, we learn to trust God in a way where we come to a place of complete surrender and stay there knowing he is with us. We learn to become patient with others, knowing that we all grow and learn life lessons at our different paces. We learn to be patient with ourselves, learning more of who we are in Christ.

It is all a discovery process.

Through patience, we learn the love of God: "Love is patient, love is kind" (1 Corinthians 13:4a), as it starts in the "love chapter" of the Bible. God is so patient with us, working through our struggles, shortfalls, and deficiencies; teaching us, uplifting us, correcting us; and slowly bringing into alignment with him so we become more and more into his likeness. He builds on our strengths too so that we can be even better stewards of what he's given us, as we allow him to do so humbly and in complete surrender. Let us learn patience and grow in it so we become more like him in this way. It will bring us all into a new level of freedom. Amen.

May 10, 2018

I am learning to not jump ahead of God. I found out last Friday that I was granted day parole. All I need to do now is wait for a bed in the halfway house granted as part of my parole in Victoria, British Columbia, Canada. The trouble I am facing now is two-fold: 1) I am beginning to understand when someone is getting close to their release date they start to develop "short-timers" syndrome, and 2) I am beginning to understand why God withholds information from us about our lives, our calling, and our future so that we stay humble, patient, and trusting him to guide us each day.

Let me explain each one a little further:

1) "Short-timers" syndrome – I see my fellow inmates as they get close to their release dates not to care as much about their jobs. They deliberately come five to ten minutes late for work, tend to do less or the minimum, and they even get a little grumpy because they'd rather be on the outside those gates, walls, and fences. Their minds are already there, already thinking about their new life on the outside. I saw this also when I was in the armed forces (I was in the Navy). Those getting close to the end of their contracts were behaving similarly. People who are close to their retirements have thought this way too, looking for a new life "on the other side." I don't know my release date, but I know it is soon, and I realized this morning I am growing impatient. So to counter this, I am going to count my blessings in here instead, for there are many – the heart transformation, the opportunities to learn more about myself and how much God truly loves me, the opportunity to journal my journey here in Ford Mountain, the friendships I have made here, especially in the Christian community, the break I've had from the distractions of the outside so I can focus on inner healing and nothing else, the blessing of an almost complete reversal of my diabetes, my relationships with the chaplain, the Addictions and Drug counselor, and my twelve-step groups, and the list goes on.

In this thinking, I will continue to be grateful, which will help my attitude to remain patient and humble.

2) Why God withholds information – can you imagine if God allowed us to know everything about our lives before it happened? Because of our sinful condition, I have reason to believe that we would be lazy, selfish, arrogant, prideful, conceited, worried, scared, angry, upset, sad, depressed, perplexed; almost anything but happy. There are times the Holy Spirit will allow us to see things in the future, parts of our calling, revelations of ourselves or of the kingdom, but only so that we are kept in line with the direction God wants us for the glory of the kingdom, bringing glory to God. Misuse of such information and such revelation and exercise our own will on it to the exclusion of God, then we run the risk of telling the wrong person, jumping ahead (or even behind) of God's timing, or using the information for selfish or improper purposes. We run the risk of the revelation itself to become our "god" instead of our worship belonging to the God of heaven only. I also have reason to believe this is also why God limits the vast majority of us to obtain massive material possessions. When God entrusts us with treasures from heaven, whether it is physical (abilities, talents), material, or spiritual, we must be responsible stewards, caretakers, and custodians of what we were given. He will test us with what we've been entrusted, and in this case for me, the knowledge of leaving well before my actual release date but not certain of the date of release itself (a bed in the halfway house I'm waiting for must become available), and we must show ourselves faithful to him as to what we've been given. And when we pass the test, he will bless us, sometimes with joy or contentment, sometimes with an upgrade, sometimes with a new trial or tribulation to refine us further, sometimes with greater or a new responsibility – whatever it will be, it will be, in the end a greater blessing to you and glory to his great name. In whatever way, trust God that he has our best interests in mind, trust in his omniscience and lean not unto our own understanding, be humble and responsible with what God

has given you, entrusted you, revealed to you and continue to walk in full surrender to him, no matter what your situation is, ranging from amazing to terrible.

We don't need to know everything, but trust the one who does.

Amen.

May 13, 2018

God can do the impossible. He orchestrates things in such a way that you can't help but marvel at what he does. I am asking him for a miracle – restoration of relationships that I, through my actions, have blown apart. They're broken because I sinned greatly, and who would want to forgive me for what I've done against them? Against society? The Holy Spirit spoke to me months ago, "I will restore some of those relationships." I believe him. I just don't know the timeline or how he's going to do it. I mean, he's going to work on their hearts and orchestrate restoration of some of the relationships I've destroyed – I don't know who either – and do this without interfering with their own wills. Now that's going to be miracles.

One of the relationships I've destroyed is the one between my mom and I. And today, being Mother's Day, I can't wish her a happy Mother's Day because we haven't spoken since October 24, the day before my sentencing. God allowed my story to be all over the news the next day and that's when my mom found out (actually my sister told her before this all reached the news, thankfully). She never heard it from me because I was too ashamed to tell her that her son committed crimes against young boys and that he was going to jail. I was petrified of her reaction and how I would be treated by her afterwards. Our relationship is already toxic, and we butt heads all the time. Thanks to being here in Ford Mountain, I've had a chance to be healed by the anger, the bitterness, and the judgment I had on her for decades. I have finally let go. I don't know if my mom has; but if my mom is one of those relationships he wants to restore it will, I believe, take a miracle. God is into performing miracles, so I can't wait to see how this will play out, without interfering with the will of my mom. I have forgiven her; it's going to take deep forgiveness for restoration be made possible – deep forgiveness in both directions – so I will wait for that day. I've done my part; I've forgiven her deeply. I love my mom unconditionally; I pray for her constantly. And now, even though she can't read today, "Happy Mother's Day Mom, I love you." I write this with tears of healing in my eyes, tears of anguish in my heart, asking her for forgiveness for what I've done. I now let go of this request and leave it in the hands of the one who can restore relationships. Thank you, Jesus. Amen.

What happened since: Unfortunately, my mom passed away on June 28, 2021, after having major heart surgery in April and during a massive heat wave (104 F or 40 C) that contributed to her death. I did help serve her from May 21 to June 8, by preparing food and running errands in the background for both my mom and my sister, while my sister was staying with her and caring for her needs once she was out of the hospital; but I never saw my mom directly. We didn't make direct amends either, so I now say, "I'm sorry mom for all I've done."

May 22, 2018

Entry: (names in bold are changed to protect the identities of the individuals)

It is so important to be obedient to the leading of the Holy Spirit. Yesterday, I was in conversation with my good friend **the lady who has always supported me**, and the conversation of my parole came up. I had asked **the lady who has always supported me** back in December and January to write a letter of support for me so that it would help me get parole. She never wrote the letter and I had completely forgotten about it until she brought it up in conversation.

She said, "The reason I didn't write the letter is because when I thought about doing it, I kept getting a check in my spirit."

My response to he was, "Well actually I didn't need it" (**The only lady in my Bible study** sent a letter unbeknownst to me, and that is in another entry of my journal book).

She said, relieved, "Oh I am glad you're not mad (or upset, can't remember exact words) about me not writing it."

I responded, "I'm actually glad you listened and obeyed the Holy Spirit. I've to commend you for your obedience." A little later she started asking about parole. I just responded, "Right now all I can tell you is I am here one day at a time and I'm still here at Ford Mountain."

It's not time yet for **the lady who has always supported me** to know when I finally leave. It's my heart's desire to surprise her with a visit at her home with **the only lady in my Bible study**. The only people on the outside that know I got day parole is my sister, brother-in-law, and my close friend and business partner **the only lady in my Bible study**. I have a peace in my heart at this time to wait before letting anyone else in my outside community know about me leaving here before my sentence is finished inside Ford Mountain. It will give me a chance to get my bearings, report to the authorities that I need to, establish the business partnership, and clear up email and other computer stuff. I believe that because of this peace, this is either what God wants, or he is saying to me, "I will honor that too." Either way, thank you, Jesus, for being my support. I choose to honor and obey you. Amen.

What happened since: I asked **the only lady in my Bible study** to set up a meeting with **the lady who has always supported me** at a restaurant, and I would come in a little later to surprise her. Well, it worked! I was able to come around the corner and say to her, "Is this seat taken?" and she almost jumped out of her skin! That was about three days after I was released from prison in mid-September, 2018.

FORD MOUNTAIN

April 11, 2018

In some Christian circles, it seems like they talk and treat Christ and the Word of God as a *magic formula*, and that to engage and walk in the Holy Spirit is like employing a *magic wand* and presto! Your miracle has come, or there is your healing. I know God has the power to do such things, but what I've learned more than ever before is that God is more interested in a deep, meaningful, loving, and personal relationship with us first and the manifestation of his presence stems from that. For instance, I've had several people pray over my type 2 diabetes for years now. Instead of getting better, it got worse to the point of taking two of one pill twice a day, two of another pill three times a day, one of a very expensive pill once a day, and insulin once a day to cap it off. At my heaviest I was almost 220 lbs. So what happened? The day of my arrest I was 195 lbs.; that was July 21, 2016. In five months, from a combination of stress, change of diet, and eating habits, plus fasting when God told me to, I dropped to 160 lbs. When I saw my doctor in December 2016, she took me off my most expensive pill altogether and then cut my insulin from thirty units a day to ten units a day. I stayed that way until I came to jail in October 2017. By this time, I was so broken in my heart that I hit a very low point in my life. But it was here at Ford Mountain I started to exercise – racquetball, soccer, baseball, and long walks with my new friends. I started learning about addictive behavior, criminal thinking, and how to remedy them, and then came the twelve-step groups.

Over the next six months a transformation began. I began to love myself. I began to make good solid food choices and stick with them. I felt loved by God. I wanted to live more abundantly. As a result and as a positive consequence of God sending me to jail (remember, he said before I came in to "trust me"), my medication of two of one pill once a day, two of another pill twice a day, and as of yesterday, the doctor took me off insulin! Is this a miracle? I believe so. It's one that is in slow progression. I am a transformed man, and it is God who is transforming me. I just want to say that miracles come in many packages, but it is still God that produces them. I love you, Jesus, with all my heart. Thank you for your healing. I give glory to you. Amen.

When your attitude changes, the healing begins.

- Mike Mahy

April 29, 2018

I give God praise for our support group for the level of transparency and the level of confessions the men are making in that room. I have never seen anything like this before, and I know that God is there with us, wanting to heal us from our wounds, our sins, our broken relationships, our broken lives. When I say the *level*, meaning "the disgusting details (but not to the level of sordid – we are all spared that) of transparency in that room" is off-the-charts honest, so much so that many of these men need tissues while they are talking. There's extreme patience and courtesy from the rest of the room while the confessor takes his time sorting through his feelings, working up the courage to speak about his next embarrassing piece, what he's done, how he has affected others, how it has destroyed his life, citing how much he's lost in all this as a result of his sex addiction. The group waits patiently, non-judgmentally. When he is finished confessing and opens up his Pandora's box, his Davey's locker, the group then responsibly gives him encouragement for taking such a first brave step and acknowledge to him that it took great courage to open up like that. Can you imagine if people in the church confessed their sins like that? I have strong reason to believe there would be a revival as a result, a spiritual awakening, an amazing renewal. Men's lives are changing for the better in this room because my support group, and thank you twelve-step groups, has provided a safe, confidential place for men to open up. I mean these are men! Being sensitive! Opening up the most horrid parts of their lives! They never thought it would ever be safe to open up for fear of being ridiculed, being judged. And after they have opened up they feel like a ten thousand pound anvil has come off their chest, off their shoulders, from their heads. And to top it off, this is being done in jail, the most unlikely of places where men would open up. But this isn't a normal jail. It's designed to help inmates (here called residents) get rehabilitated, and my support group is a welcome part of that healing process. I wish more jurisdictions in North America would emulate this model here at Ford Mountain in Chilliwack, British

Columbia. The statistics show that it has the highest success rate of those leaving here will not re-offend once they leave.

Thank you, God, for my support group and for this type of jail model; they are both amazing entities.

May 18, 2018

God is good. Another inmate here at Ford Mountain made a decision to follow Jesus. This is the third one since I've been here to make such a decision. It's amazing to see such hunger for God, and it's genuine. The tough part is when they leave here. This is a controlled environment with relatively few distractions and a strong focus and encouragement on spirituality. This is the opportunity to reap a harvest, to share the gospel of Jesus Christ. On the outside, they will face so many distractions, so I pray for them that they will commit to reading the Word of God and develop that as a habit; that they come to church and Bible study while they are in here; that they learn to pray and develop a loving, intimate relationship with God; that they foster loving relationships with the brethren so that they can grow and be equipped before they leave here. I pray for when they leave that God will bring loving Christians alongside them on the outside, supernaturally, and that the Lord leads them into a solid fellowship where they live so that the root of their faith can grow deep into the ground. So many of them here have severely broken lives, and I know it will take solid, mature Christians to come alongside them, accept them for where they are at, and then partner with God to lead them to where God wants them to be, so they can walk in the fullness of their purpose and destiny for the kingdom of God. God loves these souls, and he can't wait to use them because God has powerful ministries for so many of them. They will be used by Jesus as difference makers, and some will be game changers for the kingdom of God.

To those who are reading this, I implore you to be brave and come alongside the prison community and watch God use you for the kingdom. Be part of the transformation God wants make in others. Amen.

May 21, 2018

I am so looking forward to participating in tonight's Bible study, for we will have the privilege of hearing inmates share testimonies of how God have moved in their lives supernaturally. I have had the privilege of hearing some of them, and there is no doubt that God was moving in them, intervening divinely for them. I mean, some of these stories are crazy; they defy common sense – the perfect timing of police showing up at the door of one inmate with a warrant, while the inmate's face was turning blue from a drug overdose; another inmate collapsing from his blood sugar dropping too fast, and another inmate decides out of the blue to make a hot chocolate, which he has never made before for himself to take to Bible study and has never done since, and doesn't even so much as to take a sip of it yet, and then as he arrives to Bible study that was the exact need for the semi-comatose inmate going into insulin shock at the exact time, just to give a couple of examples.

When I have chaired a few twelve-step meetings, I have felt led by the Holy Spirit to ask the group – now I'm talking about fourteen or fifteen inmates in a meeting – if they believe God (as they understand him) has brought them here to Ford Mountain. Almost every hand goes up. Now that's the power of spiritual experience, a spiritual awakening in their hearts. My prayer is that spiritual awakening translates into a personal, loving, intimate relationship with Jesus Christ, who is himself spirit and truth, the author of our lives and the one who has the power and authority to bring transformation and restoration to those who earnestly seek him out.

Christianity is not a religion as so many people believe, even though in the book of James it is mentioned as such. In its true essence and spirit, however, it is a relationship with a personal and living God, who gives life and freedom and sets us on a spiritual journey with him to help us heal, grow, and learn to be like him. Hence, the amazing testimonies I can't wait to hear tonight so that all who listen understand that God is real, and he really moves in unexplainable ways. He is not just the miracle worker of the first century, he is the miracle worker of every century and is working still in the twenty-first century. Amen.

Speeches & Poems

April 6, 2018

Note: (names in black are the real names and used by permission)

So the Lord has closed a door here at Ford Mountain. Who was supposed to attend did attend, and who was supposed to learn did so as well. I believe God will use those he called to be businessmen for his kingdom. Praise his holy name. The last Bible study for business went last night. It was supposed to be Chad leading but he's now on the outside! Praise his holy name! Chad gave me final notes and his public speaking game, and off I went to teach, not sure how this would turn out. Pretty big shoes to fill. It went very well – lots of fun and lots of laughs, plus everyone who participated did a great job; everyone has improved.

I pray Chad uses this game as part of his teaching material for public speaking. I kept his game cards (and his pickle ball) with the intention of giving both of them back as a covenant relationship between Chad and I. Finally, I wrote a speech to give God glory for what he's done here and honor Chad and the students of the Bible study for business class. Here it is:

April 5, 2018

God opens doors, God closes doors. There is a time for everything. Back in January the Lord led me to start the Bible study for business. I didn't know how long it would last, and there was no material written for it. By the leading of the Holy Spirit, the study came together. Over the course of February and March, the study went on, preparing those who wanted to participate. Some of you here now have hope because you chose to attend, learn, and develop your business idea. You learned spiritual principles from the Word of God to help you with the premise we began with:

If you have been called by God into business and it has been given to you by revelation of the Holy Spirit, it will be unstoppable.

⋆   quote from my workbook – *Business With Purpose*

Next, Chad was led by God to put together this public speaking series as an extension of the Bible-study-for-business format, and his contribution has given each of you increased confidence to stand in front of your peers and improve your public speaking skillsets. Sadly but gladly at the same time, this is our last class in this series. Sad because Chad had planned to share more of his talents with us; glad because he has a new opportunity to resume his life on the outside. He was a blessing to us, and I pray God will lead him into the fullness of his calling and purpose for his life, as God is leading us for ours.

With that, let's start this final session and have lots of fun doing so!

Lord, I pray for all of us. You are raising up Josephs in the business world. I ask that we learn to obey you, be in full surrender to you, surrender these business relationships to you so that we understand that you have entrusted these responsibilities to us. Help us to learn stewardship, being only stewards in each business enterprise, not loving money or the businesses themselves. Help us have our hearts toward Jesus at all times, placing him on the throne of our lives, attitudes, relationships, possessions, and responsibilities. Lord, help us learn to have you be Lord over our abilities, talents, and intellect, over our mind, will, and emotions. In this, we seek to glorify your name, not afraid to build giant businesses making millions, no billions of dollars for your great name. Help us listen as you direct us as to what to do with these resources so that in full partnership with you, we become your hands and feet, your ears and mouth, that we may respond to your leading – feeding the "other 6 mountains". (Other mountains – church, family, education, politics, media, arts and entertainment) Show us how to do that for your glory, for your kingdom. In Jesus' name, amen.

April 9, 2018

I Am Loved

I am loved. I feel loved because I am loved.

I am valued. I feel valued because I am loved, and I feel loved because I am valued.

I am forgiven. I feel forgiven because I am loved and I am valued, and I feel loved because I am valued and I am forgiven.

I am cherished. I feel cherished because I am loved and I am valued and I am forgiven, and I feel loved because I am valued and I am forgiven and I am cherished.

I am honored. I feel honored because I am loved and I am valued and I am forgiven and I am cherished, and I feel loved because I am valued and I am forgiven and I am cherished and I am honored.

I am blessed. I feel blessed because I am loved and I am valued and I am forgiven and I am cherished and I am honored, and I feel loved because I am valued and I am forgiven and I am cherished and I am honored and I am blessed.

I am strengthened because of all the values God has put into me. I am loved. I am valued. I am forgiven. I am cherished. I am honored. I am blessed; so therefore I am strengthened.

April 12, 2018

Teamwork

Thank you, Jesus, for your inspiration for the closing positive message of today's hut meeting. Teaming up with you is the best partnership anyone could have. Thank you for delivering me the words to say so that others may be encouraged and you be glorified in it.

Here is today's message:

This week's theme: teamwork

Effective teamwork works in three parts:

1) Co-operation – a willingness to work together to reach a common goal

2) Co-ordination – an execution of a plan to maximize time and resources efficiently

3) Interdependence – a trusting of each other's capabilities to carry out their roles effectively and harmoniously when meshing of roles are required

April 18, 2018

This morning, I was on the list for our Wednesday morning hut meeting to give the closing positive message. This week's theme was on respect. I asked the Lord for help with it, so it would flow nicely. Thank you again, Lord, for your inspiration, your true treasures from heaven:

So here is this morning's message:

Respectful Relationships

Respect can be earned; respect can be given. The responsibility falls on the shoulders of the one whom the respect is attained.

Respect can be a one-way street, two-way street, or a multi-way street. It is to be guarded, nurtured, and used diligently so that both the respecter and "respectee" benefit from its relationship.

Respect is both positional and relational, and it exists on many different levels.

If you want true respect, start by learning to respect yourself so that in doing so you will succeed in respecting others.

Lord, teach us to respect you, honor you, respect your Word, and honor your Word. They go hand in hand. In this, we will have treasures in fostering amazing relationships, where authority is carried out diligently, responsibly, and with great care and attention. Teach us your ways, O Lord, and let us lean on your understanding so that we may grow in you, be one in you, and with you. In Jesus' name I pray, amen.

May 4, 2018

Here is the closing positive message that the Lord downloaded to me for Thursday's hut meeting, but never got to read out loud because a few inmates blew up at each other in the meeting. Tempers flared up but clearly there were deeper, underlying issues, so on my prayer walk later in the morning I prayed for the whole hut. I pray they all would know Jesus personally, but I also prayed for their protection and that they would let God help them through their issues. One of them later yesterday opened up about where he stands in his belief and relationship with God, so I see a crack in the door opening up.

I will continue to pray for them and allow the Holy Spirit do his work in them.

Now here is the message:

'D' Hut closing positive message – May 3, 2018

Accepting Change

When you choose to accept that you need change in your life to address places needed for improvement, then learning, planning, and executing those positive changes, you will discover more of who you are, what you can become, and how you can influence change to others, now and in the future. This is your hope and opportunity.

In truth, and as great as that sounds, it's better when you partner with God in accepting change in your life. When you choose to "plug in" to heaven in the process of making change in your life, you are trusting the knowledge of God's grace and truth, the power of his name, and his mighty presence by the power of his blood to bring forth transformation in your life and the renewing of your mind. That is the power and glory of Christ, choose to accept change – yes – but do it with him as your partner. Amen.

May 6, 2018

What Would It Look Like If?

What would it look like if – trust is still earned
But forgiveness flowed?

What would it look like if – we all saw a clean slate
As Jesus sees in our salvation?

What would it look like if – we never judged out of fear
Or of misinformation or misconception?

What would it look like if – we learn to love, to be loved,
And to receive love as God gives us?

What would it look like if – we showed compassion,
In the manner of the Good Samaritan?

What would it look like if – we saw the poorest, the most needy
Of our society in a way that compels us to do something more?

What would it look like if – we love our enemies,
Fed them, and gave them something to drink?

We would be more like Jesus.
That's what it would look like.

May 17, 2018

Note: this is supplemental

Who God Is to Me?

I believe in myself because I have a God
Who believes in me;

I love myself because I have a God
Who loves me;

I forgive myself because I have a God
Who forgives me;

I see myself as valuable because I have a God
Who values me;

I cherish my life because I have a God
Who cherishes me;

When I see myself in these ways, it is because this is how God
chooses to see me, and as I grow in these I will choose to see others
the same way. It is the way to growth and healing, life and liberty.

May 19, 2018

On May 17, I wrote down two things on a piece of paper: a little quote and a little closing positive message for our hut meeting that morning. The quote is this: "Inspiration that leads to transformation"

> I believe that at this point in my life, as I choose to fully surrender my life to Jesus, I have received a gift from him to "plug in" to heaven and receive words of wisdom, encouragement, and transformation from him. I know that we all possess this gift as it has to do with our choices, attitudes, and relationship to the heavenly host, as we grow in a close, loving, and intimate relationship with Jesus. He will bring you to a place of restoration, healing, renewal, and transformation in your body, soul, and spirit. Through Jesus, by the power of the Holy Spirit, opportunity to serve in many capacities will abound, and I have reason to believe inspiration will come as a result. It can come in many forms – a kind word to someone in God's perfect timing; a prophetic art; a new song; a poem or a great literary work; incredible insights in teaching others the Word of God; a new invention that has come by revelation of the Holy Spirit; receiving a commission for your calling; an act of kindness that is done selflessly and quietly; a moving of the spirit in worship; a prophetic word given; a medical breakthrough given by inspiration in the medical science community; an amazing and moving speech by one in politics who loves the Lord; a teacher who is patient and loves teaching their students; and the list goes on. But it is all about choices, which breed consequences, which leads me to share the closing positive message on Thursday, May 17's meeting:

> When good choices are made, quite often, we don't see the positive outcomes or positive consequences; but when poor choices are made, quite often we will see the negative outcomes or negative consequences in a hurry. This is because we all too often take our

good choices for granted, as they are an expectation; whereas our poor choices all too often stick out like a sore thumb, and many are quick to point them out.

I will make a good choice – I choose to follow Jesus. Amen.

JOURNAL
BOOK 5

INSPIRATIONAL WRITINGS

May 24, 2018

> *Your kingdom come, your will be done on Earth as it is in heaven.*
> - Matthew 6:10

Last night's Bible study focused on James 1:9-11, which talked about the poor who are rich in faith and the rich who ought to be grateful in the humble position of material wealth. So often, people pursue material wealth because the sin of greed is manifest, or they believe obtaining great wealth on Earth will give them status, position in the community, and influence to those around them. Although this may be true and is most likely to happen, if they pursue it to the exclusion of seeking God and all this for their own exclusive benefit, then the sin of pride is now manifest along with it. Quite often, fear of losing it all, a controlling spirit, and the fear of being manipulated by others can make those who have great wealth become misers, walk in constant fear, which ends up making them miserable people. Next thing you know, psychological issues arise, health issues, vanity, family in-fighting, and this because there is no more trust. Greed begets greed, and when it is manifested, ugly events happen. People step on toes, manipulate, lie, cheat, and even kill to get someone else's wealth. *Ugh!*

But what if God calls you to build great wealth for his kingdom purposes? First, one would be wise to obey his calling. As I have been teaching in business class: "If you have been called to business, and it has been given to you by the revelation of the Holy Spirit, it will be unstoppable." Being in business is one way to build wealth, and lots of it. Depending on the scope of your calling, your walk with God and your willingness to completely surrender the business entity completely into the care of Jesus, God will raise Josephs from within the business community to carry out his bidding.

Of the seven mountains, one is business. And God will use this mountain to financially feed the other six (arts and entertainment, media, family, church, politics, and education).

This entry is not in my journal but I must make this note:

> As some may find this teaching on the seven mountains controversial, I do not personally subscribe to the Christian church "taking back" the Earth for an earthly kingdom. That thinking does not tie in to end-times prophecy. With that said, I do personally subscribe to God raising up people on each "mountain" to work toward the timeline leading to the end-times and its prophecies to partner with Jesus to gather as many of the "elect" as possible before the time of the tribulation happens.

I believe when the fullness of the anointing falls on the other six mountains, the anointing which falls on the seventh – business – will make each other mountain almost unstoppable by Satan and his cohorts because then the operation of an outpouring of the Holy Spirit will be coming like a freight train. This is because every mountain has both the spiritual *and* material power to manifest. This is when heaven and earth converge, and salvation, transformation, healing, mercy, truth and material provision through the sharing of wealth generously, and compassion can operate at its highest level.

When God's children choose to relinquish control of their material wealth for the sake of the kingdom (Matthew 6:33), and choose to just become stewards, custodians, and caretakers of the possessions they've been entrusted in both their minds and hearts, in humility and complete surrender, then possessions and material wealth become weapons in heaven's arsenal along with all the other spiritual giftings that God provides. Our collective ministry, meaning, both the spiritual and material worlds, becomes the total package.

If we follow this calling and purpose as a seven-mountain community, we must all surrender completely to Jesus together as a single unit, united in purpose and destiny. We must operate in the Spirit, completely trusting God's omniscience, allowing him to make key decisions on the spiritual and material battlefield. The thing we need to be aware of on the battlefield is Satan's schemes. When things do go well, we need to keep our pride in check and put arrogance and conceit in park, no, in reverse, so that we can always be in tune to the guidance, leading, and direction of the Holy Spirit. We must manage our giftings, callings, and material possessions well, using our talents and time wisely, always keeping Jesus first in our hearts, souls, and minds and have him on the throne in everything in our lives. The end of the church age is coming. There is, I believe, one final outpouring of the Holy Spirit coming. We must be prepared. There will be thousands, no millions, of people, again, I believe, coming to Christ, recommitting to Christ, who are not "churched" or discipled. We need to walk in the compassion, in the Spirit, in the humility, and in the mercy as Christ had shown the fishermen, tax collectors, and prostitutes of his day. We are to be like him, and all seven mountains need to be working together at its highest level. God will bring this forth, and his will be done. But will we respond like Isaiah did, "Here I am?" Let us make ourselves available vessels for Jesus, for the kingdom; for that is what he is looking for, on every mountain. Let us heed our calling, and walk in our purpose and destiny, to his glory and great name. Amen.

May 29, 2018

Patience. Don't be afraid. Be thankful. Watch and see what God does for you and through you. Be the light, speak forth words of life, for this is your calling. Be surrendered to your Lord, and he will lift you up. Let your light so shine before men that they may see your good works, and glorify your Father in heaven.

Be a difference maker. Allow the Holy Spirit manifest change in your life through his power of love. Know who God is; he is unstoppable. No man or woman will, in the end, be able to resist him, for every knee shall bow and every tongue confess that Jesus Christ is Lord.

You are worthy. You are made in his image. You are his masterpiece. Let him bring glory to his great name by letting him change you, letting him transform you. It won't be easy; at times, it will be difficult, and sometimes downright awful, but in the end it will be worth it; for you are worth it. You are of great value to God.

You are made righteous, righteous by the blood of the Lamb. Let the Holy Spirit lead you into walking in that righteousness by his supernatural power. Read the Word, soak in the Word, allow the Word to come alive in you, and the Lord will show you the way to everlasting.

Walk in holiness. Allow your mind to be renewed. Accept change necessary for holiness. Be transformed. In holiness you will feel clean, you will feel free! Holiness is cleansing; by the blood, it will make you white as snow. You will crave after it. Taste and see that the Lord is good. Let go of your old ways that lead to death and destruction and pursue ways that lead to life, liberty, and love. You will walk in victory.

Be the victory. God doesn't know defeat. Remember what happens in the end. We win! We are victorious! Sin and death are defeated. Satan is cast out! We win! We win! Let us always remember this. Amen.

June 1, 2018

When God Turns Up the Heat

When God increases suffering and allows attacks from the enemy, he is preparing you for great works. God wants each believer to be equipped, prepared, sanctified, and set apart for service in his kingdom. One way to compare this is when I went through army boot camp; ten weeks of being yelled at, ten weeks of being told what to do, ten solid weeks of PT; ten weeks of learning, marching, firing weapons, camping in poor conditions, forced marches, being pushed sometimes to what seemed like beyond our limits. Inspections, ironing perfect shirts, shiny boots, and beds made so you could bounce a quarter off of it. In ten weeks, the weakest were weeded out, the defiant and rebellious were weeded out, and the rest who understood listened, heeded, and obeyed orders because they knew it was their duty; and it was what they signed up for. At the end of boot camp I was in the best shape of my life, knew how to take orders well, and worked within the system I was told to follow.

God wants the same thing for his army. He wants his army go through "boot camp" too. When he turns up the heat, allows you to go through trials and tribulations, and brings correction, this will lead you to exhibiting compassion to others. This is because you can relate to them, exhibit unbelievable patience and perseverance, foster a whole new character of integrity, truth, and empathy, and most importantly, an unwavering faith in Jesus, listening to the still, small voice and leading of the Holy Spirit.

Transformation, at times, isn't fun. But if God is bringing forth transformation in your life, it's worth it. He will use you for unbelievable things, do incredible acts through you, and you will experience hope, joy, peace, love, mercy, grace, truth, and compassion like never before. It will be harder for the enemy to attack you too because there will be fewer areas in your mind, will, and emotions (in your soul) of which he will have any territory. You will be confident to walk in the authority of the name of

Jesus, to stand up against the enemy. God will use you to lead others to freedom, whatever that may look like for each person and each instance. Your life will be different. You'll be counted as worthy for the Way and the name. Amen.

June 3, 2018

Last night, the Lord gave me a challenge. The challenge was to have the Holy Spirit lead me through an explanation of the spirit realm, how it basically exists in regards to angels and the enemy, and in most basic terms, how angels and the enemy influence our lives. Thankfully, to the strong believer, we understand that God uses both angels and demons to help us grow in faith and in our walk with Christ. But to a seeker or a new believer, it is paramount to introduce them to elementary teachings. Here is the challenge: in the first century almost everyone believed in the spirit realm, and many to the point of superstition, so one of the primary challenges was to present a correct teaching to steer a seeker to a saving knowledge of Christ. Most were uneducated and didn't know how to read, so oral teachings were the primary source of education for so many. Also, so many had simple faith, so the time was ripe in the first century for people to receive the message of Christ and learn about the spirit realm. Not so easy today.

In the twenty-first century, people seek knowledge, and access to knowledge has never been easier to get. So to explain Christ and the spirit realm, we have to navigate through extra layers of challenges: the layer of pragmatism, with people saying, "I'll believe it when I see it." Next is the layer of knowledge which so often slows the process of receiving Christ and understanding the spirit realm. They try to figure it out in their brain rather than receiving what they've heard and let it sink into their heart. Then there's the layer of unbelief about God's existence and the existence of the spirit realm, angels and demons. If people are not open to that, good luck trying to explain to them that angels are sent to you personally, to serve you, to deliver messages from heaven to you, to help protect you, and to help bring you to where God has directed them. And if people have a hard time believing that, good luck telling them that the enemy – Satan and his demon army – is real, and will try to lie, deceive, or tempt you, for that is all they have authority to do, and through their scheming, they will attempt to influence you in any way possible that will distract you from getting to know God personally. They will try to draw you away from tasks God wants a believer to do, drive wedges in-between families, split churches, destroy communities, and steer nations right down the toilet.

Satan and his army are set up like a regular army in the physical realm. They have a leader – Satan – and then they have a hierarchy. Think of their hierarchy like this: there are demons who lead and act like generals who report to Satan directly; they oversee commanders who oversee captains who oversee the rank and file. In the book of Ephesians, Paul describes them as the "principalities and powers of this dark world." Jesus has said that a kingdom, including its army, can't be divided otherwise it will fall (read Luke 11:16-26). Jesus also teaches here that unclean spirits (demons) can influence you; and as you allow, they can control you. Nasty stuff.

When so many in Canada and the United States struggle to believe this, we as Christians are faced with many uphill battles and challenges. Quite often, I see believers dodge the spirit realm subject almost altogether, in part, because they themselves don't know enough about it. Remember, knowledge is power in the twenty-first century. Many Christians don't have the confidence or boldness to stand up to the mockery and ridicule to those who only believe in science and in using science try to *explain away* supernatural incidents. People use *knowledge* to make a Christian look like a fool or stupid, a relic, and a buffoon. It's incredulous to see. Yet when a major crisis comes to those mockers and intimidators, it's interesting to see them coming to those same Christians for prayer, comfort, and help.

As believers, we need to stand up for what we believe with no shame. Ridicule, mockery, and persecution about what we believe will come. Jesus promised that. We can't be afraid of what we believe. We need to not have shame for what we believe. We need to let God work through us so that his glory, his reality, his power, his Spirit, and his love shine through. Consider yourself worthy for the kingdom when you are mocked, made fun of, and ridiculed for your faith in Jesus Christ and the existence of the spirit realm. The thinking of man has changed drastically in the last twenty-plus centuries – since when Jesus walked on the earth – but Jesus, the kingdom of God, and the spirit realm has not (see Hebrews 13:8). Satan doesn't want people to believe him; he'd rather be *cloaked and hidden away,* so he can do his evil deeds and destroy people. It's time to expose him and this writing is doing just that. It's time to show his evil empire for what it is – an enmity between us and God. But we have Jesus – our Savior, our victor, our redeemer, our champion. There is no other name that is above all names, that every knee shall bow, and every tongue confess, that Jesus Christ is Lord. Amen.

June 7, 2018

> *How do I know that we are just stewards, custodians and*
> *caretakers of our material possessions rather than owning them?*
> *It's because when our life is over, we can't take them with us.*
>
> — Mike Mahy

It is one year today when I made the decision to fully surrender my life to Christ, to make me his servant, letting the Lord direct me however he wishes. It's one thing to have Jesus as my Savior, when I received my salvation in March 1990, but it's another to have him as Lord of your life. Salvation is a free gift, but it costs you everything. I don't believe us North Americans quite get that. I know some do, but the rest live their lives saying they are living the life Christ wants, but to the unsaved, many wouldn't know because we Christians blend in with our society so much that our testimony of Jesus is almost non-existent. Many Christians believe in God, but don't believe the anointing and power of the Holy Spirit exists today as it did in the first century. Many Christians believe in the power of God, but don't believe he can heal them, like I did, heal their souls, renew their minds, even bring healing to their bodies. Christians are so often afraid to operate in the anointing and power of the Holy Spirit, operating in the gifts, talents and callings he's given us, for fear of persecution but, more often, fear of ridicule and being made fun of in our faith.

I'm not saying to go out there and *be an idiot* for Christ, but rather allow Christ to shine forth in you and through you as he grows and matures you in your faith in him. The supernatural power of the Holy Spirit in you will become the new norm. God will give you the strength, the wisdom, and the words, and you will be comfortable in your own skin, and you will be able to be yourself for God. He will reveal to you who you are in him, and be confident to be who you are in Christ. You will notice a fluidity in your witness for Christ because God will create the situations for you, and all you will have to do is *walk through the door* that he opens up for you. No forcing of situations unless the Holy Spirit directs you to do so; no awkward moments unless it is led by the Holy Spirit. In surrender you can be at peace, even in extreme circumstances – domestic violence, being held up at gunpoint or knifepoint, a huge argument as examples of extremes. In surrender to Christ, you will still hear God helping you, even if you are scared, angry, or bewildered. You understand in your surrender that God is in complete control of all situations, and you can trust his omniscience, omnipotence, and omnipresence, and that he will be there. Amen.

June 8, 2018

> *Known to God from eternity are all his works.*
>
> *- Acts 15:18*

This was said by James, Jesus' half-brother. So what does this mean except that God knows everything – from the end right back to the beginning and right back again. He knew that I was going to write this journal entry, and he knew I was going to let him help me write it, so that I, choosing obedience, would allow my God have a say in it. The amazing part about it is that it was never forced; it was of my own free will to yield to the leading of the Holy Spirit, so that I am not behaving like a robot, or be like a puppet on a string. I can choose to control it, or I can choose to yield.

For me, in choosing to yield, I am seeing better results. I am witnessing upgrades, I am experiencing higher quality everything because I am allowing the best flow through me, not just the good. The good is the enemy of the best, and God always wants the best for us. If we want to see the best God offers, however, then we must come into agreement with God's standard, his law, and walk in that standard. "Therefore you shall be perfect, just as your Father in heaven is perfect" (Matthew 5:48 NKJV). Sound possible? Well not while we are still in these tents of sin and corruption, but by the blood of Christ, we have redemption, the remission of sins, and the Holy Spirit now in us as a seal of that promise. With that, we can now receive supernatural help to get to the standard God wants us. We also have strength to repent, be healed in our souls, renewed in our minds, and be transformed. It is possible!

Next is understanding that God's timing in everything is perfect. So now I yield to the leading of the Lord for his perfect timing, not my own. We can't see what he sees, so it is enough for me to trust him in his leading. This may sound simple and elementary, but it is hard because it is the choice for us to make the decision to have our will come into alignment with his, not the other way around. It does bring God great joy to give us our heart's desires, answer our requests, and let us do things without asking him, like a good father to a son or daughter; but it is as a result of our son or daughter being obedient to our father's, our daddy's, listening and obeying them as originally intended. In this we know the love and care of God. Amen.

June 12, 2018

> *When He had called the people to Himself, with His disciples also, He said to them, "Whoever desires to come after Me, let him deny himself, and take up his cross, and follow Me. For whoever desires to save his life will lose it, but whoevers loses his life my My sake and the gospel's will save it. For what will it profit a man if he gains the whole world, and loses his own soul? Or what will a man give in exchange for his soul? For whoever is ashamed of Me and My words in this adulterous and sinful generation, of him the Son of Man also will be ashamed when He comes in the glory of His Father with the holy angels."*
>
> - Mark 8:34-38 (NKJV)

Our God doesn't know defeat. He only knows what victory is. He is omnipotent. He is holy. He is omnipresent. He is omniscient. This is why it is worth it to take up our cross and follow him daily. We can trust in his decisions. We can seek his counsel. All he asks us of him is to trust him and believe in him completely.

If God has given us a specific prophecy, an outcome in the future, and you know it has come from him for certain, we are to believe what he has said and to not doubt. Trust him. Believe. Obey. And don't be afraid. And we are to believe and trust no matter what life circumstances are thrown at us, no matter what smoke-screens, distractions, or deceptions are flung in our direction. We are asked to be at peace with Jesus in all situations; and when we start over-thinking, worrying, trying to take back control, trying to figure it all out, we become anxious, feel defeated, feel hopeless and helpless. This isn't the victory God has given us.

In our walk with Christ, he will test our faith, fully designed to help us grow, mature, persevere, and give us strong character so we can be fit for service in the kingdom. We must wait on the King for guidance in difficult situations, through trials and tribulations, moving deliberately forward with him – not too fast, not too slow but keeping *in step* with him. You will know when you are *in step* with him when you have that inner peace, a peace that passes all understanding. Peace in our hearts is a gift from God. We maintain that strong inner peace when we obey his words, walk in holiness, choose to delight in his Word more than anything else, believe on him, surrender to him, and walk in humility, and finally, by choosing to keep *in step*. These are all choices – free will. The choice is ours.

I choose to surrender. I choose to let God have control of my life. I choose to take up my cross and follow him. I choose to let God have control of my circumstances; I will trust him for their outcomes. I will do my part by believing him, especially if he has told me something prophetically or by revelation, so I could have confidence, no matter how rough the ride may be.

We just have to see Paul's life in the book of Acts. The same is true with Peter's. We need not be afraid. Angels came to them. The Holy Spirit gave them outcomes before they happened so they could trust the Lord on every journey they were led. Was it rough for them? Absolutely! So why should it be any different for us? We should expect no less than what Peter and Paul experienced in the book of Acts, and if we are to be completely sold out for Christ as they were, then difficulties, hardships, battles, disasters, resistance, hatred, anger, and defiance from others are going to be expected. The enemy will throw at us their full arsenal, trying to stop us. We not need to be concerned, for we are the children of God. We are his sons and daughters. Positionally, we are princes and princesses (kings and queens).

We serve the King of kings and Lord of lords.

We are given the tools of the kingdom to fight back:

- love, peace, joy
- humility, surrender, faithfulness
- truth, wisdom, knowledge
- forgiveness, compassion, healing
- the Holy Spirit and the Word of God
- kindheartedness and self-control

- prayer, meditation on the Word, spiritual warfare
- gifts, talents, callings
- the blood of Jesus and the cross
- the resurrection of Christ
- obedience, faith, no fear

There is more, but let's start with those. We have a powerful God who loves us. Let's trust in him and work in what he has given us. We have reason to live abundantly, be full of love, and walk into the fullness to our purpose, calling, and destiny. We just need to believe who God is, and who we are in him. Amen.

June 13, 2018

> *And now, compelled by the Holy Spirit, I am going to Jerusalem, not knowing what will happen to me there. I only know that in every city, the Holy Spirit warns me that prison and hardships are facing me. However, I consider my life worth nothing to me; my only aim is to finish the race and complete the task the Lord Jesus has given me – task of testifying to the good news of God's grace.*
>
> - Acts 20:22-24 (NIV)

Will I face hardships? Possibly. Will I face prison because of the gospel of Jesus Christ and for no other reason? That looks unlikely right now here in North America, but even that can change over time. What spoke to me most was verse 24 because in Christ, my life is worth nothing to me; all I want to do, feel compelled to do, is share the gospel of Jesus. I desire nothing else.

Does this mean God won't fulfill the prophesies given to me over the years? The short answer: he will fulfill them; they just become part of that surrender. I choose to let him own any fame, any fortune, any material possession that is either given me or as I choose to acquire. In everything, as I travel, as opportunities open up in business, my support groups and fellowships, speaking engagements, socials, meeting politicians, etc., I will walk in one purpose to share Jesus as my sole motive. I work for the kingdom, and God is my boss. I will do as he tells me and I can't wait to get going on it.

Here in jail he's keeping me busy too. The opportunities to share the gospel have abounded immensely. There is a genuine hunger here for God, and in doing my part as a believer in Jesus to share his message of good news, I am helping in carrying out the Great Commission, which is the responsibility of all Christians. I have had the privilege to teach Bible study once a week, teach English literacy twice a week, mentor the chairmen of my support group, and I am a peer mentor in 'B' hut, a program to mentor those who want or need some extra encouragement or advice. It's a brand-new program here in Ford Mountain and I feel privileged to be one of its pioneers. I pray for the whole camp, including the guards and staff. It's an opportunity to lift the name of Jesus, and I desire to do so. I am so sold out for Christ that abundant opportunity awaits when I leave here. I see it as a new chapter in my journey for the kingdom of Christ. In him, I have nothing to lose and everything to gain. Amen.

June 14, 2018

I give my life to Christ. I give my day to Christ. He is my shepherd. He is my shelter. He is my shield. I give him all the glory. I love his great name. He is worthy, worthy to be worshipped. I bow my knee before him. Jesus is my king. I bow in worship. I give my heart to him. He is my glory, my covering, my protector, my provider. I surrender my whole life to him.

There is no one in heaven, on earth, or beneath the earth who is greater than he. There is no one greater that every knee shall bow and every tongue confess that Jesus Christ is Lord. I shall wait on him. I yield to the Holy Spirit.

In your tender mercies you brought us salvation, redemption of our souls to restore a magnificent relationship with you. Your grace, oh your amazing grace, allows us to live a life full of abundance, for we are the children of the King.

I love you. I love you. I love you. You redeemed my soul. You are making me whole. Little by little, and day by day, my heart hurts less and less! Why? Because it starts with salvation, and in salvation comes sanctification. This is a miracle, and your miracles abound magnificently. As I confess my sins, bare my soul to you, O Lord, you then lift me up and heal the deepest black crevices of my heart. As I humble myself before you, you draw me to a place of healing. You bring forth the things of my past, where sin, pain, and trauma existed.

You said, "Forgive those whom you need to forgive, let go of the past and leave it in my hands, remember that your sins are remembered no more, and I am giving you a new identity, for I know who you are in me and in me this is what you shall become."

I trust in him. I trust in his great name. I trust who he is and what he will do for me no matter how hard things will get, no matter the trials, no matter the tribulations, and even more so when things go well, when success and living become so easy. It is here that I will need you more than ever so I do not become complacent, nor lazy, nor proud, nor self-sufficient. Help me rely on you in every way. Amen.

June 16, 2018

> *For you do not desire sacrifice, or else I would give it; you do not delight*
> *in burnt offering. The sacrifices of God are a broken spirit, a broken*
> *and a contrite heart — these, O God, you will not despise.*
>
> - Psalm 51:16-17 (NKJV)

Teach us, O Lord, those who know you, those who love you, to look past the sins of others – the unchurched, the new believers, the seekers and inquirers of God – those who are earnestly looking to find you, looking to find rest in their souls, peace in their hearts, but have none. Show us how to look past their sins, their attitudes, their foul language. Help us come alongside them and not get *religious* on them. Help us not do your job by telling them what to do, but help us, by the power of your Spirit, come into alignment with you for each person we come across who are looking for you, seeking your face, and then yield and step out of your way for you to do your job, for you are so much better at reaching people than we are. Help us to never shy away from the truth, and in sharing the truth, apply the truth in perfect balance with your grace, with your mercy, just like how you did that with the woman caught in adultery (John 8:1-11). Help us to live and walk and be true witnesses for Jesus, and in sharing the gospel, we are fulfilling the Great Commission. Teach us how to share your message of hope to those in desperate need of it. Teach us how to handle mockers, teach us how to walk in the Spirit, being full of the wisdom, knowledge, and power that come with it. Teach us not to be afraid to walk in our callings, our talents, or in the gifts of the Spirit so that being coupled by our love for one another, show the world the true riches of the kingdom. Help us become wise stewards of your resources so that by our actions and example, others will know how to be responsible, walk in integrity, and develop strong character. Help us show those seeking you true humility, true submission to Jesus, and walking in full surrender, yielding to the leading of the Holy Spirit. Teach us not to judge others outside the church, help us walk a mile in their shoes, and listen to their stories when we are being living witnesses for Christ. Help us to listen first, and then speak, for you gave us two ears and one mouth. In all these things, we will see the salvation and redemption of souls, for Jesus sat and ate with fishermen, tax collectors, prostitutes, and sinners. He is calling us to do the same. Let us, the believing community, all be good Samaritans together. Amen.

My Story

May 26, 2018

I am beginning to understand, on a small scale, what it is like to feel rejected. I understand that the rejection I am experiencing has directly to do with what I have done. I have hurt people. I have caused others anguish and trauma. And I own up to the sins I've committed.

But you hope, in spite of all that you've done, that there would be those who you would think who would stand beside you, loving you but not what you've done. And when those people whom you hope would stand beside you and don't, at least for me, the feeling of rejection goes right into my heart, my soul.

I have one powerful tool that Jesus taught me when you end up being judged, mocked, ridiculed, hated, rejected, criticized, and pushed away – and that tool is forgiveness.

"Father, forgive them, for they do not know what they do." (Luke 23:34)

Jesus did absolutely nothing wrong when he uttered those words. But he still used the moment in his pain. By now, he was up on the cross, he's been scourged and in great physical, mental and emotional pain, and he was rejected to the highest degree. His own Father had to turn his back on him and forsake him for a split moment in history, to pay for all the sins we committed.

Can you imagine then when you feel rejected, the power of forgiveness will work for you? Forgiveness will work on many levels. First, you will feel the forgiveness of God when you let him in. Second, you will experience the power of forgiveness and then choose to forgive others as a habit and a practice. Third, you will seek genuine forgiveness for yourself from God, and you eventually find the courage to forgive yourself. This powerful tool will bring healing to your soul. It will allow your mind to be renewed, and it will become a source of the transformation process in your life. In forgiveness, you will learn to let go the sting of pain when someone sins against you. Either the sting will be much shorter than normal or you will not feel it at all, and you will notice a big difference in how you handle situations when you flow in forgiveness continually. It will help you grow spiritually, help mature you more quickly, and give you a freedom never before experienced. Forgiveness sets you free. Amen.

May 28, 2018

It's interesting. As I sit here, I am realizing how much I am growing here in Christ. I am far more patient than I've ever been. I don't get angry nowhere near as quickly as I ever have. I am flowing in forgiveness to those who have hurt me, and the forgiveness is flowing so much faster, even in difficult circumstances. Lustful thinking has diminished to rare thoughts that get rebuked in a hurry. I am connected in my soul with the Holy Spirit like never before, and my heart's desire is to never be out of alignment with him. My desire is to surrender myself to the King of kings and the Lord of lords, and my desire is to yield to the leading of the Holy Spirit. I trust that he knows best, and I can act when he speaks to my spirit. I am still in the process of being made whole, but that is why the Lord is still putting me through his refiner's fire. It doesn't bother me anymore to heed correction, accept a rebuke, for I see them now as learning opportunities to grow and be more mature. One who loves and heeds correction is a wise man or woman.

These changes are a part of what transformation is in Christ. When we let him, he will make us whole. But it is a partnership. You have to do your part. Let him in by letting go. Set aside pride, fear, sinful desires, and learn to trust him completely. Jesus promises to take care of you no matter what. But that *being taken care of* is on the inside and not necessarily on the outside. On the inside, he promises to do this: transform you; renew your mind; give you a new identity in him; teach you ways of the kingdom; show you what true and everlasting love is; a forgiving heart; and he will bear your burdens. He will give you a new life in him no matter the circumstances thrown at you, how grave your situation may be, for in Christ you will learn to see things from an eternal standpoint and realize our lives here are temporal. You will run to God instead of run away from him. There is no more need to hide anything from him. You can share your deepest secrets to him. This is all part of a complete surrender to Jesus. If you choose to give your whole life over to him, he will make changes in you that after he's refined you, tried you, and transformed you, you will become and believe to be the masterpiece that he already sees you as. You are his masterpiece, a work of art, made in his image. Now it's time to walk in what he sees us as. Amen.

June 4, 2018

A Second Chance

When one is placed in a position of authority, in a place of responsibility, it is so important to carry out your duties with care and diligence.

I didn't do that. I failed my partner, my family, the victims of my crimes and their families, the church, and the community. It took my being arrested, pleading guilty, and being sentenced to jail to realize how far down the rabbit hole I have gone. I wasn't thinking straight, I allowed my lust to reign instead of my Lord in my life, and now I have left destruction behind in the wake of my choices and actions. I thought I could control the demons inside me but I couldn't. I was too ashamed to seek help, so I drove my secret life of sexual sin deep down in hope that no one would notice, and those I had hurt, I hoped would never speak up. Speak up they did, and I was grateful for it. I was grateful that they did the right thing – go to the police and report me – for the victims were now forced to relive what happened to them, and that's a horrible thing and a brave one too. It took courage on their part to give details of the pain I inflicted on them so the police could do their jobs.

When I got arrested and then came back home from the police station and told my partner the truth, she was shocked. She didn't know what hit her, but she told me to own up to what I've done, and that's exactly what I did. I pleaded guilty. Even when I had the chance to change my mind months later while living alone, the Holy Spirit spoke to me and directed me to stay on course and follow through. I obeyed even though I was scared and wanted to run. I had to face my charges and do the right thing. God was right there with me, helping me move forward each step of the way.

Now I see why God wanted this to happen. He had intentions to fix my life, make my life better. He wanted to see that justice was carried out for the victims. I hoped they have some form of closure, so they can heal and move on in their lives.

I am so sorry for how I have brought hurt and harm to them and their families. I am sorry to my partner, her family, my family, friends, church, colleagues, clients, and my community. I want to make amends where possible, asking for forgiveness for what I have done. If forgiveness isn't given, I understand. It will take deep forgiveness for what I've done. But when I leave jail, I have a second chance to do things right, for I have been given new and powerful tools to be successful and never again re-offend. And with God's help, I will never again do so.

June 15, 2018

God keeps his promises. In turn, in our fellowship with him, in our worship to him, in our love for him, he asks us, as part of our walk, to do the same. I taught a business series back in late 2015 to early 2016, and at the end of the first session, I spoke about keeping our promises as part of a series of seven "successful thinking tips" for people to remember and use. These were shared at the end of each business lesson for the first seven weeks of the course. It said, "This week's successful thinking tip, keep your promises. If you make a promise to someone, keep it. Remember; only make promises you *know* you can keep!" Whether they are big promises or small promises, keeping every promise you make shows the kind of person you are to another; it's in part a reflection of your character.

We all suffer as a fallen race character flaws, and from time to time, we fail to keep the promises we make. I must confess I have failed miserably in this department. And to this point, I must say I am so sorry to those I have failed to keep my promises.

To my partner, I am sorry for not keeping my vows to her, for lying and hiding my secret, a very destructive life from her. I may still be with her today if I set aside my pride and doused my fears about my sexuality and evil lusts; I might have received counseling to get us through this. Instead, I ignored those and went down this destructive path and left her in the wake of that destruction. Again, I am most sorry.

The same goes to her family; I am most sorry to them being deceived by my criminal thinking and hypocrisy, making them believe that I was someone who I was not.

To my mom, sister, brother and their families, I am sorry for not telling the truth – that I was sick in my head, my soul, and my lifestyle – and for failing to being a family member they expected me to be, and rightly so. I am most sorry to them.

I have already written an apology in previous entries to my victims and their families, but I will do it again here – and again, and again to never-ending. I am most sorry that I have violated your trust, broken your confidence, and set a negative path for you, all because of my actions, my selfishness, and my destructive behaviors. I don't know how anyone can ever repay for such crimes I've committed to you; again I am most sorry.

To my friends and the churches I attended, I am so sorry for my actions, my hypocrisy, and to my shame, I have wrecked so many of those relationships all because of destructive sins I've committed. I hope all that are listed here can forgive me, but I will understand if anyone chooses not to. I have broken many promises – to protect young people who were entrusted into my care, to be expected to walk in integrity.

To the community as a whole, I was expected to be both truthful and accountable in all situations no matter how shameful and embarrassing my defects of character are (or were), and to plead guilty to the charges and accept the consequences of my actions, including receiving jail time as a debt repayment to society, is the only expected responsibility I should take, considering what I've done. But here, too, I am sorry to my community for failing it.

Finally, I want to say sorry to my dad even though he hasn't been with us since April 27, 2011. I am sorry for failing you as your eldest son. In one way, I'm glad you weren't here to witness some of the darkest days of my life, of which I've caused and take responsibility for; but I am so sorry to you nevertheless. You and mom tried to raise me right, and that's all I'm going to say, except for one more thing, if you were alive I would be asking for your forgiveness too, without expecting any from you.

So where do I go from here, with the destructive path I've left behind? I've learned that my situation isn't hopeless. With the transformation I have experienced here at Ford Mountain, I have a new lease on life, and a chance to reintegrate back into the community with a new attitude, new thinking, a soul and heart that is in the process of being healed, new tools to combat my defective thinking, a support system (my support group, my sister, fellow inmates that have become friends, friends on the outside), and new business partnerships to help me become successful in every way possible, including the ability to keep promises, both big and small, to those whom I make them, starting with society.

To those in the church, I thank you for your prayers for me while I've been gone; they have been answered. God has been my main source of love, affirmation, rebuke, correction, renewal, and transformation; and most important, he has never left my side through all of this.

Jesus has given me a new identity, and I look forward to being the person who he has made me to be when I leave here, hopefully sometime in July (well I actually left September 17). With this new life, with this new hope, I will look to God to help me be my strength as I surrender my life to him, as I look to him to supernaturally strengthen my defects of character, as I choose to remain humble and with a contrite heart before him. With that help that I receive from the throne room of heaven, I will soar on the wings of eagles. I will walk and not be faint. I will fear no evil. For your rod and staff comfort me.

Thank you, Jesus, for your correction. Show me your ways of making promises and keeping them. Amen.

June 19, 2018

There Was Something Wrong With Me

It was October 2013. I cried out to the Lord, "There is something wrong with me!"

I knew there was something wrong in my head; I couldn't stop the evil thoughts crossing my mind. My attitude was prideful, arrogant, defensive, standoffish, and there was no way I was going to let anyone help me. Absolutely no way. I would say to God, whom I knew knows every thought I had, "If anyone asks me if I had touched anyone, I'm going to lie." I was prepared to lie, hide, and deceive anyone – everyone – to keep my deepest, darkest secrets from being let out. At the same time, I still wanted help from God, so when I cried out, "There is something wrong with me." I was crying out to God for help. It was an S.O.S.

Be careful what you ask for because God will answer your prayers, especially ones like the one I asked because in his infinite love he wants to fix our lives, repair the broken parts, and upright the listing ship that's about to sink. Here's the catch: he will answer your prayer his way, and in the way you would least expect. I didn't expect to lose my partner, my business, most of my friends; get sentenced for two years less a day in jail; and then have it plastered all over the news. It was a wake-up call to how God chastens his children who wish to lie, try to deceive and connive your way out of sins you've committed – both against the victims and him – and then try and get away with it.

God loves us, but he is also a God of justice. God is merciful, and in his mercy he sent me here to Ford Mountain to serve my sentence. It's still jail, run by corrections, but meant to correct thinking patterns, attitudes, and behaviors which benefit society, not harm it. God is faithful, and in his faithfulness, he has brought me transformation – to a person walking in truth, holiness, and love.

This is what he wanted all along, and he answered that prayer – "There is something wrong with me" – to the correction I needed the most, and the Lord was most gentle with me through this whole process. Looking back, even though it was painful, and now I see the pain was worth it. I now have a new lease on life, a hope, and a promise. What was wrong with me is now being fixed, and it will only get better each day, as I allow Jesus deeper into my life. Amen.

June 20, 2018

Inner healing happens at various speeds. Inner healing comes through various different forms, and true inner healing, when one allows God through the person of the Holy Spirit, leads to freedom and peace, and joy is experienced.

There have been times and testimonies of the Holy Spirit instantly healing someone in their souls, paving the way for ministry. God only knows the heart of that person, and in that case, he has determined that instant healing was the best choice. But what about stubborn people like me? Well, it has taken more than four and a half years (at the time of this writing) from that day when I said, "There is something wrong with me!" to now to experience such freedom in Christ; and over the next several journal entries will share what God has done for me to bring me to this point. Here, I desire to give an overview of the past two years in dealing with the "cancer" that God has spoken to me about on the day I asked him en route between North Fraser Correctional Center and Fraser Correctional Center:

- I had to forgive my schoolmates for bullying me.
- I forgave my family – adopted family – and asked God for forgiveness for what I've done to them.
- I forgave the sins to the third and fourth generation of my biological family through the revelation of the Holy Spirit.
- I went through a period of deep repentance. Some of that by fasting when the Holy Spirit directed me.
- Declared a Surrender Day to Jesus, as a result of Christ coming to me in person.
- I had to experience loss and rejection, and this because of my sins.
- I received deliverance, and in the deliverance, received authority over demonic activity.
- The renewing of my mind, and God giving me an amazing method on how to be brought to that renewal.

I will share some of these in the order I feel led, rather than in the order of remembrance (chronologically). Each part here has brought me to new freedom and a new experience in the realm of the kingdom of heaven. I hope and pray these can help the reader both understand the concept of inner healing with God and the opportunity it presents.

God is calling me to a life of total surrender – no more stubbornness, no more pride – a life dedicated to him in complete obedience, for this is my calling. It is also a calling to share with every person a message to receive Christ as his or her Savior. When we come to that place, God through the Holy Spirit will lead us to a place of complete fulfillment, peace, and joy. We will walk in the fullness of our calling, purpose, and destiny. It will not matter what our health is like, our current life circumstances, no matter what distractions, trials or tribulations are thrown at us, whether it is people or the enemy, or a combination of both, trying to stop us, deceive us, or lie to us about who we are in Christ and our walk in marching forward through God's strength for the kingdom. In him, we will persevere, receive strength when all our own strength is sapped out, and he will supernaturally help us and use us for his glory. That is just how God rolls when we choose to let him in fully into our lives. These upcoming stories will help many of you be given, hopefully, tools to be overcomers in Christ, as the ones that pertain to you or resonate with you can now be applied in your life.

I was a major clean-up job, but God decided to take this broken vessel and clean it up anyways. That spoke to how much he values me, and he values you the same! Our repentant, humble, fully surrendered hearts just brings added value to God's kingdom. He can then use us more, trust us more, and bring forth better and stronger results because our character, integrity, availability, and usability just became a weapon against the kingdom of darkness. And our hearts got healed, roots of sin dug up, and our minds cleaned up. These were true treasures from heaven. Amen.

June 21, 2018

Day of Surrender

April 2015 – close to the end of tax season (which is April 30 in Canada) the Lord spoke to me to fly to Calgary, Alberta for four days. So I phoned my friend (and client) out there and asked if I could stay there for those days (May 19-22). He asked me why I was coming, and I responded, "I don't know." I said to him it was the Lord that directed me to do this but was never revealed as to why. We did make an appointment to deal with business issues related to his company, plus he got me an appointment with three of his sub-contractors for the Friday morning which justified it as a business trip for my company. The trip to Calgary was set. I was going on complete faith not knowing what else to expect.

The day came, and I was on the first flight of the day from Victoria, British Columbia to Calgary, Alberta. The plane was full, being the day after Queen Victoria Day (a national holiday in Canada), except where I was sitting. Just minutes before we were about to taxi on to the runway, two more passengers came on to the plane – one who was in his twenties and another in his fifties – and settled in on either side of me; the younger on my left and the older on my right. We all settled in, and just before the stewardess announced to turn off all electronic devices, I glanced to my right to the screen of the older gentleman's tablet. He was reading Psalm 100. What were the chances of a Christian sitting beside me out of Victoria airport? Less than 2 in 100. That's the percentage of Christians in Victoria! It's the least churched city in all of North America.

I asked him where he fellowshipped, and he told me he was a priest in a parish in the Inglewood part of Calgary. So we started chatting and talked the entire one-hour-two-minute flight. I found out that he was introduced to Jesus by a couple of evangelical Anglicans (which is similar to the Episcopalian church), became a reverend in the Anglican Church, got married, and had a son, who was the one sitting on my left on the plane. He then told me that when the Anglican Church was starting to change its policies, he felt they were compromising the truth of the Word, and so he sought alliance with the Roman Catholic Church. The church agreed and gave him an exemption, so he could serve as a priest without forsaking his marriage or family. He was with his wife and son in Victoria because his wife's mother was in hospice, and they were saying their final good-bye's to her. His wife was staying in Victoria a little longer while they were headed back.

(I will continue writing this on June 22.)

June 22, 2018

He asked me why I was coming to Calgary, and I told him I didn't know, but there must be a purpose. He lifted up a prayer for me, and I said a prayer for him and his family. The flight seemed to go by fast, and we had great time of fellowship. Note: had they not arrived late for the flight, I would have moved over one seat and that *divine moment* may have never happened, as I would have not been able to see Psalm 100 on his tablet. Interestingly enough, as we were all disembarking from the plane, I heard the Holy Spirit say to me, "I told you I wanted you on this plane."

When my friend picked me up from the airport, I told him this story. He really didn't seem to react to it too much, but then he said he had to get right back to work, so we ended up driving around town to different worksites. We stopped at the first worksite, and he got out, so I just waited in the truck. Within minutes, I would pass out. I was so tired. After a while he got back into the truck, and I woke up. We would talk while going to the next job site. This went on for a couple of hours until lunchtime. We stopped at Phil's restaurant for lunch, and then he said he would drop me off at his house while he worked the rest of the afternoon. Being so tired all of a sudden, I obliged. When I got to the apartment, I put my head down on the couch and slept the afternoon away. Both that Tuesday and Wednesday, that's all I did – sleep. I slept all night, then I slept on and off throughout the day. I didn't realize how mentally and emotionally drained I was from three months of tax season! It started in mid-February, and I really hadn't slowed down too much until the week prior to flying to Calgary. So after two straight days of rest I felt I could enjoy the remainder of my time. Thursday came, and in the afternoon we had our meeting for my friend's business. It was quite productive. Later, my friend said we were going to join his Bible study group, and we were going to play mini-golf at a new indoor facility where his wife's daughter was working that evening. There must have been ten of us playing, and we had a great time. We then went to Pete's drive-in after – a famous soda shop that has been around Calgary since the 1960s. Being late May, the days were long and I didn't realize it was past 9:30 p.m., and I decided to have a diet Pepsi – a large one, which is full of caffeine. Of course I drank it all.

(I will continue writing this on June 23.)

June 23, 2018

After our evening of enjoyment, we got back to the apartment around 10:30 p.m., said good night, and I retired to my room they had for me. With the caffeine in my system, I started waking up; but when I woke up, a song kept coming into my head, sung by Francesca Battiselli – "Holy Spirit you are welcome here, come flood this place, come fill the atmosphere," and it kept repeating in my head until I would fall back to sleep again. This happened three or four times, and at the last time it happened, which was around 2:00 a.m. of that Friday – my last day on the trip – I thought to myself, *Well! If I'm going to keep waking up, at least, I get to hear this amazing song in my head!* So I contentedly rolled to my right side and proceeded to go back to sleep. Within a minute, I felt a presence come in from behind me, getting stronger as it came, moving from my feet to the center of my back. It stopped, and from within that presence, I heard these words, "I want all of you!" The presence then proceeded to leave away from my head gradually. The voice – it was soft but strong; firm but gentle – was not demanding but sounded like a firm, solid request. He wanted all of me, end of story. As soon as the presence left, I rolled flat on to my back and started repenting of everything I could think of, hoping that in my repentance, it would solve that request. I didn't know that this was the beginning of a journey that would bring me to today, but we will talk more about that later.

I got up at 6:00 a.m., went to my meeting with the three sub-contractors, and then went back to the apartment, with the night's events still in my mind. I couldn't figure out who came to me. Was that an angel? Was it the Holy Spirit? I mean, the song in my head would certainly lead to the conclusion. Who was it? Then it dawned on me. That was Jesus, my King of kings and Lord of lords, who came to see me in person that night! God in Jesus pulled me out of Victoria, gave me a short rest, allowed me to enjoy my time in activities, fellowship, and prayer with my friends and their friends, then came to me for the final purpose of that trip – meet me in person and give me his message. I will never forget the morning of May 22, 2015; it's a turning point in my relationship to God and a signal of changes in my life, starting right then and there. What I didn't know, and was about to find out over these next few years, is what his request meant.

(I will continue writing this on June 24.)

June 24, 2018

The Arrest

On July 21, 2016, three days before my fiftieth birthday, I was doing my weekly Thursday morning housecleaning routine. I didn't remember what time it was but I believed it was close to 9:00 a.m. There was a knock on the door. It was the Victoria police, one male and one female officer. I opened the door, and they asked if I was Michael David Mahy, and I said yes. They asked if they could come in, so I invited them in. I didn't have a shirt on, so they asked me to put one on, and after I had done that, they read me my charges and put me in handcuffs, right in the front room entranceway. I was then taken out to the police cruiser. What I noticed during all this was God's mercy. The police were gentle with me. I glanced to the right and left of the house, and there were no cars in the driveways. There were no cars passing by on the road, and no one was walking by. It was as if blinders were put on to everyone around me during one of the most embarrassing but important times of my life. I was taken to the station.

When I got processed and put into a holding cell and waiting for my interrogation, I was allowed one phone call. Remarkably, I barely remembered the name of a lawyer whom I had received advice from a few years earlier (up to this point, I had never been charged formally for anything even though I should have been put in jail for crimes committed decades earlier) and asked the officer to call him. Within minutes, the officer came back and handed me the phone. My lawyer then told me to do the following: don't answer any of their questions and say to them, "I will not answer any questions until I have received counsel from my lawyer." So I agreed with my lawyer to do what he asked. Lawyers were busy, and I was shocked to talk to him so quickly, another showing of God's mercy to me.

After a few hours, I was taken up for questioning. I was with a female officer, and she started the conversation nicely, and then started asking about my past, starting with my time in the Navy. I answered the first couple of questions during this point, but as soon as I realized she was starting to dig deeper, I remembered what the lawyer said, "Don't answer any questions until I've seen my lawyer." She did, at the beginning, ask me if I talked to a lawyer, and I said yes. She also asked me if I understood what I should do, and I said yes, so she pressed on, and the interview intensified, asking me questions about the allegations made against me, showing me videos of the interviews of the victims making their allegations, only highlighting the allegations in the videos. She must have asked me five dozen questions. My lawyer also told me to respond to every question politely, so my response was almost always in the same ballpark, "I will not answer any questions until I have talked to my lawyer." I was always calm and always polite to respond. The thing was, I was so scared, never being in this position before. I wanted to hide. I wanted to lie, and I wanted this to all go away. I thought God was helping me with that. He wasn't. He was instead carrying out a plan to draw the truth out of me, including sharing my story here, but he was doing all this in an incredibly merciful way.

Finally, the questioning ended and the officer said, "Well obviously we are letting you go; but we will find more." After six hours from the time of my arrest to that statement, I finally was able to head back home. I grabbed a taxi, and when I got home, I was now being forced to face the truth of my sins, of my crimes, and one of the first people I had to face was my partner.

When she got home a few hours later, I told her I was on bail, and I showed her the allegations against me, including four counts of sexual interference against four young males under the age of sixteen. She asked me if they were true, and I said, "Yes they were."

She just sat back on the armrest of the couch and said, "I'm in shock." She didn't know what else to say.

I started bawling and told her how sorry I was for all of this, and that I was taking full responsibility for all of it. This was the first time I had to face the truth – no lying, no hiding – and now I had to face taking responsibility for it all. Everything after this over the next twenty-four hours was a blur. I did remember that we still slept in the same bed that night. I did work the next day, and I cooked dinner for our evening meal. She also made me promise to plead guilty to the charges, of which I told her I would. That Friday at dinner I said to her and her mom, "This is getting very awkward. I am going to leave and if I could have ten days to find a place and move out." After dinner, she packed a bag, and I saw her walking down the driveway in tears, going to her girlfriend's house to stay. She pretty much stayed away until I was gone, except on my fiftieth birthday. She met me briefly to talk about separation, I agreed to everything she wanted then I asked her if she would have lunch with me for my birthday. In her mercy, she said yes. We went to Red Robin for lunch. I thanked her deeply for coming with me. We then left, in separate cars. My life as I knew it was beginning to unravel.

(I will continue writing this on June 25.)

June 25, 2018

Finding a New Home

Now I was alone for the first time in close to twenty-seven years and only the second time in my life. But I had to find a new place to live. Victoria is a tough place to find a house to rent, but it is even harder when you have bail restrictions on you – can't be close to schools, parks, playgrounds and recreation centers – anywhere where youth under sixteen would be expected. So I started this search asking God for help, with less than a one percent vacancy rate in the city and being the busiest month to move of the year, it was going to take God to provide the miracle. I just had to do my part and start looking. It was a frustrating experience. I was online every day, trying to find a place to live, and I thought the price range of under $1,000 a month would be where I had to be financially. I remember finding one place under $900 per month, and I went to check it out. I met the owners and asked them if they had kids. They said they had teenagers but they were older than sixteen, so I obliged to look. The place was only 400 sq. ft. for $900! Victoria is an expensive city, and this place I could have swung a cat by its tail and hit all four walls! I tried to imagine how I could put my office, bedroom, and personal living space crammed in this single room. I didn't know where the front room ended and the kitchen began. But if the Lord would grant me this place, then I would be content to live there. I phoned back and found out they had rented it out.

Back to the drawing board, running out of time, and part of that ten-day window was a long weekend – at the tail end of that period of time. It was now Thursday, and looking at dozens of places to live all week, I heard the Holy Spirit speak to me, "Raise your price range." So I obeyed that voice and upped the range to $1,500 and started looking, thankfully with more choices. I found a place and phoned, the lady said there was an open house the next day at 2:00 p.m., so I went. I determined in my mind that I would take it sight unseen. When I got there, there were three people leaving, so I was beginning to panic. It was the Friday going into the long weekend. It was a little 795 sq. ft. two-bedroom unit in a duplex, which would be perfect – one room for me to sleep and one room for my business office, so I could work. It had a small dining area, perfect for a table and four chairs, a nice small kitchen with plenty of counter and cupboard space, plus an area for a front room. I looked at the property manager before she could barely say hi, and I said, "I'll take it!" She handed me an application, and I started filling it out there. She then told me I needed to fill that out, provide references and financial information, then scan and email it to the person in charge of vetting new tenants. I said thank you, raced home, and did everything exactly as she said before 3:00 p.m. Thank the Lord I had a scanner and knew how to send all that documentation on such short notice. Once it was done, now it was time to wait for a reply. It was late in the afternoon, going into the long weekend in the middle of summer. I would need a miracle.

My heart was in panic mode because I didn't know if I would get the place. I was running out of options, and I promised my partner I would be out in three days. All I was doing was looking to God and desperately looking for a miracle – three-thirty, four o'clock, four-thirty, five o'clock. No phone call, and I sensed the office would now be closed. At five-thirty, I, out of desperation, called the property management office.

June 26, 2018

Finding a New Home (continued)

Someone answered the phone! I asked the guy on the other end if my application had been looked at for the rental unit, and he told me that someone else was handling the processing of applications and that he would call her right away. Within five minutes, she called me back! I felt there was a little hope. I introduced myself on the phone and asked her if she had a chance to look at the application.

She replied, "I just got in the door, I've been run off my feet all day (it was a hot day to boot), and I haven't even looked at my computer. Just give me a second and I will look."

I waited patiently and quietly while she looked. She then replied, "I see your application, and it looks like you have everything here, but it's late Friday afternoon, going into a long weekend. I'm tired from inspecting so many units, and I also will need to do a credit check on you. I can look at this on Tuesday after the long weekend. The unit occupancy is August 1, right?"

I replied, "Yes." My heart was starting to get deflated.

She said, "Okay, I can talk to you again on Tuesday."

Out of desperation, I garnered the strength to reply before she hung up on me. I said, "I know this isn't your problem and not that I expect anything, but I just separated from my partner, and I have until the end of the month to leave here. I just want to say thank you for the opportunity to take this place. I do have the money for first month's rent and the damage deposit. I will hear from you on Tuesday."

She replied, "No problem and try to have a good night." Then she hung up. I just sat there in disbelief, not knowing what to do. I just stared at the TV – the baseball game – mind-numbing TV to pass the time. I couldn't think because I didn't know what to do. I was too ashamed to ask my partner for more time to move out; she by this time had been through enough. I couldn't burden her with anymore inconvenience. She wasn't where she was supposed to be – home – and patiently waiting for me to leave.

Around 7:00 p.m. my cell phone rang. It was property manager! I answered.

She said, "Hello Mike. I've taken the time after a small break to review your application. Everything seems to be in order, so I've decided to tell you that you can have the unit on Tuesday afternoon. We'll do an inspection around one o'clock, and if you could please go to our office Tuesday morning with the first month's rent and damage deposit."

I started crying. While in tears I asked, "Thank you so much for this! This is great news! Thank you! But, what made you change your mind to do this tonight?"

She replied, "I had a long day today, and when I called you I was finally coming home to rest. But then when I had a moment to finally relax, I decided to see your application. I have been where you are right now, and I know how hard it is to try and start all over."

By now I was bawling. She actually understood my predicament. She had compassion on me. God chose the right person for me to be in contact with. This was his mercy and compassion on me too.

Over the long weekend, I started packing up my stuff. I was taking my office, personal belongings, my clothes, and I left everything else for my partner to keep. I was starting all over. No furniture, no bed (I had my dresser), no dishes, and just my griddle. The one other challenge I had to face in the short term was Tuesday, August 2. I had to be out August 1. I ended up calling a friend who knew of my allegations and marital situation and, in her kindness, put me up for the night. She had a spare room, so I was very grateful. I asked my partner if I could leave the boxes in the front room overnight and then be allowed in the next day to load up in the U-Haul that I had rented for the day. I also had one good friend help me move but to unload when I got the keys to the new place. With a dolly, I was able to move my filing cabinets, dresser, and stack boxes to wheel them into the truck. Again, and amazingly, no neighbors to see me leave. In God's infinite mercy, it was like I was invisible, which was fine by me at the time. I still wasn't quite ready to face the truth, face reality. All I knew was massive changes were on their way, and unbeknownst to me, God was orchestrating this all. At that point, I was just grateful for the miracles. So Tuesday afternoon, I met the property manager, did the unit inspection together, and she handed me the keys, and my buddy and I moved everything in. Not much stuff to move in, lots of empty spaces to fill, just like it was in my heart. For the first time since 1989, I was living alone again.

June 27, 2018

A New Beginning to Grow in Christ

It is now August 2016. I now had to face a whole host of new challenges that I have either never faced before or haven't had to face in years. First, I had to face being alone, living alone. I was so ashamed of the exposure of my sins, my crimes that I didn't want anyone else to know – or as few as possible – so before I moved out I shut down my Facebook, Twitter, and LinkedIn accounts. For the first time in years, I was completely off social media. I wanted no one else to live with me either. I was on bail and had many restrictions. People were slowly beginning to find out what happened to me, so I noticed a significant drop in people contacting me, texting me, and as the gossip spread, I started only closing in on those friends who openly supported me. Then there was my family who had no idea what was going on, and I was too ashamed to tell them. My partner was kind enough not to tell them either, which, looking back, was amazing considering the seriousness of the situation. I didn't know how to face them about our separation; they just thought our marriage was stale, and therefore it was all over for us. I just couldn't tell them the truth. I was prepared to lie, deceive, and lead them away from any notion of what was really going on.

Next was the financial situation. When I got arrested we only had our car loan of $5,700 left. That was it. No credit-card debt, lines of credit all cleared. Two incomes coming in, both of us making about the same. Oh, and no taxes owing either. I bore the burden of the car loan because I was taking that car. She had the other one; the money on my line of credit was used to pay off the loan. Then there was the cost of buying food, a bed, furniture, dishes, pots and pans, plus other necessities. Then came the cost for two lawyers; one for my separation and one for my criminal case. With all these expenses, plus ongoing costs for gas, rent, food and the like, within a few months I racked up more than $20,000 in debt. Finally, there was my faith, or lack thereof.

Before all this went down, one of my brothers in Christ told me my faith and walk with God was stale. He was right; it was. On top of that, I would say to God about those crimes – the secret sins – "I know you know, but if anyone else inquires of it, I'm going to lie." He had different plans about that. But now, being alone, and very soon after feeling lonely and isolated, I started praying like I have never done before, confessing my sins. As I was confessing them, I would feel nauseous in my spirit and would gag, dry heave, and sometimes puke up into the kitchen sink. This went on for weeks, even months. The pride, arrogance, selfishness, self-pity, hate, anger, critical spirit, judgmental heart, lying, deceiving, double-mindedness, divisive mind and soul I had was being prepared by the Holy Spirit to be overhauled. The Lord was preparing for surgery, and he was preparing his child, whom he loves very much, to be chastened, corrected, rebuked, delivered, sanctified, and transformed into what he intended for his purpose, calling, and destiny. He isolated me and put me into a corner deliberately, so he could perform the changes necessary in my life to prepare his son for what lay ahead. This is the goodness of God. I started praying for hours on end because, with the exception of work, there were no more distractions – no marriage, much of a social life, no social media – to stop me from reading the Word of God, pray for at least one hour every morning, reading books, and watching videos and YouTube to help build, or rebuild, my faith in Christ.

June 29, 2018

Note: (names in bold are changed to protect the identities of the individuals)

One of the ways the Lord wanted to bring transformation in my life was the renewing of my mind. One of my closest friends (**my good friend who has been my support throughout all of this**) during the time while I was on bail (and she still is an amazing support for me today and still very close to me) introduced me to a minister of the gospel who shows scientifically that the mind can change! The teacher's name is Dr. Caroline Leaf, who specializes in the science and study of the brain. I learned many things from her videos that God designed our brains for love, and anything else that invades our brain is considered toxic and poisons our brain function, generally speaking. What else I got from her is that it can be proven that our brains can be re-wired through the process of confession, renouncing our sin, and asking God to take it away. This process of confession was to be done for at least seven minutes a day over a twenty-one-day cycle. And if you did it in three cycles of twenty-one days, you would experience renewal in your mind to the confession of sin you were making! I was sold on this (I love science)! So being convinced scientifically that my mind could be renewed, I just had to try it!

My first round of this *new* method I chose to bring to the Lord some of the toughest sins I had, ones that I knew for sure that were holding me back in my growth in Christ – pride, arrogance, and conceit. So I started my first twenty-one-day cycle with these sins. The first few mornings I was confessing these to Jesus I was running to the sink, dry heaving, feeling nauseous, and sometimes puking. It wasn't fun, but I also started noticing that my heart was beginning to soften up a little, so I kept at it for the three weeks. When I finished this first cycle, I could believe in the process, so I chose to keep it going. I knew God was helping me change. I could see it. I could feel it. I started a second cycle of this twenty-one days of prayer, and I also chose to add another layer – the confession of a judgmental heart and a critical spirit – as part of a first cycle. Now this became fourteen minutes of this type of prayer daily; again running to the sink feeling nauseous, dry heaving, sometimes puking. I knew something was happening. Something had to be happening because I was experiencing changes in my thinking and in my heart. Once I finished that second cycle of my first set of confessions and first cycle of the second set of confessions, I chose to add a third set of confessions – anger, hate, bitterness and rage – and for three weeks I was praying like this for at least seven minutes, sometimes up to twenty-plus minutes, depending on the day. I finished each set a full sixty-three days each. My thinking was starting to seriously change; experiencing renewal and transformation. God was showing me that change was possible, and that he could orchestrate it. I was beginning to see a ray of hope in my life.

June 29, 2018

Note: (names in bold are changed to protect the identities of the individuals)

From the time of my first arrest to my first court date, I was under a lot of stress. I told my lawyer already that I would be pleading guilty to the charges. He said, "Fine but allow me to do my job for you. Otherwise you will get six years the way you're asking me. Just allow me to do my job." At that point, I chose to trust him. God gave me this lawyer, which I understood was a provision from him; so I just let him do as he has asked me. But the court date, by the time I moved into my new place, was just under a couple of months away. The waiting part and not knowing what was going to happen was the hardest. I was still relying on my own strength to get through each day rather than trusting in God's power. He wanted all of me, so he *turned up the heat* on me, so I could start relying on his power, presence, and knowledge. I did ask **the prophetess of our church,** "Where do you see me?"

She said, "I don't see you going to jail."

In the time that she said that, I probably asked her at least three more times, and she patiently told me the same thing. I was double-minded. I believed in Jesus but I couldn't believe in his power, or the power of his name, not to the level of faith he wanted or expected of me.

Trials and tribulations are designed to build faith, character, and in the end, help you better relate to others empathetically because you can then associate with someone else's pain. So here I was now praying more than ever, in the Word more, reading Christian literature more than ever, and staying so close to the Christian community like glue. I did tell the leadership of my church what was going on, so they were aware and were holding me accountable. But I had three close friends that met with me every Tuesday in my new place faithfully. At that time, all they knew was about my separation but not the criminal allegations. I was petrified that if they found out, they would abandon me. They did eventually find out months later because the Holy Spirit told me to share the truth with them individually, but right now, I was just grateful that I was having the equivalent of church in my house with my close friends every Tuesday. This was because I wasn't allowed to attend church while on bail. I was amazed at their faithfulness when it was less than a week away for my court date (they did know about that but not as to why) we decided to have a prayer session.

It was an amazing time of prayer! I still remember some of the prophetic utterances and words that were given. **My buddy the gardener** received this word from the Holy Spirit: *a big, giant wheel barrel with gold coins and cash piled up in it*, which for him was amazing, considering his business was lawn and gardening, so this signified that God was going to grow his business. **The fourth one in our Bible study** received a word that he was standing just outside a door. The door was open just a crack, so he could see just inside, and inside was a big cake with candles, balloons, and streamers. It was all for him! All he had to do was go through the door, and it was all his! Another one was given to **the only lady in my Bible study**, but the word was more solemn – she was dealing with bitterness and wanted more clarification for her direction at that time. Then I was given two prophetic words. The first one was there a giant silo, and that silo represented me, at that point in my life. She said, "God is going to blow it up to smithereens, and in all the chaos, God will send an angel and lower you down gently." When I heard those words, I got so discouraged. I thought for sure I was going to jail at the end of the week. About ten minutes later, she gave me another prophetic word. She said she saw me with a big brown Bible, expensive shoes, and travel. That second word encouraged me more. That would be our last Tuesday study for the next little while, but I now needed to face this court date. The night before the date of the court appearance, I was so scared I ended up on the couch in the fetal position; I don't ever remember doing that before.

The next day came, and now I was waiting for a phone call from my lawyer to appear in court. No phone call. Morning came and went and still no phone call. After lunch, I finally called their office. About 3:00 p.m. someone got back to me. I asked what happened, and she said I wasn't on the court docket. It had disappeared! She said she would look again and call back to confirm. She called back and said it looks like the charges were dropped. I asked her if I was still on bail, and she said to check with the bail office. I called the office, but being late Friday, they couldn't check but to check again Monday morning. I was scratching my head as to what happened.

Monday morning came, and I sensed the excitement of the Holy Spirit. He was urging me to go quickly to the bail office. He was so excited! I was doubting his excitement, but he urged me to keep driving. So I did. I got into the bail office and asked the first available clerk if I was still on bail. She looked into the computer couldn't find my name! She said I was free to go and I just started to tear up. Then she said to me, "I hope you've learned your lesson." In tears, I nodded and said thank you. I got what I thought was a reprieve. I also thought that my secrets were safe, and I would never tell anyone. God had something else in store. This was just a small emotional break. That was it.

Ford Mountain

May 27, 2018

I can hear the Chilliwack River from my room when I open up the window.
The sound is so soothing. I can hear the birds chirping. Out my window
is a forest, leading down to the river, and on the other side, the forest goes
straight up the mountainside, a sea of evergreens. Here at Ford Mountain
Correctional Center, I am not locked up in a cell, but I have a room, with
my own key. This is still jail, and there are guards still doing their jobs.
But this jail is a unique concept, and it has caught the attention of the
other correctional centers throughout the province. I have heard that what
the other correctional centers are doing is designating a single unit for the
"Right Living Community" concept to be implemented and run.

Here in Ford Mountain the concept works well, and inmates experience
positive life-change because the following is in place: a spacious area (I
am talking many acres) where inmates roam freely from within the spaces
they are allowed to be, semi-autonomously; a field with a track to allow
soccer, football, and baseball to be played; education programs to allow you
graduate from high school or college and also programs to give you essential
skills; programs specifically designed to help inmates to change criminal
thinking, behaviors, and help deal with emotional, mental, and psychological
issues deeply rooted in their being; anonymous support groups such as AA,
NA, and SAA; even a generic twelve-step group to allow inmates to speak
openly among themselves about their addictions and associated struggles;
faith-based groups such as Bible study and church, yoga, meditation class
(run by Buddhists), and the freedom to exercise faith openly in such
environments; a community designated just for aboriginals so they can
experience and practice their culture, and its open to anyone who wishes
to practice with them; meetings with guards (both as a whole community
and within our cell units) to share and promote "right living community"

standards, and through shared facilitation, guards and inmates together help us inmates create goals, share thoughts, and encourage everyone to seek personal positive change in our lives which will, in turn, benefit our communities when we leave. Then we have the recreation room with two pool tables, a large weight-room, and a gym where I've seen hand-ball, racquetball, volleyball, basketball, and indoor soccer being played; a dining hall where inmates sit together and food is served on plates and bowls and with silverware; health care and mental healthcare are on the premises; all the supports where parole and probation officers come and meet us on-site; an integration plan can be done with the help of a correctional officer for repeat offenders; and the list goes on.

For this concept to be duplicated elsewhere, all these components (plus components that I haven't mentioned here that exist and are part of the RLC operation) have to exist for it to succeed. I believe that without every part of what Ford Mountain offers and operates, the other RLC communities trying to be implemented throughout the rest of the province will not realize the same results, and I'm concerned some will be doomed to fail. First, the staff who are trained to do this have to *buy* into the concept.

Ford Mountain is isolated and a stand-alone camp where the guards have much less influence from their peers in the regular institutions who could possibly mock, ridicule, tease, and undermine such an operation. I mean, this is jail, and guards are human, not superhuman. They are a key part of this success. I just hope that Corrections BC learns well from this model and duplicates it most similarly to this one. I believe private enterprise may step in and run it instead because private enterprise has less of a tendency to *muck up* things that are functioning well; and quite often are able to bypass all the bureaucracy governments have.

This is a great concept. My understanding is that Ford Mountain has the lowest rate of re-offending in the entire province. This saves tax dollars, helps our communities be safer and better, and is a beacon of hope to those who are sent here. Change is possible, and we need to pay close attention to what is going on here, see its success, and hopefully duplicate this model properly both here in British Columbia and in other jurisdictions throughout Canada and the United States. This model works, and works well; I am one life that has been positively influenced by it, and this has been by far the best place for me to change. The environment Ford Mountain has supplied helped give me confidence that change is possible. Oh! And I forgot one important aspect of this camp – we are all put to work here. We all *do* something!

May 30, 2018

Well, how soon does one forget that after being set free in Christ, with complete renewal in your heart, that there are fellow brothers and sisters in Christ who have their salvation but are struggling in their walks, hurting inside, struggling in their faith, struggling to feel loved, and can't remember the last time they felt a touch of the Holy Spirit. Such an occasion arose last night.

Three of us went for prayer up at Holloway House, and one of us was earmarked by the Lord to receive such a touch from him. When we all sat down, we started talking instead of praying. In the course of this discussion, the Lord had us two *more mature* Christians just listen to the one who had a chance to pour out his heart, shared some of his deepest thoughts, deepest questions he wanted to ask God, in a safe place where he could speak freely, and feel so safe to talk without feeling judged or feel stupid because of what he didn't know or understand. What he received was a listening audience who were sensitive to his words, his needs, and his questions. And when it was time for one of us *more mature* Christians to speak, we chose to yield to the work of the Holy Spirit to speak through us so that his agenda was carried out, his words of wisdom be spoken, and what parts of his Word would be appropriately shared. Interestingly, our young brother in Christ spoke about control and worry and needed to be the one who had *the answers* for others, but didn't know how to release and let go of the burdens he carried for all these people who *dumped* their problems on him plus carrying his own.

My other brother and I piped up and with smiles told him that he was "preaching to the choir," and we briefly each took a turn to let him know that we also struggled in the same area and that we could relate to him. Then we took turns sharing with him how God transformed us in those areas, then let him know how much he was loved by God, and he wanted to teach him how to let go. We also were led to answer one of his questions of how can God love everyone, and through the guidance of the Holy Spirit, he was God's creation, his work of art, his masterpiece and that is why he loves every one of us. But he leaves us to choose him or not, and that's his love too.

The main thing is us *mature* Christians chose to be available vessels to the Lord, allowing him to work through us rather than us trying to control the situation for God. For me personally, this is a huge departure from how I used to witness, counsel, and share with others:

- I now choose to listen before I speak, and in doing so, I am now hearing their personal stories, personal pain and tragedies, victories and triumphs, concerns and questions.

- While they are speaking, I now yield to the counsel of the Holy Spirit, having my "antenna up," hearing what he has to say, if anything at all.

- God is teaching me patience through this whole process, just as he is patient with all of us.

- I now respond with gentleness, compassion, and wisdom — even if God wants to bring correction, a rebuke, admonition, or exhortation — and bring such counsel to that person who is desperately wanting change, counsel and/or encouragement.

- I allow the anointing of the Holy Spirit to flow, instead of me trying to control it, and now I personally benefit too as I feel the presence of the Holy Spirit fill the room.

- When it comes time for prayer, there is, most frequently, an openness to receive God's counsel, God's love, and God's favor.

It's an amazing experience to have Christ as the center of the whole process, keeping him on the throne, and relinquishing all control in complete surrender. We all benefit from this, and the one who is struggling, learning, and growing receives in abundance the true experience of God in his presence and gives them a fighting chance to become the believer God intends them. Amen.

June 2, 2018

Here in jail, we have every walk of life. It has become for me a perfect training ground to grow and learn to walk in mercy and compassion for those who are deeply hurt by life's trials and tribulations. Here, I have learned as a Bible study teacher to listen to each inmate as they speak, seek out the Holy Spirit for guidance during the course of conversation, and be ready to answer with Scripture when called upon. I have learned to show empathy and concern when called upon. I especially have learned to challenge gently when someone "hijacks" the study, whether it be talking on and on about nothing, expressing their personal thoughts and, sometimes personal agendas, about their personal beliefs that do not line up with the Word of God, including the belief that God does not exist, without raising an ire by the speaker or others in the study when called upon.

It's a delicate balancing act because, in jail, there seems to be a much greater interest in God and spirituality than I've seen on the outside. Since I have been leading or participating in Bible studies here at Ford Mountain, we are graced with strong believers, "weaker" believers, new believers, seekers of God and spirituality, honest inquirers, and those who come in to "kick the tires." They keep you on your toes. Their questions at times are "zingers" and they are expecting real answers, not fluffy ones, and look at you sideways and in confusion the minute you start speaking in "Christianese."

So many of the inmates are simple, have no church background, and it's important that you speak always to the lowest common denominator. When someone doesn't understand something you've just explained and says so out loud, I thank them with deep gratitude and then attempt, for their sake, to simplify the explanation without making them feel stupid. This is so that the student will feel empowered to ask more questions because they feel safe to do so in a Bible study environment. This is true discipleship. When the outpouring comes, we, as a church, will be faced with the same task as I have experienced here in jail. We need to have study leaders, pastors, elders, deacons – the whole church community – to be ready for those who are unchurched, don't speak "Christianese," but desperately want God and to be in his presence. They are looking for Jesus; and it's our responsibility through the power of the Holy Spirit to bring forth the message of salvation, the message of hope, in its simplest form. Give milk where needed. Amen.

June 5, 2018

Note: (names in bold are changed to protect the identities of the individuals) (names in black are the real names and used by permission)

This was interesting. The dream I had on the morning of April 20 was partially fulfilled! Yesterday, the kitchen staff were told that we were all moving from 'D' Hut back to 'A' Hut. 'A' Hut has traditionally been the hut to house the kitchen staff of the camp, but because of hut renovations in the last six months we have been asked, not once but twice, to move out of 'A' Hut to facilitate the completion of these renovations by the contractors. So when the call to go back to 'A' Hut came yesterday, I was curious to see if I was going back there too because of that dream I had.

At the end of roll call, 'D' Hut residents and 'A' Hut residents were told to switch, room for room, by room number (i.e. D1 switch with A1, D2 switch with A2, etc.). But when it came to my name, I was told I was going to B4 ('B' Hut)! I was now separated from the rest of the kitchen staff, including Milton and **Andrew**, just like in the dream, even though I still worked in the kitchen too! There is more – since that writing on April 20, I had also said that I qualified for both day parole and full parole. Since that writing on May 4, I received a decision from the Parole Board of Canada: I got day parole! There is a waiting list for a bed in a halfway house to where I am going back (Victoria, British Columbia), and now I am just waiting for a bed. It will be soon when I leave here at Ford Mountain.

All this just confirms that the dream I had came from the Lord. Here in 'B' Hut I was asked to be a peer mentor, helping inmates in this designated hut with challenges toward having good social skills and life skills, and just for the mentees to have someone to talk to. I was only one of two such mentors in the camp. We are called to have the patience of Job, the wisdom of Solomon, the leadership of Moses and King David, and the grace of Jesus to fulfill this mandate. It was an awesome opportunity to give back to a camp that God has used to help me so much.

Thank you, Jesus, for the gift of service. Help me be the steward and servant you've called me to be. Amen.

June 10, 2018

Note: (names in black are the real names and used by permission)

The Invitation

Behold, I stand at the door and knock. If anyone hears my voice and opens the door, I will come in to him and dine with him, and he with me.

- Revelation 3:20

Last night, we had an impromptu prayer session, and eight of us showed up for it with two of them seekers of God, two of them who received Christ as their Savior here in the camp. One of the seekers participated in our prayer time by praying out loud for the first time, probably either in his life or in decades. He told us that he only prayed silently before, and he wanted to try by praying out loud. One of the newly saved believers was in tears, confessing his shame and being very humble before God. We prayed for the whole camp – the inmates, the guards, and the staff. We prayed for ourselves; some of us prayed for our loved ones. The presence of the Lord was thick in the room.

Thanks to Milton's desire to seek Jesus, he shared, "Hold on to him no matter the circumstances, no matter how hard life gets. You will see transformation in your life." Milton said, "If you follow Jesus, your life will get harder, not easier." I agree with him. Milton also said that, "The enemy will attack you because he doesn't want to you share the message of hope."

At the end of our prayer session Milton shared about the cost of following Jesus, and in doing so your life circumstances become more difficult, especially if you ask for more faith. While Milton was talking, the Lord led me to read Psalm 51:1-13 after he had finished, describing mercy, repentance, the refiner's fire, forgiveness, and the desire to be in the Holy Spirit's presence – all in one Scripture passage. Upon leaving prayer time, we all had joined hands together, thanks to Milton's leading of that, and pressed in together for one final prayer. Everyone said they were touched by our time together. God truly blessed us all.

In closing, I just want to say how dear a friend Milton is to me. But most importantly, I know God's hand is on him mightily, and I can't wait to see what ministry God has for him. I sense a strong anointing on Milton, and I believe God will use him mightily for his glory and for the glory of the kingdom. I feel privileged to be his friend. Amen.

June 11, 2018

Note: (names in black are the real names and used by permission)

It was another day of amazing events. Yesterday morning, (this was *after* I had written yesterday's journal entry, which was finished by around 7:30 a.m.), Milton came to me in the morning shift in the kitchen to tell me that he was woken up last night to his four bags of Doritos, which were stacked neatly at the back of his top shelf, being thrown down on to the floor at around midnight! His window was closed, his door was locked, and the guard came by on his hourly rounds a few minutes after the incident, so neither the wind nor another person could have done this. He also said he experienced some nervous twitching in his body at around 10 p.m., but he shrugged that off and went to sleep until the chip event. Clearly, it was an enemy attack. So Milton was a little scared and wanted to run, but instead, he put his Doritos back up on the shelf, went back to bed, and started praying. He fell back to sleep.

When he finished telling me this story, I smiled, told him we will talk when the shift was over, and then the Holy Spirit told me to tell him, "Don't be afraid." So I passed that along. When we met outside later, I brought my journal back with me. He gave me more details to his story, and after hearing him, I shared with Milton June 10's journal entry, pointing out the part of the enemy will attack. Milton started to smile and asked me to read the middle paragraph again, so he could understand its significance. I then told him that since our prayer time, the enemy attack and me being led by the Holy Spirit to write about Milton specifically. There was a direct correlation to it all. Milton wanted to tell Terry this as well, but I asked him I needed to share with him what I had to say to him alone first. But within minutes of finishing our conversation, Terry walked by! Perfect timing yet again! So we updated him of these events as he was at prayer the night before.

In the evening, it was church service, and I asked the chaplain if he could see Milton, Terry, and I after the service. He is a spirit-filled man, a man who truly loved God. The chaplain said yes as he had no scheduled visits after the service. So after the service, the three of us went into chaplain's office, and we all took turns sharing with him everything that had happened, starting with our prayer time the night before. Once we all finished sharing, the chaplain picked up on something we missed with Milton.

Milton was Guatemalan, and in Central America, people have a tendency to be more sensitive to the spirit realm than here in Canada and the United States. The chaplain surmised that this attack might have come as a result of something that happened to him while he was living in Guatemala. As the chaplain was talking, it was brought to Milton's memory that one of his aunties practiced witchcraft and that she had put a curse on him to bring harm to him and to be in jail, which had come true. The chaplain then had us all join hands together to bind the enemy and then in Jesus name break the "money curse," for this curse had to do with Milton not paying back money to his auntie as payment to a coyote bringing Milton across Mexico to the American border, as the Lord showed me (I wrote "money curse" down and gave it to the chaplain, so he knew exactly what the curse was). Milton was in tears because prior to this encounter, he completely forgot about what happened to him with his auntie.

Then the Lord asked me to help lead a prayer with Milton to forgive his auntie for the curse, of which he did. I believe this was a major turning point for Milton and for all of us because we learned amazing lessons about prayer, the spirit realm, how to deal with the breaking of curses, knowing and understanding the authority God has given his saints and his church, and to do all this in submission to the Lord Jesus and in humility.

God's hand is on Milton, Terry, the chaplain, and me in this camp, and we recognized it.

God has his hand on others here too; they just don't recognize it yet. My prayer for them is that Jesus is revealed in such a way that they recognize him, and choose to follow him; which takes me back to finishing with what was written at the beginning of yesterday's journal entry: "Behold, I stand at the door and knock. If anyone hears my voice and opens the door, I will come in to him and dine with him, and he with me" Revelation 3:20 (NKJV). Amen.

June 17, 2018

There has been a spiritual battle in this camp, and with the camp being small (on average ninety inmates, give or take, at any given time) and with it a controlled environment, one can see the fruits of prayer. When I mean controlled environment, I'm talking about having no electronic devices to distract us. You see the same people every day. Changeover (inmates coming in or leaving camp) is relatively slow, and the camp itself is extremely unique because it is the only jail in British Columbia with a full-blown "Right Living Community" model operating that fully encourages inmate participation, self-help and self-awareness programs, education, twelve-step programs, trades skills development programs, a work environment for all inmates, and what I feel is most important, an opportunity for a spiritual experience. We have Native and Buddhist programs available, but my focus will be on the Christ-centered ones: church every Sunday night and Bible studies on Mondays, Wednesdays, and Fridays of which I have the privilege of leading the Monday one.

About three months ago, however, I felt led by the Holy Spirit to gather a small group of believers (four of us) to start praying for the camp primarily. The thing was, we tried to pray on a set day and that's where we experienced difficulties meeting. Out of the blue, a random heated argument came from one of the kitchen staff and me and one of the other prayer warriors. Next thing we knew, was chef changed our schedules around and separated us from having that same day off. At the same time, one other prayer warrior was starting to receive personal attacks from family members on the outside, which caused quite a distraction to his concentration, and then a fifth prayer warrior who was supposed to join us all of a sudden got muscle cramps in his back, which caused neck pain and headaches. All this in one week!

The enemy was trying to fight back for its territory. Over the next three to four weeks, I was seeking the Lord on what to do and how he wanted us to proceed. None of us were interested in giving up because God loves this camp and the people herein – inmates, guards and support staff – so we just started gathering randomly at different times on different days when we sensed the Holy Spirit was leading us. We started seeing breakthrough in the camp. My support group had experienced phenomenal growth in the last eight weeks from averaging twelve to fourteen to having twenty there at last night's meeting. That's more than 25 percent of the camp! Bible study is being solidly attended every session too with the average attendance being between nine to twelve guys. What was most remarkable about that is the studies don't start until close to 8:30 p.m. and run right to the horn at 9:45 p.m. when everyone is tired from a busy work and program day. That's solid commitment!

I see a spiritual hunger in this camp, but I believe our prayer time – our last prayer meeting had eight inmates praying together with three of them being non-believers praying to Jesus – is making a difference. We are praying for the camp, praying for the programs, praying for ourselves, praying for loved ones, praying for healing, and asking God for revelation. There is also the laying of hands to those inmates who wish to receive a direct word from the Holy Spirit. The presence of God is thick in the room. Inmates are open to spiritual experience, and they are getting their fill of it directly from the throne room of heaven. The change of spiritual interest in the camp has certainly increased, and I have every reason to believe there is a direct correlation between the active participation of both my support group and Bible study – the two best-attended groups in the camp – and the prayer group.

We pray for the other groups too, and we pray for breakthroughs with them too, for the other twelve-step support groups are spiritual in nature as well. We will just ask God to continually break down those barriers so that inmates will understand that they are spiritual beings first, and that their need for God's help becomes paramount. From that, I pray they come to a saving knowledge of Christ and have the ultimate spiritual experience being renewed in their minds and transformed in their hearts and know the fullness of the true love of God, walking in their purpose, calling, and destiny. The enemy can't stop this freight train; I'd like to see him try. Well, he will try. We need to be in continual prayer, in complete humility and full surrender to Christ, in order to move forward, taking back territory for Christ. We can't stop. The momentum right now is amazing and too great for us to become complacent and just sit back on our laurels. We just need to seek the Holy Spirit to guide us to our next prayer time, find out who he wants in that prayer group, and then listen to his voice, supplicate our prayers to him, and be blessed by his amazing presence. Amen.

Speeches & Poems

May 23, 2018

I Will Wait On the Lord

I will wait on the Lord, for he is worthy.

I will stand in his presence, for he is great.

He gives me revelation, a hope, and a dream.

Visions come forth from the glory of the Holy Spirit.

I love his name, his great name – the Lord Jesus.

I bow down in worship, lay prostrate in his presence.

Surely the Lord will do great things, great things he will do.

Through his people, for his people, he will do great things.

And I desire to serve him, and serve him only.

All the days of my life, for he has brought me salvation.

May 25, 2018

Untitled

How much the love of God is manifest in us. He reigns in our
hearts and our lives. There is none like him.

I worship you, I worship you, O Lord

You set forth time and space, you brought forth stars and planets,
the universe is filled with your glory.

You made man in your likeness; in your love, you gave him choice.
Free will you blessed him with.

But man fell because of free choice,
so you set forth a plan to redeem us.

In our trials, you gave us faith, a trust, and a hope,
to trust in you oh my Savior.

In Abraham, it was faith, in Moses, the law.
In Noah, a promise; and David, kingship forever.

But is was through Jesus, your blessed Son,
A new covenant came forth, by shed blood on a cross.

You made promises, and you've kept them all.
So we trust in what you will do and say in the future.

The future is very bright 'cause it says, "We win! We win!"
You restore us to the glory you first intended.

We will know both good and evil, just like you
for eternity; for it was your will for you to share this if we wanted it.

But now we know. Now we know that you are good,
and we choose to follow you, Lord Jesus, forever.

So all I say, to hope and pray, that whoever reads this
Will come to the same conclusion.

May 31, 2018

It is hard work to build your faith. In building your faith you must learn to let go and let Jesus reign in your heart. As Hebrews 11:1 says, "Now faith is to be sure in what we hope for, and certain of what we do not see" (NIV – from memory). It takes hard work for faith to grow. God expects you to do your part in trusting him, even though you can't see him. It is a partnership. It takes hard work to stay humble, it takes hard work to be slow to anger, quick to forgive; and it is hard work to look for God in everything you do. Faith is like a muscle; you must work at it in order for it to grow and be healthy. Think of going to a workout gym for the first time. To many, it looks like an insurmountable task while looking at yourself for where you are at that time and visualizing of where you want to be. But you go into the gym anyways. You start working out your arms, your chest, your abs and your legs, then your back. You keep going back, steadily learning along the way, receiving instruction from others as they encourage you to keep going. You keep going back. Soon, you slowly start to see results. Your hard work is paying off! Muscles are building, getting stronger. So it is the same with faith. But faith has one extra beautiful component to it – you are plugging into a supernatural connection. You are *plugging* into the kingdom of heaven. It's one thing to have faith in your family or friends; it's another to have faith in Jesus. That faith requires a lot of work, but it's worth it. And now, here is the closing positive message for our hut meeting this morning:

'D' Hut Closing Positive Message on Hard Work, May 31, 2018

It takes hard work for you to become a better person. It takes hard work to keep a promise. It takes hard work to walk a life of integrity. It takes hard work to plan and build a house.

But in all these things, as you plan, you visualize the final outcome. You look at the details and cost of what it is going to take. But in the end, you work hard because what you are doing is worth it. Who you do it for are worth it. And importantly, you are worth it.

June 6, 2018

'B' Hut meeting closing positive message, written by me but read by one of my hut mates:

'B' Hut meeting June 5, 2018
Changing Attitudes

We most often think what we believe. Our attitudes reflect that. If you feed your mind positively, that will reflect on your attitude. A positive attitude will feed what you believe, therefore creating a prosperous cycle, which leads to positive successes.

It's up to us to foster a good attitude, a positive attitude. It's our part in our partnership with God. How do we feed it? As Christians, it is given in many ways: the Word of God, where truth in grace and mercy is given and taught in perfect balance. In Bible study, where one comes and grows into being a disciple of Christ. In prayer, where you have an opportunity to talk to God directly. In worship, whether at home or with friends, with music or at church.

"Do not forsake the gathering of the saints," so be in fellowship with like-minded believers. Read books, watch videos, or search online for good Christian commentaries and material on various subjects of our faith, but be careful! If in doubt, get a second or third opinion to ensure what you are reading or watching is biblically accurate.

And after we feed our minds, hearts, and spirits with these truths, we must then take what we've learned and put it into practice. This is our part, and when we put what we've learned into practice, God will then supernaturally empower us by the Holy Spirit as we choose to yield to him. This is how we flow in the anointing – to walk in love, be rich in good deeds, possess an amazing faith, have your mind renewed and your soul healed. This is amazing grace, and God wants to pour out, no, lavish us, with his goodness, mercy, and love. He wants to give us all that he has, give us all of who he is, in abundance. Our part is to have a good attitude, choose him first, and come into full agreement to walk in his ways, and receive Jesus as our Lord and Savior. Amen.

JOURNAL
BOOK 6

INSPIRATIONAL WRITINGS

July 2, 2018

Training in Righteousness

Note: (names in bold are changed to protect the identities of the individuals)

Even though I have been arrested twice by now, God was still wanting me to change my ways for his glory. He still had a plan to use me for his kingdom. This is his good pleasure and no one else's. God looks for repentant hearts – hearts that are willing to change, willing to be transformed. Sometimes he will put his child into a corner to get their attention. **My good friend who has been my support throughout all of this** actually told me that shortly after my first arrest.

She said, "God has put you into a corner."

He also knows the end from the beginning and therefore holds a distinct advantage over sin, over time, and clearly over the enemy. But even in that comforting thought, what I find even more comforting is that he will not interfere with our free will, which is, in my opinion, one of the most precious gifts he's ever given all of us, aside from the gift of salvation.

To anyone who is reading this, there is hope for you. God gives us this hope and his promise. It is a choice then, to partner with him on it. Despite what I've done, despite the horrible sins I've committed, despite the damage I have caused, God still wants to use me for his kingdom. And, no matter what we've done, big or small, absolutely disgusting or seemingly harmless, whenever we choose to surrender our lives to Christ, he will want to use our lives and our testimonies to the benefit and glory of his kingdom. He will train *any* willing heart in righteousness in order for us to be fit for service in the purpose, calling and destiny, to those who choose to be obedient to him.

If he can use Apostle Paul, a murderer; and Apostle Peter, a simple fisherman who denied his Lord three times, and then used them to turn the known world up-side-down in the first century for the kingdom of God, because of their repentant hearts; then he can use someone like myself, one who would be labeled by many as a pedophile, for his kingdom in the twenty-first century.

God is looking for repentant hearts, willing and available vessels for the kingdom, and like the woman caught in adultery, he will not condemn us but tell us to leave our life of sin and then ask us to follow him wholeheartedly. That's the disciple he is looking for – a willing, available vessel, desiring to be humble, repentant, and fully surrendering our lives to him. Then he, in his great wisdom, can train us for righteousness and carry his message to the world.

July 6, 2018

Strive In Step

Now I beg you, brethren, through the Lord Jesus Christ, and through the love of the Spirit, that you strive together with me in prayers to God for me.
- Romans 15:30 (NKJV)

So many times I have gone too far ahead of God, assuming things, making decisions without his counsel, not being patient in allowing his vision, dream, or word unfold supernaturally. In other words, I was the one trying to make what I heard from him happen, running into the danger of stealing his thunder, taking his glory away from him, showing a false humility of giving praise to him when all along, I wanted to take credit for what happened if the very thing God showed us came to pass. It's a dangerous game of which the devil can use to bring us down – *fast*.

God intends to show us visions, give us dreams, answer our prayers, but he also wants us to wait on him, be patient as to how events and circumstances unfold, the *when* he calls us to do our part, that we *strive in step* with the Holy Spirit. In this, we bring glory to his great name, stay humble, yielding to his power and direction, listening intently and be ready when to move and when not to move. It's an amazing partnership we have with God. But when we *strive in step*, not to be complacent or lazy to fall behind because he expects us to carry out what he said to us, nor to go at "a million miles an hour" and jump too far ahead. We've heard the saying: "Don't put the cart before the horse." When we do that, we all too often fall flat on our faces.

Strive in step with the Holy Spirit. Walk diligently with him. In doing that, we will see great things and see his glory. That's what he wants when we co-labor with him. Amen.

July 23, 2018

Loss and Rejection

"It is well with my soul," the writer wrote when speaking about loss. I have experienced loss on many levels – material, financial, death of a loved one, relationships, position, authority, business. Each comes with its own level of emotions too: grief, sadness, anger, and bitterness come to mind. I've written in previous journal entries about loss and how I've come to terms with it in the Lord. One item I haven't written about as part of my inner healing process is the subject of being and feeling rejected.

Back around Mother's Day, I was talking to my sister and read to her my entry to my mom for Mother's Day. I teared up as I read it to her, and it really moved her too. She asked me if she could pass on a happy Mother's Day to her, and I said, "Do it if you feel compelled, but please, be wise." I sensed deep down it would not be received well, and my mom would react angrily.

The next time I called my sister I asked how that conversation went. She explained that it didn't go too well and tried to minimize the details of what transpired. Typical of my sister. I pressed in on the issue and asked what happened, and she finally told me that one of her responses was, "I will never forgive him for what he did." I thanked her for telling me the truth and for trying. What I didn't tell my sister was how deep the rejection of a mother's unconditional love pierced through my heart. Instead, I said to her that was pretty much what I expected. After I hung up the phone, I now had to deal with something I never expected – rejection from my mother. I had to go through a grieving process, as if she died, but knowing she was still alive. I looked to the Lord Jesus for help because I knew through reading the Scriptures the ultimate rejection: his own Father turned his back on him in his greatest moment of need. Jesus bore the sin of the world – past, present, and future – on him just before his death on the cross. I knew Jesus could relate to me. I sensed his comfort for me and helped me come to terms with this rejection; that my mom isn't perfect, not flowing in forgiveness, for not loving me unconditionally (loving me, not what I did), and letting the pain and sting of rejection go. It took many days for this process to happen, and now that I have experienced such a thing, I pray it be used to help others overcome similar experiences; as Jesus did and still does today.

2 Corinthians 3:17

Now the Lord is the Spirit, and where the Spirit
of the Lord is, there is freedom.

- 2 Corinthians 3:17 (NIV)

When we come to Christ, when we make an open confession of him, there lies beneath in our hearts a freedom no one can take away from us. Not the enemy, not persecution, nor mocking, idle threats, trials, or tribulations. Nothing. And because of this power of freedom, we become transformed more and more into the likeness of Christ, and becoming more like him, the old self passes away. For some of us, as a result of this amazing, abundant freedom in Christ, we experience change quickly in our lives, and for some of us, it can be painfully slow. Either way, from within this freedom, change still happens when we allow the Holy Spirit operate in our hearts, yielding to his love, correction, and transformation. But this transformation doesn't come into its fullness until we choose to come into agreement with his Word, and then yield both intellectually and spiritually to allow the fullness of the spirit of God operate in us. We are spirit beings in human bodies, we must not forget that!

Will *crazy* things happen?

Will I *babble* in tongues and make a fool of myself?

Again, possibly, especially if God asks you to be a *fool* for him. God confounds the *wise*, the *intellectual*, and the *pragmatic*. God is not just asking us as believing Christians to just believe his message of salvation, even though that is the cornerstone of our faith, but he wants us to walk in the fullness of his power, whatever that looks like for each individual. God wants us to experience the fullness of freedom, not *blend in* with society, rather to *stand out* as the first-century believers did! Read the book of Acts, and you'll see what I mean. The Holy Spirit is operating today in the twenty-first century as he was starting with that amazing day on the day of Pentecost. If anyone tells you differently, then I challenge you to find it in the Scriptures where it ends. Miracles still happen, as do *divine appointments*, visits from angels, healings, speaking in tongues, interpretation of tongues, spiritual warfare (driving out demons), prophecies, distinguishing between spirits, just to name a few things that happen in our spiritual freedom in Christ. This all anchored by the blood of Christ – the source of our freedom. We then have the fruits of the Spirit – love, joy, peace, patience, perseverance, and self-control. We will have a renewed mind and a transformed heart, and a liberty no one can steal. Finally, we have the promise of the Holy Spirit, our seal of redemption.

July 27, 2018

Live in the light as he is in the light. That's a tough challenge for us saints. We combat sin; circumstances in our lives that are beyond our control; the enemy who will try to lie, deceive, and tempt us; and people who influence us. Sometimes all of these working against us at the same time. So how do we walk in the light as he is in the light? Praise be to Jesus, he has given us tools.

First, we have his magnificent presence. He is always with us and will never leave our side. We can take great comfort that we are never abandoned. Next, we have the Word of God so we can learn to walk and live in his ways – regarding his salvation; how to live holy lives; prayer; relationships with family, friends, in the church, strangers, and even enemies; how to trust God and walk in the power of the Holy Spirit. We have the fellowship of the saints, those we can talk to, pray with, and learn from. We have the weapons of God – prayer, the Word, love, compassion, truth, armor of God, righteousness, humility, surrender; and in all of these we have the different gifts through the Holy Spirit so that we can stand firm, build up, and edify the church.

We can be confident to walk in the light as he is in the light. We, in humility and surrender to him, put Jesus first in everything in our lives, relinquishing control to him in all aspects of our lives. You will witness healing in your heart, a renewing of your mind, a transformation of your life, and be a living witness for Jesus, one who lives in the light. Allow the Lord to shine his light on you, for it is glorious, it is cleansing, and you will be made whole and pure. This is the power of the blood of Jesus, shed for you. Then you will be an agent of change on earth for the glory of the kingdom of heaven.

July 29, 2018

> *For godly sorrow produces repentance leading to salvation, not*
> *to be regretted; but the sorrow of the world produces death.*
> - 2 Corinthians 7:10 (NKJV)

I have had to learn to not feel sorry for myself during this whole time of change and transformation, but to truly repent of my sins, and then trust the mighty hand of God bring forth the changes necessary so that life in the Spirit can be made manifest. Godly sorrow means you realize what you've done wrong, and you are able to see the shortcomings as the light has been shone on them. You then take steps to ask God to heal and remove and forgive them through a process of confession (1 John 1:9), renouncing of sin (2 Corinthians 4:2), and seeking forgiveness of sin from God as well as you forgiving others, including yourself (Matthew 6:14). This is a godly process, a holy interaction between you and God, and brings glory to his great name and life to you.

You belong in the land of the living – the land where the kingdom of God resides – where the abundant riches of life and liberty flow. Out of these rivers come joy, love, peace, prosperity (not necessarily material but also it can be immaterial), kindness, truth, life, and self-control. Self-pity or feeling sorry for yourself robs you of all these things. It is a thief, a liar, and a cheater, taking away from you rather than giving. Sin is a thief. Selfishness is a deceiver, a smoke-screen of joy, robbing you of true treasures from heaven. A critical and judgmental spirit steals your better judgment and can destroy relationships, sometimes with just one comment. A religious spirit can turn people off and lead people away from the most spiritual part of the gospel, speaking the truth in love and in perfect balance. Then there is pride stopping us from being able to move forward in the process of godly sorrow, sometimes out of fear of having to swallow our pride, sometimes out of sheer arrogance "I just won't do it," sometimes out of ignorance, and the list goes on. In humility and surrender, repentance brings forth fruit that God can till, prune, and produce in you to be an effective weapon for the kingdom. You will then be his delight, his *favorite* child, his blessed one, the apple of his eye. Show yourself worthy for the kingdom using the process of godly sorrow as the Holy Spirit shines his light on you, leading you to a repentant heart and flowing in you his living water, cleansing you to purity and holiness and renewed mind, and a restored heart – one that is made whole. Amen.

July 30, 2018

When There Is No Boasting

Thank you, Lord, for breaking my pride, my arrogance, and my conceit. Thank you for delivering me from the need to *lift myself up*, for you lift me up instead. You have brought me to a place where I can trust you wholeheartedly, where I can leave the will of my life safely in your hands, for I feel safe inside your loving arms. My life – it's all about you now, and I don't care if others think I am crazy to follow you the way I do. I know I hear your voice, and I trust it.

Show me more, Lord; show me more so that in all the days of my life, I walk in surrender to you. All the talents, all my abilities, my intellect – I surrender them all to you. I choose to be a good steward, an amazing custodian, and a fantastic caretaker of these gifts, so that I use them for your kingdom. This is my prayer – that I walk in complete submission to you and know that your ways are higher than mine, your thoughts are higher than mine – so that there will be no boasting but great joy instead. You are my rock and my salvation. You are the strength of my life, and I worship you. I will not be afraid. I have the joy of the Lord in my heart.

I now ask that you take my brokenness, take my pain, take my evil thoughts, and heal your child. Bring me to that place of wholeness so that I may experience the fullness of your joy in me; that I may experience the fullness of your love. In you, I have everything, so I know you see this request. You will bring me to the place and you know how to do it, for you know what is in me and you have a plan to bring me to that place. You will "pull out the roots" of sin as I allow you, and it will be glorious. You teach me to listen and be a good listener, both to you and to others. You bring me to your safe places – places where I experience the magnitude of your grace, the depth of your mercy, and the abundance of your love. I have never felt so loved; I have never felt so forgiven. I bow in humble adoration to you. You are my

King, my Lord, my Savior. There is no one like you. There will be no equal to you. You are worthy and I give you my heart – all of it!

To him be the glory, to him be all power, to him I shall worship – the One who reigns everlasting. Amen.

July 31, 2018

*If you need wisdom, ask our generous God, and he will give it to you. He will
not rebuke you for asking. But when you ask him, be sure that your faith is
in God alone. Do not waver, for a person with divided loyalty is as unsettled
as a wave of the sea that is blown and tossed by the wind. Such people
should not expect to receive anything from the Lord. Their loyalty is divided
between God and the world, and they are unstable in everything they do.*
- James 1:5-8 (NLT)

God is a great teacher, giving everyone who truly asks him for wisdom.
When we come to know Christ as our Savior, both your spirit and mind
"wake up" to his truth in the Word of God. It's like the words you read
in your Bible *come right off their pages*, breathing life into your very soul.
Someone with an unstable mind can throw you right off those tracks, not
only for him or herself but also to those who are listening. Listening to
worldly thinking mixed in with Bible references is the devil's trap; he does
not want people to listen to sound doctrine and will even use the Bible as
one of his weapons against them. Heck, he even tried that with Jesus when
he tempted him in the desert. If you are growing and learning about Christ
and you know deep down that your roots in your faith in Christ are not as
solid as you would like them to be, here are some suggestions to help you:

1) Get wisdom from God – pray daily and ask God for wisdom, and
just believe he will give it to you. Everyone will receive wisdom
at different paces, different ways and at different times; therefore
making your journey to obtain wisdom exciting, trying, and
eventful.

2) Read the Word of God – make a habit to read the Word of God
daily. Learn from the Scriptures about God's nature and how to
live as a believer of Jesus. Memorize Scripture so you can remember
what he is teaching you.

3) Attend Bible study – find yourself a good Bible study where you feel free to ask questions about God and where you are able to learn and grow in the Word, where you can pray with others. Bible study can also be a safe place to open up about your life, so you can receive healing, forgiveness, and restoration. Not every Bible study will offer this, but if you are looking for such a fellowship, don't stop looking until you find one that best suits your needs and wants.

4) Surround yourself with positive *spheres of influence* – find a strong Christian brother or sister who will encourage you, hold you accountable, teach you, help with good and effective Christian living, and pray with you – all this is called discipleship.

All these will help you grow in the wisdom of God, but God will be your primary source of teaching, inspiration, growth, and maturing. God is your key to being a stable, strong, balanced believer, giving you liberally his Spirit. He will bring healing in your life. He will teach you what it is like to live a life in the Spirit. He will fill you with the fruits and the gifts of the Spirit. He will teach you how to love, how to forgive, how to walk in grace and truth in perfect balance, and will teach you to live at peace with others, even with your enemies. He is a gracious God and will bring you into his glorious light. You just have to allow him in. It's your choice. Do as the Scripture in James declared: ask for wisdom, believe on faith in God alone to provide that wisdom – however the methods he delivers them to you; be unwavering in your faith to receive; and finally, be loyal to God and not with the world. In this, you will receive blessings in plenty, a bountiful supply of wisdom, love, favor, and peace. There is no match and no equal for what God gives his children who love him wholeheartedly, in humility, and complete surrender.

MY STORY

June 30, 2018

I was now allowed back into church, it was now October 2016. I stayed quiet about my allegations to the rest of the church, and God seemed to bless me over the next six weeks. I belong to a charismatic group of believers who love to walk in the Spirit and in the prophetic. And during this time, whether I was in a Bible study, at church, or even one-on-one in prayer, on six different occasions, it was prophesied over me pertaining the responsibility of building wealth. One saw a vision of a money tree where anyone could just pull money off its branches. He shared that with me twice over this six-week period. Another saw a vast acreage that I would have. Another prophet thrust his hand to my stomach and yelled, "Wealth! You will give a million dollars to that church! Inventions!" Another prophet wrote down for me that he saw me in a red sports car, and the only fuel it would take was premium gas, and one other that I remember and was written down for me from a prophetess was I would reach my hand into the darkness and take back to what was stolen from the light.

God was using this time to remind me of my calling, which was encouraging. I still hadn't clued in, however, the cost and demand he was making on me in order to receive that calling. At that point, my heart was still too hard and my thinking not right, to have any greater responsibility than what he was allowing me at that point: nothing. Notta. No ministry whatsoever. Still not ready. God did allow me to go to a conference in November. The group leading these conferences titled them "Island Rain." I had been invited to attend all of them, but when they came up, I couldn't. I was being sent to Calgary, Florida, or Vancouver during the same weekends of the conferences. It was like I was being deliberately blocked from going to them, and to this day I still don't know why.

Over the past four to five years, prophets or high-profile Christians from all over the world (from Canada, United States, Australia, U.K.) have been drawn to Vancouver Island, and while they have been here they have confirmed prophesies of an outpouring of the Holy Spirit will start here, and from here, will spread across North America. So these "Island Rain" conferences were being held from Port Hardy, one of the most northern communities to Victoria, the southernmost community of Vancouver Island. This one was held in the oldest church in Victoria – The Church of Our Lord – an Episcopal church and a spirit-filled and God-fearing church.

There was discussion as to how they felt led by the Spirit for this outpouring – that it would start with the aboriginal community and spread from there. There must have been close to fifty, maybe even sixty people at the conference, representing communities from Port Hardy down to Victoria and many communities in-between. There were even speakers who came in from the Lower Mainland (Greater Vancouver). They were all together for this one purpose. The conference ran all day and ended close to 4:00 p.m.

The Lord finally let me know what he has in store for us. He wants to pour out his Spirit, and I'm believing for one last time, to give us all a chance to repent of our sins and come into a saving knowledge of Jesus Christ as our Lord and Savior. He is speaking to his church ahead of time, so we can be prepared for the massive influx of new converts to Christ. But will we? It will require massive humility, amazing patience, great perseverance, and a very large dose of character to deal with people who are completely unchurched, don't understand "Christianese," have experienced a great move of God in their lives, but don't know what to do with it? Are we prepared? Can we get ready in time for the final outpouring God wants to give us?

I pray in Jesus name that he raises up great teachers who will be able to both train the believing community and then the masses to love one another as Christ loved the church, just like how that responsibility was laid on the apostles in the first-century church, now with twenty-first century challenges – distractions like never before, especially because of such a great increase in technology. We have our work cut out for us, but God is preparing us to be up to this task.

So God finally allowed me to go to this one conference, and it would be the last one I would attend at the time of this writing. I suppose one was all I would need to see. This time of grace – my grace period – was about to come to an end. The Lord in his infinite mercy was about to plunge me back into facing my sin; the lies, the deceits, the double-mindedness, and pave the way for a huge operation of deliverance, taking the "cancer" that he saw in me out of my soul. No more hiding.

July 1, 2018

In October, when I was free of any allegations against me, I planned to go on a trip to Phoenix, Arizona, and stay at my sister and brother-in-law's second house down there. I chose by the recommendation of one of my old pastor's to go to counseling. I went for six weeks, and they were very helpful. The last session would end in the third week of November, so I booked my flight for the day after the last counseling session. Two days before that last session, I was spending time with my friends for prayer and fellowship, and two of those friends were from Port Hardy. They decided to stay behind for a few extra days after the "Island Rain" conference that God allowed me to attend. It was after 9:00 p.m. when I left the fellowship and headed home for the night. I got home, and I don't believe I was there twenty minutes when I got a knock on the door. It was the police!

They said, "Are you Michael Mahy?"

I answered, "Yes."

The front officer replied, "We are here to arrest you."

I replied, "Again?! What did I do now??"

The officer replied, "I just have orders to come here and arrest you."

I went numb. I invited the officers in, but I looked past them outside the door. I saw two sets of headlights on in the driveway, no siren lights and, being November on an overcast evening, it was otherwise pitch black outside. Again, for the second time my arrest was being done inconspicuously. My neighbors would have no idea what was happening. God, in his infinite mercy, was shielding my most embarrassing moments once again. I was brought to the station and held overnight. They did contact my lawyer for me, so when I had to appear before the judge, this time there was a representative from the office there on my behalf. The judge told me the charges (they were no longer allegations) were the same charges as before.

The judge told me I was back on bail, and I was to report to the bail office. But I really didn't hear the bail office part. I had to take a taxi again home, and now I was facing my sins once again. I didn't call in the bail office the next day, like I was supposed to, and the day after that, I went to my last counseling session, told him what happened to me, and he just listened. I told him I was still hoping to go to Phoenix.

In the early afternoon that day, I got a call from the bail office and said I better report immediately; otherwise, I would be in breach. So I went. I brought with me my flight itinerary and asked if I could go on the trip while on bail. They flat out said no. They also said there would be a good chance that I would be turned back at the border because of the charges against me. I was in tears, pleading with the bail officer. So she said a supervisor would call me later to explain things to me. She did call and gave me a clear explanation, and I had to accept it. At this point I was still in total denial as to what I've done, the atrocities that I've committed to my victims, and the delusional thinking that I had.

How could I think that touching young boys wasn't so bad?

How could I possibly justify in my head God wouldn't carry out his justice for these crimes?

How could I possibly think that his *grace* was making me more special than others and therefore exempting me from correction?

That was how dark my heart was, how delusional my thinking was, and how deep I was in denial and in hiding. God made sure he wasn't going to have me *rewarded* with a trip to Phoenix. And now looking back, thank you Lord for taking it away from me. I thank you for taking everything away from me actually.

I had to unravel my trip. Cancel my flight. Cancel the car rental. I lost money on the two hockey games I purchased and go see while I was down there. Then I had to come up with some explanation to my family as to why I did an *about face* and not go. I just told them I wasn't ready to go after my separation and all. It would take to the following spring the real reason I didn't go to Phoenix to my sister and the rest of my family hearing from my sister about my situation on the day of sentencing, which was October 25, 2017.

July 3, 2018

Entry: (names in bold are changed to protect the identities of the individuals)

The Woman of Niagara Falls

It was now early December, 2016, and **my good friend who has been my support throughout all of this** told me a friend of hers was flying out to Victoria from Niagara Falls on to stay for at least two weeks. (She ended up staying for more than three months!) Up to the day, before she flew in, I never knew much about her. I had met her a few times over the years, and I knew she had a gift of walking in the Holy Spirit, but I was a little wary of her doctrinal accuracy went it came to her walk and beliefs lining up with the Word of God. When the night came to pick her up, I had a desire to come along, but my friend's brother was asked to drive. So I just chose to step back, say nothing and hoped to see her soon. I was over visiting and having tea, intending to leave around 9:00 p.m. because the flight was going to come in late, after 11 p.m. Around eight o'clock, my friend's brother called her downstairs to tell her that he wasn't up to staying up to go to the airport. She came upstairs to tell me this. So I said I would be more than happy to drive out. My friend looked at me ask if to say, "Really?! You would do that for me?"

I just looked at her and told her I had a desire to meet her friend, and this was a perfect opportunity to do just that.

She said, "Thank you so much!" And continued fellowshipping until we had to leave around ten-thirty. We got to the airport, and the flight was a little bit late. She finally arrived, and we grabbed her bags, headed to the car and went back. The **woman of Niagara Falls** was very talkative. She talked all the way back, telling us how things were up to when she left Ontario. This was the beginning of a unique relationship I had with her over the next few months, as I got to know her better. God used the gifting she had – walking in the Spirit, distinguishing between spirits, speaking in tongues, waging spiritual warfare, walking in the prophetic – to help me develop a newer, fresher relationship in Christ Jesus. God used her to help me come to a new level of repentance, a new level of trust in God, a new level of humility, a new level of surrender. She was tough on me when she had to, taking no guff or excuses from me. God showed me in a vision that she was like a big, yellow bulldozer, smoothing the land over everything it bulldozed. It became a blessing to me during this time of my life. She even bought me a nice plain, brown cross from the Christian book store to put up on my wall, above my bed. It was about six inches long, three-and-a-half to four inches wide, and less and one-inch thick. I taped that up on my wall in my bedroom instead of using a nail. My home was rented, so I avoided making new holes in the wall.

July 5, 2018

Note: (names in bold are changed to protect the identities of the individuals)

> *For we do not wrestle against flesh and blood, but against the principalities, against, powers, against the rulers of the darkness of this age, against spiritual hosts of wickedness in the heavenly places.*
> - Ephesians 6:12 (NKJV)

Christmas 2016 had now past, I was now spending a lot of my time with my two sisters in Christ, **my good friend who has been my support throughout all of this** and the **woman of Niagara Falls.** They both have the gift of walking in the prophetic, like I have said before. Being on bail meant there wasn't a lot of things I could do, and one of them was attend church. I was restricted from that. So when it came to New Year's Eve, these two amazing ladies had dinner at my house and visited me, so I wouldn't be alone.

Looking back, I think I put even more restrictions on myself than what was placed in the conditions of my bail, and again looking back, I have reason to believe in part this was why I was never bothered by my bail officer or the police, ever! I recall one former pastor of mine saying that with how I was living, I had already put myself in jail. I was so strict on myself. Hmm, now to get back on track to this part of the story.

The **woman of Niagara Falls** knew how to wage spiritual warfare, as did my other good friend. They both prayed over my home to bless it, which was awesome.

However, just after Christmas, *stuff* started happening in my bedroom, as there were four separate demonic attacks on three separate occasions over a span of approximately ten days. The first one was between Christmas and New Year's Day. I was in bed sound asleep when I got woken up to the peeling of tape off the wall. Then I felt my little brown cross, which was taped up firmly, fall on my bed. I got up and turned on my light, and there it was; the little brown cross facing down, with the pieces of tape facing up, lying flat on my bed. I wasn't too happy about that, but I put the very light cross (it couldn't be heavier than five ounces) back up on the wall and tugged on it firmly to ensure it wouldn't fall off again. It stayed stuck to the wall. I turned out the light and went back to bed, not falling asleep right away and contemplating what had just happened.

Not twenty minutes later, I could hear the rustling of plastic in my bedroom closet. I always kept the closet doors wide open, and still being awake, there was no mistake as to what I was hearing. In my closet, on the floor was the Bounty paper towels, the giant bags of twelve rolls that you buy at Costco. I could hear the giant bag falling over! I had had this bag sit in my closet, unmoved, for three months, and the only time it did get moved was when I swept the floor, as it was on the floor, or when I needed to get a roll out of it. I went through only a roll a month, since I lived by myself, so there were nine rolls left in that giant bag, firmly standing upright. The bag, when I turned the light on a second time, was listing over to its side. Now I was angry. I stood in the doorway straddling my bedroom and the entrance to the dining area and started taking authority in the name of Jesus over the enemy. I commanded him to go and declared the house holy for and in the name of Jesus. I stood there for only a minute or so doing this and then went to bed.

Now it is January 2017, the first week, and I went to bed again. I couldn't fall asleep right away, so I lied there, eyes wide open, staring at my bright white bedroom door from what little bit of moonlight that came in through my window. Next thing I saw was this black shadow move across the doorway quite slowly. I knew right then and there that "thing" was back. I also, right there and then, remembered what Kris Vallotton had wrote in his and Bill Johnson's book *The Supernatural Ways of Royalty* of an encounter he had with the enemy when he showed up at the foot of his bed. Kris finally said to his enemy, "Oh, it's just you." Then he turned over to his side and fell asleep. I decided to do the same thing. I said to him, "Oh, it's just you." I then ignored it, rolled over to my side, and fell asleep.

In the morning, I woke up, but not to my alarm that was set for 6:15 a.m. on my iPhone. I knew I had set it. I went to grab my iPhone off my night table, touched the screen to swipe it on, and nothing! The battery was completely drained! Before I went to bed, the battery was at 74 percent, and I had no programs in the background working to drain it. Any other night, the battery wouldn't drain more than 5 percent of battery life. That "thing" drained my battery! I was choked. I didn't pray or wage any warfare at this point because what was done was done, and whatever had come into my room the night before carried out what it wanted and was probably long gone by now. This wasn't going to be the last encounter. I would receive one more, and that was the very next day, in the daytime.

I had my bedroom door open, and it was quiet in the house. I didn't have any music on, and I was in the very next room. Next thing I could hear was tape peeling off the wall. Again! There was my little brown cross, lying face down, again in the exact same spot it fell the last time, except this time my bed was made. I took my little cross, took off the six pieces of tape off, re-applied seven pieces of tape on to the back, prayed over the cross, and asked God to put two angels sentry over it, taped it back to the wall and made sure it was firm. Nothing else ever happened again to that cross, my iPhone, or the house the remainder of the time I lived there. But I asked God why he allowed this to happen. He actually spoke to me back in my head. He said, "I allowed you to experience the dark side of the spirit world to remind you that it really exists and that you have the authority in my Name to cast them out."

This is a set of events that I hope I'd never forget. The Lord was building my confidence in trusting his omnipresence and his omnipotence – the things we can do in his great name. I did tell my two friends each event, and they prayed for me and this wonderful little home that God found for me to live. I was slowly learning and growing to trust him, but I had a long way to go.

At the end of January (January 28, I believe it was) the **woman of Niagara Falls** and I decided to go for a day-long drive up Vancouver Island. The

Lord had me write down on a piece of paper for her to read about what God wanted us to do on this trip. It was a task God wanted us to carry out – pray for each community we drove by in the Spirit. So we did just that! For six hours, we prayed; sometimes stopping and getting out of the car and sometimes while driving past each community while on the highway. In a couple of places, we felt the presence of the enemy at the same time, but we didn't stop praying – praying for healing, for restoration, for repentance, a praying against the principalities of each region we felt by the Holy Spirit to do. So we started in Victoria and finished right at CFB Comox, an air force base halfway up Vancouver Island. We were exhausted when we were done. We then proceeded further north to Campbell River, then enjoyed our three-hour drive back from Campbell River, back to Victoria. We did as God asked us and it was our pleasure to obey.

July 7, 2018

Note: (names in bold are changed to protect the identities of the individuals)

The Storyteller to Be

It was now February 2017, and I was spending between one and two hours a day reading the Scriptures and praying. One morning while I was pacing back and forth from the door entranceway to the end of the front room, I heard the Holy Spirit speak to me, "You are going to tell your story!" When I heard that, I was petrified! I mean, I was trying to hide at this point everything that was happening to me! I was off social media completely. I only spent time with my closest friends, plus the **woman from Niagara Falls**, and talking with my family, who at this point had absolutely no clue what was going on in my life. I wasn't interested in sharing my two arrests, my crimes, my sexual preference, my past, my life. Not interested in putting it on display for others to read, to judge, or to even comment on: positively, neutrally, or negatively. Just not interested.

Well, we know when God tells us he wants to do something with us, he'll eventually get his way. But this day, fear poured over me, and my gut reaction was to crawl under a rock and hide. *Why does he want me to do this?* The selfish side of me was starting to get angry. How dare he put me on display, for all to judge! The pity party was starting to kick in. All those days of growing in humility and surrender seemed like they were about to be thrown out the window. I was ready to take my life back, get back into the driver's seat and take back control, just like I did before. I used to say to Jesus before all this part of my life was seemingly looking like it was spiraling out of control was, "I love you Jesus," then in my head I would imagine me straight-arming, "but that's as close as you get!" That's what I felt like I wanted to do at that point. But something else happened instead. I kept praying. I kept seeking his face. The Lord had brought me so far in a new walk with him that I reasoned, "If you want me to tell my story, you have to have a purpose for it." I was still scared about the notion of sharing disgusting details of my past, my sins and awful choices, but as I write this today, I didn't see the level of humility he was going to bring me to and carry that on into even deeper humility and surrender this day forward.

God knows what he is doing, and he allowed time to factor in all he intended so that a message of hope can be brought to others who are hiding sexual sins, hiding their sexual identity, helping people who will judge us harshly to take a good look in the mirror and learn from the Lord how to balance grace and truth in perfect balance just like he did. This is so the church can be equipped to handle the serious matters of sexuality and all its pitfalls: adultery, fornication, pedophilia, pornography, uncontrollable sexual thoughts, and the different kinds of sexual identity – homosexuality, lesbianism, being bi-sexual, being transgendered, wanting multiple sexual partners, even dealing with things like bestiality. The church seems to be ill-equipped to handle such matters, and in so many cases would rather *run away* from these issues rather than tackling them head on.

Jesus sat with the *outcasts* of society. He said, "It isn't the healthy that I came for, but the sick."

As part of the Great Commission, Jesus is calling us to be his hands and feet, and no one – absolutely no one who claims to know Jesus as their personal Lord and Savior – is exempted. We are to help those who are victims of sexual touching, rape, sexual violence, unwanted pregnancies, and child pornography. We are to co-labor with Jesus to see all these people healed by the power of the Holy Spirit, regain confidence of who they are, allow God's love to fill their hearts, and learn the powerful tool of forgiveness, forgiving those who have hurt them sexually so that their souls get healed from the sting and pain of sexual deviancy and sexual sin.

To those who have committed such acts, like I did, they need a place for confession, a place where transformation, the renewing of the mind, and inner healing can take place – again with the perfect balance of grace and truth and even justice if necessary, however that looks. Our example is in John 8:1-11, where the woman was caught in adultery. So how can the church be prepared? Well, we all, including me, need to stop judging each other, so we all need to come to the Lord with repentant hearts, some asking for forgiveness for judging, sometimes too harshly, to those who have committed sexual sins beyond the capacity outlined in the Word of God. Some need to ask for forgiveness for gossiping to others about the conduct of those who committed such sins; and then those asking for forgiveness for judging those who have judged them too harshly because they have committed the sexual sin. These sins are cancers in the church, and they need to go. Satan just loves it when he can drive a wedge into the church and render it ineffective because of secret sins, because of the bitterness and hate associated with the sin of judgment and then gleefully watches the church mishandle these situations. The church instead has a great opportunity! First and most important, we have the Gospel, the Word of God as a weapon against the kingdom of darkness and to restore people back into the kingdom of light. We also have all kinds of books and materials that are balanced and inspired by God to help the church learn to tackle the sexual sins and sexual issues of today. This is an opportunity to take back what the enemy has been stealing from us: sexual purity, restoration of healthy sexual relationships, and where necessary, holy justice for those who have been acting out in a criminal manner as I did. The church can also bring in support groups into their fellowships, such as an appropriate twelve-step group for Christians and/or Celebrate Recovery exclusively for sexual addiction, which more information can be found through the ministry of Rick Warren and Saddleback Church in California.

Recovery for sex addiction and coming to terms with sexual identity requires, as AA famously puts it, the power of fellowship and the power of spiritual experience. We, the church, can do both of those so well when we want to. But we need to allow God to do his part in order for victory to become real in people's lives. The power, no, the supernatural power of the Holy Spirit to bring forth healing and transformation while we do our part in presenting the truth with grace, mercy, and in great humility and surrender. This is our opportunity. This is our time. We can be witnesses and co-laborers in Christ to see a sexual reformation. It will take prayer; it will take spiritual warfare, and great patience, waiting on God, to execute a massive shift back to sexual purity not seen since the early 1960s. We also need to show grace and mercy to those who struggle in their sexual identity or even to those who comfortably identify themselves as gay, lesbian, bisexual, or transgendered.

As of this writing, my sexual attraction is toward men, of which I would be identified as gay. But I love Jesus, know his Word, believe his Word, and walk in his Word. His Word is holy and perfect. If the Word says that my body is the temple of the Holy Spirit, then I come into agreement with that truth declared in the Word. Therefore, I will not smoke, overeat (I have lost more than 60 lbs.), do drugs, drink excessively, nor engage in any sexual activity – no dating, no sexual encounters, do nothing sexually that goes against the Word of God – as part of that to honor him who gives me life, liberty, renewal, and transformation. This is my promise to him who has promised me salvation. I am saved. I am born-again. No man can judge me or take that away from me just because I am identified as gay. But if we want to see the outpouring of the Holy Spirit, we as a church need to clean up our act in preparation for it.

July 8, 2018

Note: (names in bold are changed to protect the identities of the individuals)

My Sister Now Knows

It is now April 2017, and I'm coming near to the end of the last tax season in the name of the company God asked me to form more than twelve years earlier. Easter was a week away, and my court date to plead guilty to my charges seemed to be getting pushed back every month. I had no idea what my lawyer was doing, but I could intuitively trust him, so I did. Then came this random phone call from my sister. She said she wanted to come and spend the night at my house before travelling over to the mainland to visit family over the Easter weekend. The thing was, and like I said before, no one in my family knew what was going on. All they knew was that I was separated. I was living by myself. They even knew I wasn't attending church. They just didn't know why. By the grace of God, no one who knew the real story, which was very few people, said anything to my family, and my sister didn't indicate in this phone call that she knew anything either.

A little while after the phone call and trying to figure out why my sister was coming to Vancouver Island from the Sunshine Coast, I worked up the nerve to ask the Lord. The Lord replied, "You are going to let her know what is going on with you." I was now petrified again. Thoughts were racing through my mind, and my heart was melting in fear. My sister, who has stood beside me all my life, through thick and sometimes very, very thin, was about to be told my deepest, darkest secrets, and God (as far as I was concerned at the time) was giving me *marching orders* to let her know – everything.

So all week, as each day got closer, the fear would escalate, then de-escalate. What was the Lord Jesus doing? Was my sister going to reject me? Was she going to stop loving me? Was she going to judge me, hate me, and push me away? What I did know, as each day passed, was that I had to tell her because the Lord spoke to me and told me to do so. I knew that, in the end, it was in my best interests to obey. I wasn't coming in on blind faith either. By this time in my walk with God, I understood better his omniscience, and even though I didn't know the outcome ahead of time and even though I could have said no, I knew I could trust God.

By now, I was coming to a place to understand that he knew what was best for me. So the day came when my sister arrived. I picked her up at the bus stop, and the Lord gave me an overwhelming peace and calm until it came time to tell her. We went for dinner, and at one point, my sister started talking about how she would be prepared to stand up for what she believed in, get handcuffed, and put in jail!

The Lord was using our general conversation to drop some pretty major hints that I needed to tell her! She was not even a Christian! No one in my family is at the time of this writing. Just me. I kept, in my head, promising God I would tell her, just not at the restaurant in the middle of eating dinner. After we ate, she wanted to go to Old Navy, because they always seemed to have clothes that fit her for really cheap. So we went in there and all the while, the Holy Spirit was pushing me to tell her what was going on. I replied to him that I promised to tell, but I wanted to tell her when we got back to the house. I had to keep this promise to God. So when we got home, my sister sat down on the couch while I sat down in my oversized chair I loved so much. She opened up her bag and was going through all her purchases she made, giddy like a kid in a candy store. I finally worked up the courage to do what God had asked me to do.

I said to her, "I hope you enjoyed shopping and the clothes you bought because I'm about to put a damper on it. I have to tell you the real reason why we got separated and why I am living alone."

She just stared at me, intently listening. I started to tear up, my mouth quivering as I spoke. I was looking to God for courage. I said to her, "I have been charged for sexual interference, for touching young boys; and I'm probably going to jail for it." I just started sobbing when I told her. She just stared at me like a deer caught in headlights. Nothing was said for maybe ten seconds, but it felt like an eternity. I didn't know how she was going to respond. She didn't show anger. She didn't show sadness. She didn't show rage.

Then she finally spoke, "You know I love you unconditionally. Unconditionally! I knew there was something wrong! I just couldn't figure it out."

I was sobbing uncontrollably by this time. And I said, "I am so sorry that I never told you before this. I've been so scared and so ashamed of what I've done. I just couldn't bring myself to telling anyone what was happening to me."

It was finally out. I wasn't rejected. Judged, yes, and rightly so, but not rejected by my sister. This was huge for me because God had me tell the truth to her and he knew she would be important in my path to healing and restoration of my life. We talked about details and questions she had and a bowl of ice cream to go with it. I then said to my sister I wanted her to talk to **my good friend who has been my support throughout all of this,** so I called her, and the two talked so my sister could confirm from someone else that I was telling the truth. The next day we headed to the mainland, and she said, "We'll keep the matter quiet and try and figure something out to tell the rest of the family in the future." Well, needless to say, they got shell-shocked instead.

July 9, 2018

Note: (names in bold are changed to protect the identities of the individuals)

My Three Close Friends

My sister wasn't the only one the Lord wanted me to *spill the beans* to in person. The three close friends that stood by me and did Bible study with me during my first arrest and knew about my second arrest didn't know the details or the reason why I was arrested. Since the early fall of 2016, I also hadn't spent much time with them either. During the fall, winter, and early spring, I spent most of my time with **my good friend who has been my support throughout all of this**, the **woman of Niagara Falls** until she went back to Ontario, my pastor, and **my buddy the gardener** who was one of the three.

My buddy the gardener – I told him first; and early on after the second arrest because during the winter, spring, and summer of 2017 I would go to his house once a week to pray with him and his roommate. He never judged me, which I found most amazing. God must had given him peace about our friendship and to stand by me. I am forever grateful for his friendship.

The next person the Lord wanted me to tell was **the only lady in my Bible study**. The Holy Spirit wanted me to contact her, so we got together shortly after I told my sister. I was starting to gain a bit of confidence in telling all, but I was still very nervous. We were in the car and I said to her, "I need to tell you what is going on with me."

She replied, "I was praying today and asking the Lord, 'What is up with Mike?'"

I smiled a little, and said, "Well, God is about to answer your prayer today."

I gave her details of the nature of my charges, how I have been handling it, and that I finally told my sister and that she and her husband were the only family members that knew. She was so graceful, and she said that she didn't judge, and that God was giving her an opportunity to grow in the Lord with someone like me for reasons I can't disclose here.

She also said to me, "The Lord has told me to come into alignment with you so that's what I'm going to do."

She is an amazing woman of God, full of faith and walking in the Spirit, as does **my buddy the gardener.** Two now know, and now I needed to tell **the fourth one in our Bible study,** and he was the one I was so apprehensive to tell. I was certain he was going to judge me, but a month after (now it's May 2017), the Holy Spirit told me to call him and have coffee with him. Then I was to tell him the truth. I was scared again, but not as bad as it was with my sister. When we met, I remember it was a Saturday afternoon, and we sat down across from each other. I didn't wait long this time to start *spilling the beans.* I was in tears, going through a bunch of napkins, while telling him what was going on.

He replied after I finished, "No Mike. I don't judge you."

I just gave him a big hug, and talked for another hour. I had my three friends back, and we started up our little fellowship again. They would be right there with me, right up to our last Bible study together at my place the night before the day of my sentencing.

July 10, 2018

Day of Surrender

It was now June 2017, and I was facing the date of pleading guilty to my charges. This date had been pushed back several times since December. And at this point, it was set for June 7. I thought I had fully surrendered to God, but this wasn't true. I was still holding back part of my life from him, part of my identity. I thought I was going to lose that completely and therefore not know who I was anymore. I was afraid God was going to make such massive changes in me, and I just wasn't prepared to let it all go. So now, it's June 7. No phone call from my lawyer. *Hmmm.* Better go online and find out what time it's supposed to start. The date was moved again to June 21! Now I was starting to get frustrated. When was this going to end? When was this part of this process going to be over with? In the frustration, I finally cried out to God, "I'm done. I fully surrender to you. I give you all my life." At that point, I didn't care about my life anymore. I chose to hand it over completely to Jesus, whatever that looked like. It was this day that God was waiting for – complete surrender, the day he asked me for more than two years earlier. I was about to find out on no certain terms what complete surrender meant.

It was now a few days before my court date. I finally got a phone call from my lawyer to have me come in to see him. When that day came, I sat down in one of his conference rooms, and he started talking about the court process, what to expect, etc. Then he asked me how are we going to proceed. I asked what he meant, and he said, "Are we going ahead with the plea of guilty or not?"

Out of curiosity, I asked what the process of pleading not guilty looked like. He said that it may be possible that some or none of the witnesses may show up to testify of which I could possibly walk out a free man. That choice wasn't sitting well with me, and I checked with the Holy Spirit for confirmation as part of this new experience of surrender to his will. I felt him speak into my heart with conviction, "Plead guilty. This is what I want you to do."

I obeyed his voice. I started to tear up, started shaking my head slowly as to say no to the lawyer and responded, "No. Pleading not guilty isn't an option. I can't force those kids to live this out again." The lawyer slightly smiled. He then ended our meeting by saying, "See you on the twenty-first. We need to be there before nine a.m."

God was pleased with me because he loves me so much and was leading me to do the right thing. Before, I would have lied, hid, and run. He was putting that new identity he has planned for me into me. I was slowly beginning to understand that surrender means – surrender all of me, not to be a coward but to be inwardly strong and face the truth; and this not only by my own strength, but with the help of Almighty God who strengthens me.

July 11, 2018

The Plea

The morning came for my court date. Thankfully, I wasn't physically alone this day. I had a good friend who knew my case and stood by me, who came with me in support. A fellow believer, someone to pray with, someone to talk to. He was originally from Colombia, and at this point I had known him ten years. Before going into the courthouse, we went for a quick coffee. While we left the coffeehouse and were walking the one block over, the Lord gave him a word for me.

He said, "Mike, the Lord is going to put you through the refiner's fire."

Not quite what I wanted to hear, but what he said in the Holy Spirit was important because the Lord used this very time to prepare me for what he had in store for me in the near future.

We got into the courthouse and waited for my lawyer to arrive. We found out what courtroom we had to go to and waited just outside of it. Lots of people were streaming in, about two dozen, then my lawyer arrived at five minutes to the hour.

He said, "Wait here. I need to talk to the Crown," which, in Canada, is the prosecutor. He went into the courtroom and, within a couple of minutes, came back out. He said, "We're moving to another courtroom. This guy who is presiding is the Justice of the Peace, and since you are pleading guilty, we're going straight before a judge."

He led my friend and I down the hall to a much, much quieter courtroom, of which I felt relieved. He said to wait there and we would start shortly. I was very nervous but took comfort that the Lord and my friend were both here, and that my lawyer was here to represent me. When the time came to go inside, my friend and I sat down in the front. In my heart, I just wanted this over with. The Crown and my lawyer came in, then came in the court clerk, and the sheriff. Everyone started talking about whose case was going to be first, who was coming in via video court, and file folders were being shuffled around into the order as discussed between everyone else and the court clerk. I found out I was second in order, so I thanked the Lord for the opportunity to get this over with quickly. Then came in the judge.

"All rise!" shouted the Sheriff.

"Please be seated," remarked the judge. We sat down.

Then the clerk read out, "The Crown vs. Mahy."

I looked up quickly as my head was down. I was first up! My lawyer motioned for me to stand beside him, so I did. He then said, "Your Honor, in the case file number (blah, blah, blah) and in the charges numbered one, two, three and five (something like in that order), my client pleads guilty."

The judge replied, "Very well. We will set a date for August 24 for sentencing."

That was it! This was done and over with in about eighty seconds! I was put in first instead of second! And I didn't have to say a word! Not a word! Furthermore! I believed the near-empty courtroom, going first, my lawyer doing all the talking, and making this whole ordeal almost painless was orchestrated by the grace and mercy of the Lord Jesus Christ. He cast favor on me that day when I didn't deserve it. Furthermore, they did not put me in jail at this time either but allowed me to live in my home, work in my business, and still follow the bail conditions until the day of sentencing. My lawyer gave me instructions right after the court appearance and told me what to expect in the upcoming weeks. I had to have a psychological assessment and a pre-sentence report (PSR) in July.

My friend and I went for breakfast afterward and talked about how good God was this day. Then I said to him, "I should let my partner know what happened but I don't know what to say."

I knew only to text her as the last time we communicated was back in early March where I emailed her to let her know I was doing one more tax season. Our text and emails throughout this whole time have been, thankfully, very cordial. She was never mean nor malicious to me. My friend suggested to keep it short and apologetic.

So I wrote, "I plead guilty today. I am sorry for all I have done to you, and I hope one day you will forgive me."

A few minutes later my iPhone said, "Read," but she never replied. From that point until the writing of this, I have never attempted to contact her, nor has she attempted to contact me. I pray for her all the time. She is the only woman I'd ever truly loved and probably the only woman I will ever love. I just couldn't believe the damage I've caused to her and to others, the lives I've hurt, and the souls I've crushed all because of my sick, selfish, destructive behavior.

It will take a miracle to make amends with any of the people I've hurt, but I am still repentant as to what I've done, the sins I've committed. Maybe one day I can say sorry to the ones I've hurt. But only if it doesn't damage them further. That's step nine in my twelve-step program and all the other twelve-step programs that stem from AA's model.

After breakfast, my friend and I parted ways. I thanked him for being such a support to me, and went home to go back to work. The next few months would prove interesting as now I had to face the reality of sentencing. The thing is, I still didn't believe that I was going to jail. My thinking was still delusional in some areas. God was about to bring reality to that too.

July 12, 2018

Pre-Sentence Report

The pre-sentence report was set for July 17. I was in deep prayer that morning, looking to the Lord for guidance. I was still in this place of surrender before him; in fact, I made it a habit by now to open up my heart in prayer daily saying, "I surrender to you." It was getting easier. Little by little, the Lord was chipping away at my hard heart, and today was no exception. After a while, laying down flat on my back in deep meditation, the Lord spoke to me, giving me instructions for this afternoon's PSR report with the probation officer.

He said, "Be very humble, be very truthful." Then he said, "Tell her about your grooming."

I got scared. I now had to tell a complete stranger the embarrassing and horrible deeds I've committed, then tell that I, in fact, groomed them, which is all true. I gained the trust of these boys and young teenagers, used "my faith" as a source of gaining trust for both the youth and parents, then abused the authority of my position of trust to touch them inappropriately. I had disgusting thinking, a warped mind, and evil intent. Looking back this now makes me sick to my stomach. Plus I wanted to lie, run and hide from taking responsibility, and ask God to protect me from it! Again, very disgusting thinking. Today, God had a different plan – he was making his son tell the truth and tell all. He wasn't letting correction go. In his mercy, but also in his justice, he was now forcing me to face the truth, tell the truth, and in the end, heal me because of the truth, and then exact chastisement, rebuke, and correction in his truth and justice. God will correct those whom he loves.

So when I got to the probation office (same office I had to report to while I was on bail), I got called in for the pre-sentence report. There I was questioned about the details of the crimes I committed, and there were also questions about other things – family upbringing, professional/ career, friends, even personal interests. She even asked if I was gay and I answered yes. She said it was no wonder with my faith in God, another subject she covered with me, why I was so confused, why I had such a hard time reconciling my sexual identity with my faith. I had to correct her on that! I told her my faith has nothing to do with my sexuality. As I love the Lord and walk according to his Word. I can accept my sexuality and God's Word. It just means I follow what it says, "No sexual sin." Therefore, I didn't date, no intimate relationships, and abstain from immoral sexual activity. She didn't like these answers but I stood firm on them and wouldn't budge from the biblical position. She had an agenda about homosexuality and Christianity, and I don't think she liked how I presented my faith, sexuality, and no compromise. That's probably one reason why I didn't get such a nice PSR report when my lawyer told me about it more than a month later. Enough of that.

When it came to the question of grooming, she asked me to express in my own words how I felt about what I did to them. I said, "What I did was wrong. I have no excuses for what I've done. I've hurt them and their families, and I'm ashamed of what I did."

She replied, "So, would you say you groomed them?"

I replied, "Yes I did groom them, they came to trust me and I took advantage of that trust, and violated it."

She read part of the report out loud to me. She then said, "In each case, the victims all said they were scared and didn't know what to do." When she said this, it finally cut down to my heart, and I broke down crying. It finally broke through the hardness, the walls of my heart. I couldn't stop crying. I hurt innocent children. I scarred them, probably for life. I forever changed their lives all because of my selfish needs and selfish desires. God was using this time to face the truth of what I've done, and he was holding me accountable for my actions.

Praise his name. He's the righteous judge and will judge according to my sins, this is his grace and mercy. To judge my sins here and now rather than judge me eternally. This is the expression of his goodness to show justice to those who seek it. My victims sought it and God delivered.

God has a bigger plan for this too. He has a plan to use people's lives as an example to bring conviction, correction, repentance, deliverance, and restoration. May the Lord Jesus bring glory to his name in using us as examples of how he can bring forth truth and justice, love and healing, mercy and grace, all in perfect measure so that he can transform our lives and use his children powerfully for the kingdom. In this, that we can be obedient to his calling, as I am doing here in this writing.

Let us all be obedient. I wasn't. I disobeyed his Word, I disobeyed his standard, and I repented of it. I ask for forgiveness for the horrible sins I committed.

I depend on the blood of Jesus to cover my sin and cleanse me from all unrighteousness. I pray that in each day, I walk humbly before him in complete surrender that I walk in truth, and be obedient to his Word and his standard. And where I fall short, I receive his strength in my weakness, so by his supernatural help I can be strong in Him.

July 13, 2018

Note: (names in bold are changed to protect the identities of the individuals)

The Lady of the North Island

I am so grateful that on this journey to transformation, God has brought me so many people in support during these darkest days of my life. I wasn't able to attend church for fear of breach of my bail order, but one particular church, one I helped found, was supporting me in such amazing ways. The pastor, his new wife, the elders, and a few congregants were *in the know* of what was going on, and they all made an effort to keep in contact with me, go for dinner, have coffee, and even visit me in my home. Seven of them came with me to a pub restaurant to celebrate my fifty-first birthday. I don't celebrate my birthday as a habit, and I haven't for years, but they made me feel special. This special church group prayed with me, visited me, took me out, and supported me, and I am again so grateful. There were a few others, like my Colombian friend and his family, plus one of my old pastors and his wife too; they all stood by me and were amazing instruments of God, along with the others I've already mentioned.

There was another special person that God used as a key person during this time. I will call her "**the lady of the North Island.**" I met her for the second time at the "Island Rain" conference and got to know her and her husband quite well. We just clicked. We kept in touch in the following months, and both her and her husband knew what was happening to me too. I really felt safe sharing this part of my life with them even though I didn't know them very well at this point in time. Of course that all started to change, and they both became such a blessing to me.

During the summer of 2017, she had an opportunity to do community work experience in Victoria as part of obtaining her degree in counseling. She lives in Port Hardy, one of the northernmost parts of Vancouver Island, more than a seven-hour drive to Victoria, which is the southernmost part.

When this opportunity came open, she jumped at it, and everything fell into place. She stayed for more than two months with **my good friend who has been my support throughout all of this**, this amazing woman of God who also housed the **woman of Niagara Falls**. God was using her mightily, and I got to see the blessing as I became a direct benefactor to each stay of these anointed ladies.

The lady of the North Island is also a prophetess, sees dreams, and receives visions and words directly from heaven. Since we are to test all things in the Spirit (1 Thessalonians 5:21), she has been found as worthy of the calling she has received; as the visions and words received have been both accurate and/or have come true. She has a true anointing in the Holy Spirit. God used her to help me transition from where God was protecting me in the first home where I started living alone to where I needed to go prior to my sentencing. I also hung around these two ladies over the summer. I'd be there three or four nights a week, hanging out, watching worship videos, talking, and praying together. God used her to help me find a storage space and be ready to pack up my belongings, as I had been given notice to vacate my residence as my lease wasn't being renewed. I did try looking to buy a condo in a fifty-five plus building so that I would have somewhere to live, whether or not I was going to jail, and **the only lady in my Bible study** was instrumental in trying to help me with that, even though buying a condo never panned out.

Close to the end of June, she gave me two words from visions she received. One was for me to live with a couple of good friends until my sentencing, and the other was to put my stuff in storage. I heeded both of her words, and they both turned out to serve God's purposes for very different reasons. The vision of the storage was interesting, as she saw the storage place with an orange door. I'll get back to this in a minute. I asked my two buddies if I could live with them, and they said yes. I, over the course of the fall, winter, spring, and now summer, I would meet with them at least once a week to pray. One was **my buddy the gardener** and the other was his roommate and good friend. I had to tell his good friend what was really happening with me, and he reluctantly allowed me to live with them, not that he judged me because he didn't, but because his grandchildren regularly visited, and I wasn't allowed to be around any children while on bail.

So now that I had somewhere to live I now focused on finding a rental truck and a storage space. Good luck in Victoria! Storage space was at a premium in the city, and I left it to the last second to rent a truck in the busiest moving weekend of the year for the second year in a row. But who had a storage space with orange doors? The only place I knew was U-Haul, famous for its orange trucks and storage spaces with doors painted orange. I went in at 7:00 a.m. on July 27 to get both, believing the vision received from **the lady of the North Island**. I finally had my turn and asked for a truck for Sunday the thirty-first.

He laughed at me and said, "You are asking now for a truck on the busiest moving weekend of the year?"

I just looked at him and said, "Yes. Is there anything?"

He took a deep sigh and said, "Let me just look." He scoured his computer, sighed a couple of times, then said, "Okay, I found one truck for Sunday. You have it for only four hours – from 10:00 a.m. to 2:00 p.m. That's it."

I said, "I'll take it!" I did the paperwork, bought boxes and packing supplies, paid for it all. Then I asked him, "Do you have any storage spaces available?"

He just said, "Unless you want a four-by-four-feet space we have nothing available here or at the Queen Street location."

Well, so much for that idea. I know I still needed to find a storage place that had orange doors. So I left U-Haul and drove to the next place that I knew, Adams Storage. I got there, but this location had green doors, and it was still closed; it wasn't even 8:00 a.m. yet. The Holy Spirit told me to go home and Google *Adams Storage* in my PC. So I did, and guess what came up? The other location with orange doors, not five minutes from my house! I called at 9:00 a.m. when it opened, and the lady said there was one unit left for rent! I jumped in my car and was there in less than five minutes. She was so shocked to see me so fast.

She said, "Let me show you the unit we have available." So we walked inside a building, and all around me were lockers with wooden doors. I was getting a check in my spirit. She opened up the available unit and it was huge, too big for what I needed. I hummed and hawed about it. She said, "Is this unit too big for you?"

I replied, "Yes, it is too big." She paused and thought for a second. Then she said, "Come with me. I do have one smaller unit available but it's outside."

I nodded and said thank you. We walked back outside, and there they were, units with the orange doors as described in the vision. We walked up to unit C4, and she opened it up. The Holy Spirit said to me, "This is the one." I said to her, "This is perfect! I'll take it!"

It was a seven-by-twelve-feet storage unit, and it fit all my belongings perfectly, including easy access to bookkeeping and tax files as I needed them. Thank you, Lord, for your provision – a truck rental and storage unit within a few hours. I now had to go home, pack and then move on the Sunday most of my stuff to storage, and the rest to my friend's place. The move took three hours and we had time to spare to return the truck from within the four hours we had. I then settled in.

Things were going smoothly, but I forgot to do one important thing – tell my bail officer where I was moving to *before* moving and not after. With all the visions coming to pass, I just assumed it would be a cinch that this place would pass inspection. I was in for a rude awakening and a lot of stress to go with it. Two bail officers came on the Tuesday and failed the place. Toys in the back yard and in the house indicated children being present, plus lots of children in the neighborhood, not good according to my bail conditions. My bail officer told me I was in breach. When I heard that, I thought I was going straight to jail. He said he'd give me two weeks to find something. I had three other people help me look for a place. The vacancy rate this year was worse than last year, from less than 1 percent to less than 0.5 percent. The real estate market was at its hottest ever, and people in my price range, which is the lowest – around $300,000 for a single bachelor suite, were bidding $15,000 to $20,000 over the asking price. I just couldn't compete with that. Couldn't rent anything, couldn't buy anything. I didn't know what God was doing. Why would he give her a vision like that?

I went to my bail officer saying, "I found something, finally," but it failed too. To make things worse, I had to pay a damage deposit, plus a full month's rent before it could be inspected. I lost the whole month's rent of $850 because the landlord couldn't find a replacement until the beginning of the following month, but I got my damage deposit back, and he broke my lease. My bail officer gave me two more weeks and said to me, "You present yourself well. You'll find a place." Then he stuck his hand through the opening of the plexiglass window to shake my hand. As I shook it, I started tearing up, knowing he was sending grace to me, because I was still in breach, and had the power to put me right into jail. I had to keep looking. My dear friend, **the only lady in my Bible study** group, was on the computer looking for both rentals and a condo unit to purchase. I told her to stop looking to buy but just to rent. The days went by. Still found nothing. I phoned the bail office after looking at a trailer to live on a five-acre property to tell her that I couldn't find a suitable place to live, and with this unit there was someone living there under sixteen and right beside a church. I was ready to give up. I dropped off my friend as she was with me after I told the bail office I couldn't find anything and asking for yet another extension. I was driving home when my friend called me back.

"I found it!" she exclaimed, "I found it!"
"What?"

She then said, "The Lord told me not to give up, so I went on the computer and guess what? I found the perfect place for you! It's in a fifty-five plus building!"

She gave me the name and number and told me to call right away. I did that and made an appointment to see him in one hour! I phoned my friend back to see if she wanted to come and she said, "Yes!" So I turned around and went back to pick her up. We got there ten minutes early so we prayed in the car before going in. We asked God to open the doors. Then we went in.

July 14, 2018

Note: (names in bold are changed to protect the identities of the individuals)

We went upstairs and was greeted by the landlord and his (what we thought) girlfriend. He showed us around the apartment, told us how much it would be for rent, and it would require a full month's rent as a damage deposit as well. Facing sentencing in seven weeks and coughing up $3,200 to meet my bail conditions, I had a peace finally because God was financially providing and giving me a safe place to stay in an adult building. My lady friend spoke highly of me to the landlord saying that I am neat and clean and would take care of his place. The thing was, he was leaving me with all his furniture, so I wouldn't have to take any of mine out of storage. God was clearly in control of my destiny towards jail, even though at this point, I still didn't believe he was sending me there. We finished our meeting. He said there were a few more interviews but would let me know by Saturday, which was the next day. By the late afternoon the following day, I got a text from the landlord; he picked me over six other people! I was elated and relieved. I could tell my bail officer on Monday I found a place, but I would move in September 5. When I talked to him, he told me again that he knew I could find a place, and he'd send someone to inspect it the day I got the keys. On that day, I got the keys, got the inspection, then they said I could have it as long as I could prove it was an all-adult building. How could I prove that? I asked my bail officer to email the council for confirmation but there was no reply. The Holy Spirit then told me, "You find it." I wasn't comfortable rooting through my landlord's personal possessions, so I brought with me **my buddy the gardener** to come with me as a witness. Before we left the house, we prayed and asked God to open our eyes to find it. When we got to the apartment I said to my friend, "If the Holy Spirit is asking me to find it, then it has to be in an easily accessible place."

So logically speaking, we should start in the office where the books were on the shelves along the wall. The Lord started guiding my direction upon entry into the office, down to the center of the shelving unit, down to the bottom shelf. There was a green binder. I opened it up, and lo and behold! The council minutes and strata info! I started flipping to the pages to where I found the specific by-law – a member must be fifty-five plus to live here and no one under nineteen is allowed to stay! Bingo! Found it! God opened our eyes and made it easy for us! Even though I was fifty-one, they made an exception for me to live there. Praise God. I went to the bail office, and they took a photocopy of the page. I was cleared to live there.

July 15, 2018

Note: (names in bold are changed to protect the identities of the individuals)

Although the Lord provided this miracle of finding me a place, it didn't seem to quite line up with the vision by **the lady of the North Island**. But her vision served a very different purpose that I would not see fulfilled for another ten months. You see, the Holy Spirit on January 15, 2018 told me to apply for parole, and he directed me through a process where I saw his hand guide me through that one week period, which I will explain in a later entry. One thing I did know in my heart, however, was I only wanted to have day parole and not full parole, even though I applied for both. The parole process moved along fairly quickly, and on April 20, 2018 the parole office said he was recommending me for both day and full parole, and a decision from the Parole Board of Canada would come in two to four weeks.

Fifteen days passed and the Parole Board came with their answer – they only approved day parole – exactly what I wanted! This way my sentence would be shorter than full parole serving only sixteen months total instead of the two years less a day which I would have to serve in full parole, plus they would feed and house me for free, so it would give me a chance financially to get back on my feet. Then I read the reason why they denied me full parole; it was because of the housing fiasco back in August of 2017, and I was in technical breach. That made them decide to disallow full parole. I now see that God gave her that vision, and that vision served his purposes, and his purpose so happened to come into agreement with my heart's desire.

Praise his name and thank you, Lord.

The lady of the North Island did give me one more vision, one that I had a hard time accepting and, at the time of it being given to me, wouldn't. She said to me, "I see you with a pair of clear, blue eyes looking out of a jail cell window. The clear, blue eyes represent purity."

Over the next several weeks that she stayed down in Victoria I kept telling her I believe I was getting house arrest, but not jail, even though my lawyer was also telling me the same thing as she was saying. I wasn't listening to her; and I wasn't listening to my lawyer. I was delusional, but at the same time, I was so scared to go to jail. I was in complete denial to that reality. At one point, I sounded so convincing to her that she repented of giving me that vision in the first place. The visions she has received from heaven have always been deadly accurate, and this one would be no different. After I went to jail, I asked **my good friend who has been my support throughout all of this**, the one whom **the lady of the North Island** lived with over the summer of 2017, to thank her for the correct vision, and let her know that I loved her (I actually got to see her in person and did that one week after I got out!) Now I needed to repent and ask for her forgiveness for casting doubt on a vision that was accurate, which I have also done.

God gives visions, and they serve a purpose for his kingdom, and they are designed to show his power to build up our faith.

July 17, 2018

Entry: (names in bold are changed to protect the identities of the individuals)

Judgment Day

Now it's the day of my sentencing. I asked my old pastor to come with me for moral support, of which he was more than happy to. He was the one who helped me get counseling too. Before I go any further into this day, let me dial back five days and share a couple of events.

It was Saturday. I still didn't believe I was going to jail, and I was trying to convince everyone that I wasn't going either – my sister, **the only lady in my Bible study** group, my colleague **Corrina** whom God had on standby to take over the business as soon as I was sentenced, **my good friend who has been my support throughout all of this, my buddy the gardener,** even the **woman of Niagara Falls** and **the lady of the North Island** – all of them. While I was sitting in the chair, where I was now living – the fifty-five plus building, I prayed. However, the Holy Spirit spoke to me and gave me these four words of understanding, "Trust me. Believe. Obey. Don't be afraid." He was preparing me for such a huge change that all he wanted me to do was focus on him. His speaking to me that morning has had such an impact on me that these four words he gave me I still use when I am feeling down, doubting, feeling anxious, or want to be rebellious. I started using what he told me right away.

The next day, I went to what would be my last luncheon fellowship before my sentencing date. It was a house meeting where there were no children, so I could attend. The couple who ran it walk in the prophetic, and they are an amazing couple. Their hearts are so big that they exceed the size of the Grand Canyon. The wife actually was used by the Holy Spirit one day to help me with my sexual identity and come into a deeper place of repentance and deliverance from my shame and guilt. Like I said, amazing couple. But after lunch, another man of God, one who doesn't always attend this fellowship (actually I think I only saw him come here once or twice before) was sitting by me, and when everyone else left the table, it was just him and me, chatting away. He then said to me, "The Holy Spirit keeps saying to me to tell you, 'I am so proud of you!'" He must have in our forty-five minute conversation said this at least seven times, or maybe eight. Every time he said it, though, I would have a hard time receiving it.

What did he mean by saying, "I am so proud of you"? I mean, I was facing a sentencing. So by the sixth or seventh time this man of God was saying this, and unlike the amazing couple who knew of my situation, this man of God didn't. I broke down into tears, just sobbing. I can't even remember if I told him or not what was going on – I think I did. Either way, it didn't matter; he just kept encouraging me.

Just before my sentencing, before when my life was about to blow up, as was prophesied thirteen months earlier about the silo being blown up into smithereens, God was speaking to me, to stay his course of living a life his way, not mine, and letting me know he was with me through this whole thing. I don't know why, but in his grace and mercy, he was standing by his son, when so many others would abandon me, judge me, and scorn me – all this understandably, but God in Christ was still standing beside me, guiding me into his correction for my life. I can't change the past, but in complete repentance, humility, truth, grace, and surrender I can walk with Jesus and, together, reshape the future for the glory of his great name.

Now back to October 25, 2017. My old pastor met me for coffee, and was a huge encouragement for me, standing by my side this day. He was the only person available to come. We went from the coffee shop to the courthouse, where we met my lawyer, just down the hallway from the courtroom. This is where I now had to face reality. My lawyer said that the final outcome of my sentencing was finished just the night before, where he and the Crown prosecutor came to an agreement for my sentencing; and that they were co-submitting a sentence on my behalf for two years less a day, three-year probation, and to be on the sex offender registry for life. This would keep me in provincial jail rather than federal jail, which is much harder time and where harder criminals tend to go, and also a recommendation for my jail time be spent at Ford Mountain, where I could be rehabilitated instead of just being incarcerated. My lawyer fought for all that, and it was an answer to prayer I had for him four months earlier. In the spirit and in prayer warfare, I was led to have my lawyer fight for me in June. I did so, but I thought it was to get me out of jail, so I prayed for him to fight for me quite earnestly. After he finished talking, I now knew I was going to jail. When we went into the courtroom, one of the parents of the three of the victims was present, with his girlfriend and his aunt. I couldn't look at them as I had such shame for what I did to him and his children; they will never be the same because of my choices. I kept looking forward except once where I saw him and his girlfriend staring straight forward and his aunt was just sobbing into a handkerchief. Before all this, I gave my pastor a thank-you for being there for me and then gave him my wallet, keys, and phone. I then walked up when my name was called and stood just behind my lawyer, just facing forward. They started the proceedings, and the Crown submitted a joint-submission to the judge. At some point, in all this, I was handed two impact statements from two of the four victims. What I remembered reading in one impact statement was that he couldn't sleep, was having constant nightmares, and didn't live a normal life anymore, all because of what I did to him. The other impact statement had much less in it but what stood out was that he said he was frightened of me if he saw me again. Now I was reading of how the consequences of my actions had altered the lives of two people, possibly forever. I felt like a monster, corrupt, evil, and sinister. My heart got so cold at this point I couldn't cry, I was so afraid. I didn't break down crying until after I was taken out of the courtroom. Now came the sentence – two years less a day, three-year probation, lifetime on the sex-offender registry. The sheriff stood behind me as the judge read out the sentence. He asked me to put my hands behind my back and then handcuffed me. I was now being carted off to jail.

July 19, 2018

Note: (names in bold are changed to protect the identities of the individuals)

First Days In Jail

I was scared. I mean, really scared. I was sitting in the truck, handcuffed – both hands and feet – going through downtown Victoria, then onto the highway, seeing outside through a small window with bars. Off to Wilkinson jail. Down a ramp into the jail basement, they processed me, changed into reds from my street clothes (inmates in British Columbia wear red), gave me only the absolute basics – small toothbrush, clear tube of toothpaste, soap, towel, and an extra change of clothes – that's all I remember. They brought me up to November unit, a protective custody (PC) unit for inmates who had committed crimes like I did. Had I been put into the general population, I probably would either be maimed for life or dead. Either way, I don't believe I would be writing this as God has asked me to, so I now knew he knew what he was doing. He saw the final outcomes, I didn't. He's asking me to trust him, as this was his correction, trust his justice for those I have harmed.

When I got into the unit, there were no other inmates mulling around. It was our unit's turn for gym time, so many of them went down, and the rest were staying in their rooms. The female guard took me to a room right across from the bathroom, opened the door and asked the inmate who was going to be my new cellmate, "Would you like a new cellmate?"

He replied, "Sure!"

He was a young aboriginal fellow, twenty-seven years old, and he was super nice to me. He introduced himself as did I, and we just started conversing. We hit it off right away! Here I saw God's grace. I don't know why, but he was protecting his child. We became good friends, and we both went to Ford Mountain two weeks apart from each other and maintained our friendship over there. I started to calm down a little. In the first few hours he told me what our unit was like, how to behave and what to expect – all very valuable information. As soon as all the other inmates came, I started getting scared again, not knowing what they knew of me or if I would get hurt. Nothing like that. So far so good. Dinner time had now passed, and I've been there for quite a few hours. We had TVs in our rooms, but I wasn't watching anything. Then came med time. Being diabetic, I had to go down for my insulin shot so there were about twelve of us that had to go into the elevator.

Once the door shut one of the inmates piped up, "Hey! I saw you on TV tonight! You were the star of the show!"

I just sunk my head down low. Other inmates started asking him what he saw, and he just shut up and quietly said sorry to me right there and didn't open his mouth again. So I was the first news story of the night. There was now no hiding from anyone about my crimes. They hit the newspapers and went all over social media. Even though I kept oblivious to it by not watching TV, everyone else was letting me know what was happening, including the inmates in my unit. So that one inmate's comment sparked interest with the other inmates, and sure enough, it was on TV the next day too. The next day, when I went down to meds in the elevator, it got even more uncomfortable. All eyes were laid on me, like darts going into a dart board. Then came the comments: "How could you?" "Wow!" "How can you live with yourself?" "Eight years old!" but no one lifted a finger on me. All I could do was stare down at the floor, embarrassed, full of shame. I wouldn't lift my head up. I just laid low, all the time, and kept my head down, not looking at anyone for a couple of days. I always ate in my cell alone too, just to avoid everyone. I wasn't too welcome to sit with many people anyways. Except for my cellmate, I felt pretty isolated. There was, however, a giant angel standing in the middle of my cell. I could see it, almost like a holographic image, like you would see in an episode of "Star Trek: The Next Generation." He was tall, and his head almost went to the ceiling, so he had to have been close to nine feet. He just stood there and didn't move, almost as if he didn't have to as his presence there was enough to stave off anything that would try to attack me, whether in the spirit or through other people. For quite a few days, I would be able to catch a glimpse of the presence of this angel, from my first full day in jail, through three other inmates staying with me until the sixth day. The first one got sent to Ford Mountain within forty-eight hours, the second one came in then got sent to seg for not swallowing his meds, so he lasted forty-eight hours, then another came in and only stayed with me overnight, then he got shipped out to a jail work camp in Nanaimo. On the fourth day, I finally got money deposited into my trust account by my colleague and friend **Corrina**, who took over my business, so I could use the phone and buy canteen. She was the only person to visit me in jail too. I didn't stay long enough locally to have any other visitors come, and the jail I'm in for my rehabilitation is too far away and too expensive for anyone to come and visit. I put money on to my phone card and called the lady who was **the only lady in my Bible study** group. She has this gift for asking God for angels and calling them down from heaven. When I got a hold of her, I asked her bluntly, "Did you by chance call down for a big angel to sit in the center of my cell? Because he is standing there from floor to ceiling and doesn't move."

She let out a loud sigh of relief and said, "Yes I did! I asked God to send down an angel to protect you! Thank you for telling me!"

I replied, "Well your prayers are answered and thank you very much."

A couple days later, however, the angel seemed to disappear when I was asked by another inmate if I would like him to be cellmates. I said sure because he was Roman Catholic, liked to read his Bible out loud and recite prayers out loud. I was game for that! The Lord provided me with fellowship until I left. He was in his seventies and didn't care about what I did; he didn't judge me. No one lifted a finger on me. For twelve days I was pretty much left alone, no verbal bashing, no fist bashing. I knew that God was guarding me, I just didn't know why. On the morning of the twelfth day, a female guard came to me and said I was being transferred and to pack my things and get ready for the move. Now I was being transferred to

North Fraser on the Lower Mainland in Port Coquitlam, which is located in the Greater Vancouver area.

North Fraser

I left November unit in the early afternoon to go downstairs, get processed, handcuffed both hands and feet, put in to the truck to be driven out to the Victoria airport where we would get boarded on to a single engine propeller plane to be flown over to Abbotsford. It was an interesting ride, never flying before while in handcuffs. We got to the Abbotsford airport, and I was the last one to get dropped off as other inmates were taken to other correctional centers first, including one female prisoner.

In the truck, on my way to North Fraser, I heard the Holy Spirit speak to me, "Lay low." That's all he said. When we arrived and after I was processed, a female guard walked me to the unit where I'd be staying.

She said, "This is a remand center, and the inmates get excited easily, so be careful. You already have received your sentencing, and they are waiting for theirs."

When I got to the unit, the guard assigned me to a cell with a cellmate. When I walked in, I said hi. But he just glared at me, then walked out. I think I found out why I was told to lay low. After I settled in, he came back in and just ignored me. He was watching a hockey game, so I just stayed up out of his way, out of his line of sight, and didn't say a word to him, and he to me. After the hockey game was over, I turned in for the night. The next morning, I heard him get up and leave, so I used the washroom, had a shower and then I came back from the shower, and I came back into our cell, and was brushing my teeth when he came in.

He finally spoke to me, "Breakfast." That's all he said.

I replied, "Thank you."

I finished brushing my teeth, then went out to get my breakfast. About fifteen minutes passed, I finished what I could eat of it (these days I didn't have much of an appetite), and then went to my cell, not knowing what to do next.

Right then my cellmate came back, "Guards want to see you. You're leaving this morning."

He's a man of many words! I went to the guard, and he told me to pack up my tote box as I was leaving for Fraser Correctional Center in Maple Ridge very shortly. Thankfully, I only had to spend one night there. Processing. Handcuffing. In the truck. Off to the next jail – Fraser.

Fraser

I am now en route to my third jail. But why wasn't I going to Ford Mountain yet? I wasn't even sure if I was going there at all. I sought out the Lord two questions while en route to Fraser:

1) Why am I going to Fraser?

   The Lord replied, "To get the cancer out of your soul."

2) And then I asked about Ford Mountain to which he replied, "Ask the clerk about it."

When I arrived, I got processed, new clothes, then sent to unit 3C – Fraser's protective custody unit. I got there shortly before noon, and all the other inmates were out on some recreation time. The guard asked if I had a preference for a cellmate. There was a young fella and an older fella I could bunk with.

I surrendered this one to the Lord and then asked the guard, "Which one do you think would be best?"

He replied, "The older guy is a bit grumpy, but you might be a good match with him."

I said, "Okay."

He let me into the cell, and I looked into the locker I had to share with him, and I saw a Bible. This looked promising. I then looked over at the desk, and there he was reading Christian books! I was bunked with a Christian! Thank you, Lord! Shortly after, he came in, and we introduced ourselves. I told him I noticed he was reading Christian materials, and he confirmed he was a believer. He was in his late seventies, and he was really nice to me. We ended up having a nice little Bible study that night, and we prayed together.

Now back to that clerk I asked the Lord about. When I saw her, I asked why was I in Fraser, and she said that this jail was the intake processor for those going to Ford Mountain. She told me I qualified to go, and I should be there in about six days. I could accept that – less than a week. I heard many good things about Ford Mountain so it would be worth the wait.

The cool thing was that three hours after I had arrived at Fraser, the guard came to me and said, "Got good news. You're leaving for Ford Mountain first thing tomorrow morning."

I was shocked! That was way faster than waiting six days! God's hand of favor was still sitting on me.

July 21, 2018

The Lord has asked me to write about my dad. My dad – I remember him as a very hard worker – a workaholic actually – and was the breadwinner at home. He was a longshoreman most of his working life, and when he finally got into the union, which took over eight years for him to get into, there was always steady work for him down at the waterfront. He would go wherever the work was – Vancouver, North Shore, Burnaby, Port Moody, and sometimes he'd go as far out as to Squamish. In the early 1970s, my dad had to have a major operation and couldn't work for, what I recall was, months. My mom had to help him recover, live off of what little money was coming in, and stretch our food out to make it last. I am sure this time was hard on both of them as my brother was just a toddler and my sister and I were very young too. I couldn't even imagine how Dad felt, not being able to provide the way he wanted. All I remember as a kid is that he always kept a brave face in front of his kids. I couldn't remember him crying in front of us while growing up. But he was funny too!

At the dinner table, we would all sit down together as a family every night and Mom – almost always, would be the one he would tease and make us kids laugh. What made it funnier was how Mom would react; she would always get sucked right in to his teasing and Dad would know exactly what buttons to press to get her going. Us kids would join in teasing Mom with Dad and get her really going. These were very fond memories of our family being together. Dad was like the glue that kept us all together. Our family wasn't without our problems though. There was a lot of arguing and fighting between Mom and Dad, but I don't ever remember my dad ever hitting my mom. Even when it came to punishment for us kids, he did use the belt but never beyond anything that would be considered abusive. Most of the time we would just get grounded.

Growing up, I was a compulsive liar, and I am certain that grated on my dad's nerves. When I was 11 years old, I discovered my sexuality and that I like both boys and girls. But because my dad was a very stoic man – he really didn't show his feelings of love and compassion – I felt ashamed that

I liked boys, so I would, through my teen years hide this from both my parents deep down and hid it from them. I felt that I would let them both down if they knew. I mean my dad, I perceived, had this tough-guy image – a can-do Dad, do-it-yourself "renos" (he "renoed" our patio, kitchen and bathroom mostly on his own), longshoreman, family man, breadwinner. How would he feel if he found out I was gay? We're talking 1977 here!

My sexuality and feelings just got stronger in the 1980s. I focused on things I knew that would make my mom and dad happy – playing sports, refereeing soccer, volunteering, doing well in school, and being on the student council. I became a people-pleaser, an attention-grabber, and a goodie-two-shoes during my teen years – all in part to divert everyone away from the truth of me feeling like a monster, full of shame and deceit. I never shared or confided in anyone about how I felt about myself, I just locked it down.

Growing up and even being an adult, I just wanted one thing – I wanted my mom and dad to be proud of me, but I didn't know how. I kept blowing it, a form of self-destruction every time I tried. I joined the Navy, then got kicked out for touching a young fifteen-year-old boy and for being a homosexual, as stated in my release papers in 1989. The next ten years, I mainly stayed in the restaurant industry, but I did try a business venture in the East Kootenays, which failed. I asked my parents for financial help, but they wouldn't. They said it wasn't a good business idea and didn't support it. I thought this idea would make them proud of me for trying something, and my best friend and I, along with our partners at the time, headed back to Vancouver Island after one month, running out of money and relying on welfare to pay the next month's rent, so we could break the lease on the house we rented in Invermere.

My parents were seemingly disappointed with me, as I kept making mistakes and, although they never said it to my face, felt that I was an underachiever and hid myself behind religion to escape my reality. But it was Dad whom I felt the most disappointment because he wasn't like Mom when it came to personal issues. He rarely talked about them, and when he did the conversation was usually short and to the point. He never expressed himself openly until just a couple of years before his death; otherwise, he would seem distant emotionally, sometimes mysterious, but you knew clearly what he wanted out of you – do your best, be honest, be faithful, and be loyal. Those are what I learned from Dad; very good values.

I do wish he was more affectionate. But he wasn't. I loved it when he would play-fight with my brother and me, but I don't remember much more of my dad hugging me closely. I don't know, but for me, that might have helped in my emotional development, or maybe not. I do know was that my dad wanted the best for me all my life, and deep down, he has always loved and supported me, even though he never knew the deepest, darkest parts of my life.

The best gift I received is when he passed on that night in April 2011. I was there when he took his last breath. That is one thing I'll never forget.

See you in heaven, Dad. I love you and miss you. Sorry for all I've done to you and the family. I hope you can forgive me.

July 26, 2018

During the spring of 2017, after tax season had ended, the Lord brought me forth to forgive in two different ways – to forgive my biological family of their sins and then forgiving my elementary school classmates for bullying me.

When it came to forgiving my biological family; it was tough; I had never met them nor had any knowledge of them. It would take the revelation of the Holy Spirit to break bondages and generational sin, so the healing could be made manifest in my life. This process went over a couple of days, and I wrote down the different sins and bondages into my iPhone, so I could remember what was broken. I prayed for each sin and bondage, then forgave my parents, grandparents, great grandparents, and great, great grandparents, so the sins were forgiven to the third and fourth generation. It was an amazing experience because with each time where I would forgive each sin and bondage, it felt like a shackle was falling off my feet, and I started to love them, even though I didn't know them or ever met them. I now began to understand the power of forgiveness from God's standpoint in this area: my bloodline is my bloodline and there is no erasing that.

God called me to forgive their sins so that the linkages of generational sin could be broken, and therefore, by the power of the blood of Christ through the Holy Spirit, be set free. To this day, I had no malice, no bitterness, no hatred, and no anger toward them. I am free indeed.

In writing this on December 14, 2018 into the computer and now out of jail, here are the generational sins that I had written into my iPhone: general curses broken today: poverty, anger, hatred, embezzlement, stealing, robbing God of tithes, pride, arrogance, Ponzi schemes. These were entered into my iPhone June 18, 2017.

Another experience of forgiveness God had me go through was forgiving my schoolmates of bullying and teasing me. Until I was twelve years old, I would walk on my tippy toes, so I guess I would look like I was flamboyant.

Starting around grade 6, I would be called May-gay, rhyming after my last name. It would put me into tears, which of course, fuelled the fire. So they didn't stop. It wasn't until my parents saw me with the school counselor and gave me tools to help with the teasing – to laugh with them when they said it. The counselor said they would eventually stop. Guess what? She was right and it finally stopped in grade seven. But the wounds in my soul stayed until God called me to forgive them at age fifty. He had me go into prayer, and one by one gave me the first name of each schoolmate and asked me to forgive them. I remembered their names – 38 years from the time of the teasing like it was yesterday! It was totally the Holy Spirit bringing each name forward. What an opportunity to let go and forgive every one of them for teasing, bullying, and name-calling. God lifted me up and healed my soul each time. We're talking dozens of people. Again, no more anger or bitterness to my old classmates. Another amazing healing by our Lord Jesus!

FORD MOUNTAIN

July 4, 2018

There is such a hunger in this camp. But what I've noticed is that those who come to Christ, in terms of comparing them to the four soils, are either "springing up" and receiving the good news at first with great joy, and then their faith withers out the minute any heat (ridicule, mockery, enticement with sin) is applied to them, or they get caught up in the "thorns and thistles," and their walk in Christ is compromised with no tangible transformation happening in their lives. It is our duty as strong believers in Christ to disciple new converts. Here in jail I see these new converts to Christ every day. Two of them are in my hut, but trying to engage with them on spiritual issues sometimes is like pulling teeth – slow and painful. I pray for them when we meet for prayer, and when we are at that time praying for the whole camp. I sense I should be praying for them more, asking God for breakthrough in their lives, asking God for divine appointments, so he can speak his truth, life, and love into their lives. These are important for discipleship. I will not stop inviting them to prayer time, to Bible study, and to church, then allow the Holy Spirit take over so he can do the hard part – bring truth, renewal, and transformation to them.

Lord, teach me patience, coming alongside those who have only known the ways of the world and nothing else. Teach them your Word and the willingness to yield to your Spirit. Teach them that friendship with the world draws them away from you and not toward you. There are so many voices, so much white noise in the world to distract a new believer. Draw them by your Spirit to your truth; your Word is truth. Bring clarity to what they need to believe so that they do not learn false doctrine. Help them grow to become strong believers, hanging on the hope they have in Jesus.

Teach them that life circumstances, material possessions, money, or even relationships – whether it be intimate, friendship, family, or work – pale in comparison to you – a loving, intimate relationship with you, praising and worshipping you; that they acknowledge your great name. Amen.

July 20, 2018

Forgiving and Being Forgiven

One of the hardest things I've had to learn was forgiveness. We all need forgiveness from God, as the Bible said, "For all have sinned and fall short of the glory of God" (Romans 3:23 NKJV), and even the vilest of sinners, God will forgive. My sins were vile, and even with my upbringing, knowing that I was adopted (my parents told me at the age of three years old), made me fill my mind full of excuses that I was the only one needing forgiveness, and that there was nothing positionally of which I should forgive them. In my mind, it was as if being adopted made me feel like a second-class citizen. Why did I feel that way? My parents never told me that; they never exhibited any favoritism that way to me. We all went on the same trips together, fed the same food in equal portions, given the same opportunities for sports, education, etc. Heck, my sister and I both got cars for graduating! So why did I feel so different? Well, I believe that my personality had something to do with it, and it grated on the rest of the family, especially between my mom and me.

The relationship between my mom and I grew more and more toxic as I got older; neither of us would back down in our attitudes, our position, "one-upping" each other, always having to be right. It was worse than a competition; it was just plain toxic. Being here at Ford Mountain, I had to learn an important lesson in completely forgiving my mom for our toxic relationship, and in turn, asking for forgiveness for my part in it. That won't be easy – the asking for forgiveness that is, as my mom currently isn't speaking to me. The fact that she has chosen to not forgive me is irrelevant. I just didn't have the opportunity to communicate to her how sorry I am for what I did, how I hurt her in all this, how I embarrassed her and the whole family and her friends, and I don't know if I'd ever get that chance. On the other hand, I had chosen to forgive her completely for our toxic relationship, and in that forgiveness, I felt a great healing on the inside of me, like a ten-thousand-pound weight has lifted off of me.

I love my mom unconditionally too, but that means, I will love her no matter what, in spite of any circumstances between us. It doesn't mean that I will stand and put up with a continued toxic relationship. That will put us back down the slippery slope of a co-dependent relationship. So boundaries must be put into place if any relationship is to be mended. It needs to be mended properly. As for the other members of my family – my dad, sister, and brother – I have forgiven them all months and months ago. My dad was gone since 2011. My sister has forgiven me, but my brother hadn't. He and my mom discovered my sentencing the hard way. They saw it on social media and the newspaper; but my sister told them first by phone so that they would know what had happened to me beforehand.

I hope one day they will forgive me, but I have no expectations; it's up to them. I'll leave it here. Talk tomorrow.

July 22, 2018

First Days of Ford Mountain

The very next morning, at seven, I was packed up and ready to leave Fraser for Ford Mountain. This would be the last time I would be in handcuffs and being processed to change jails. There was one other person coming with me up there, and they put us together in the same holding unit in the truck for the trip up. We didn't talk much at the beginning, but after about a half hour, we started to talk. He never alluded to having a faith in Christ while en route, so I didn't bring the subject of God up. After approximately ninety minutes, we arrived at Ford Mountain. It was November 8, 2017. One final processing, set of clothes, set of bedding.

My first sight at the camp was a couple of inmates shoveling snow around the office area. This was different. They weren't locked up like we were in the three other jails I stayed. I looked around quickly and saw that we were surrounded by mountains, and no jailhouse building was on the grounds. In about an hour, we were released into the inmate population, and my travelling mate and I were given an orientation and tour of the camp by a resident inmate. We were both given keys to our room, and I found out that my travelling mate and I were going to live together as "cellmates" but not in a cell! After our orientation and tour, we dropped off our bedding and clothing, then went for lunch. I was still scared, so I didn't really speak up much but was soaking in the environment. This place was beautiful! My travelling mate and I were put into 'B' Hut, and after lunch, we went to our room to settle in. This is when I found out that he was a Christian! Wow! Three believers provided for me in three separate jails! God was certainly providing me with fellowship openly, where there was someone I could talk to about God. There were two other incredible events that happened to me in those first few days of being there in Ford Mountain. One was meeting one of the kitchen staff while getting a tour, and the other was being introduced to the support-group chair who just happened to live in the same hut. I believe both were divinely orchestrated by the Lord.

The Kitchen Application

While having our tour, we came down to the kitchen and laundry area, which are beside each other. While waiting to get our clothes and bedding, one of the kitchen staff stuck his head out randomly and said, "You are the new guys? Do either of you have any experience in the kitchen?"

I quickly responded, "I spent ten years in the restaurant industry."

He then replied, "I tell you what, meet me in an hour. I'm in 'A' Hut. I will fill out a special request for you, and you just sign it. I will put it in the request box for ya."

Now that seemed random. Somehow news got out before I even arrived that I had kitchen experience. Well, sure enough, as I was walking by 'A' Hut after lunch, one hour later, he came out with that special request, got some info off my inmate card, then said, "Sign here." Done. Request in the box.

The first place you work when you get to Ford Mountain was the woodpile. On the first day you arrive, you didn't work, but being ready the next day. So when we lined up for morning count on the parade square, I was ready to work in the woodpile.

The guard pipes up, "There is no work today."

Another day off. The next day would be the Friday leading into the Remembrance Day (Veteran's Day in the US) long weekend, as it was recognized as a statutory holiday in British Columbia. Again, no work that day too. The following three days was the long weekend. I still hadn't seen the woodpile yet. But on November 14, this would be the day.

I sensed the Holy Spirit speaking to me, "Work hard in the woodpile!"

It was like he was cheering me on and getting excited for me.

The guard piped, "We are working today!"

So off to the woodpile I went. I was ready to go – boots on, gloves on, jacket on, rain gear on. When we arrived "up top," as it's called in the camp, we were put to different assignments. A couple of guys grabbed axes; some stood to wait to load the cut wood to the wheel barrels. I grabbed a wheel barrel to take the cut wood to the sheds where they'd be stacked. I did that until coffee time. After coffee, I was asked to help drag three-hundred-pound, fifty-feet-plus logs over for them to be chain-sawed into both twelve-inch- (short) and eight-foot (long) lengths, depending on what logs the guards wanted cut. Yes this was jail with axes and chain-saws! I must have moved twenty logs over to be cut, and out of the twenty-plus guys available to help, only five of us were actually moving these logs over. I didn't look at who wasn't working. I was just focusing on what the Holy Spirit said. By lunchtime, I was getting tired, sore, cold, and wet. The temperature was in the mid-40's (about 8C), and it was raining on and off that day.

Lunch. Yum. I was hungry. The food here is pretty good, and the portions were plenty, quite a bit more than regular jail, but then again, we're working too. Lunch was over, and after twelve-thirty roll call, it was back to the woodpile. Here we go again.

Just as I was about to lug more logs over to be cut, one of the guards came over to me, "Mahy! The guard in charge of the kitchen wants to see you. You are off the woodpile."

I went off the forestry grounds and walked down the causeway, whereby the office building I met the guard in charge of the kitchen, who just happened to be walking in my general direction.

"Are you Mahy?" he asked.

I responded, "Yes I am."

He said, "You applied for the kitchen, right?"

I said, "Yes."

He said, "You are starting today."

He then took me to the supply shed, gave me a couple of sets of kitchen whites, and sent me off to clean up and change for the three-o'clock shift. Within a couple of days, I was also transferred out of 'B' Hut to 'A' Hut, which is the kitchen hut. I lasted a total of three hours in the woodpile! The next day, I found out why. At med time, there was a guard administering my insulin shot, and he asked me how I liked it in the kitchen. I said I liked it, but I noticed he was still grinning when I spoke. I then said, "You got me into the kitchen, didn't you?"

He now grinned from ear to ear, "I saw you working hard, so over lunch I mentioned it to a few of the other guards, and they decided to pull you off the woodpile."

I gave him a hearty thank-you!

Thank you too, Lord!

The Sex Addicts Anonymous (SAA) Chair

In those first few days at Ford Mountain, I lived in 'B' Hut and again, it was by design. One of the people the Lord wanted me to meet right away was the SAA chair. I didn't know what this twelve-step group was, nor was I familiar with any twelve-step group. I did attend one Celebrate Recovery meeting at one of my old churches a few years ago, but that was to bring along a client who had a drinking problem; that was my exposure to such support groups.

I got to know this guy in our hut. He was friendly, personable, and a little bit older than me. After a couple of days in the camp, I felt safe to open up to him about why I was in jail. He didn't judge me!

He finally said, "There is a group I lead every Saturday, and I think it might help you. I'd like you to come. It's called SAA."

I cautiously agreed to it. "I'll pick you up tomorrow, and we'll go up together. I have to go up a little early to set up, so I'll grab you from your room."

Again, I cautiously agreed. The next day, he did exactly as he promised. He came and grabbed me, giving me details of what to expect while walking up to Holloway House. He put on coffee, and then people slowly started trickling into the room. Everyone settled in, and we were about to start. We went around the room one by one, *checking in* and introducing ourselves.

Now came my turn, "Hi, I'm Mike and I'm a sex addict." As soon as I said that, I thought, *I am a sex addict!*

Sex addicts aren't just nymphos; they are people who have problems with healthy sexual boundaries, sexual thoughts, and sexual activity. In SAA they teach you through a twelve-step process (thank you AA!) to discover healthy sexual boundaries and sexual relationships and behaviors. The power of fellowship and the power of spiritual experience are all part of that, with God leading the way. After that first meeting, I never looked back and didn't miss a support group meeting here for nine straight months. God ensured my healing and growth here in Ford Mountain.

Speeches & Poems

I give you praise, I give you my life.
I relinquish control, make my heart right.

You lift me up, and give me strength.
You bring me joy in endless width and length.

Your love abounds, and it never dies.
It keeps me steady through the lows and highs.

Your name is great, as you are our King.
So we rejoice, we praise, and we sing.

Sing Hallelujah! Lord Jesus you reign.
Reign in our hearts by your own great name!

July 28, 2018

I was blessed with the opportunity to give the closing positive message at Friday's RLC meeting in the gym. The part in parentheses was added after the speech was read but added here for clarification.

RLC Meeting: July 27, 2018
Theme of the Week: Social Networking

This week (in our hut meeting) I have had the privilege to provide a closing positive message on the subject of social networking. This is what I wrote:

> Here at Ford Mountain, we are placed in a unique position to network socially using more traditional methods: face-to-face contact, walking to make an appointment with someone, even looking at time using a clock. Let us never lose sight of these valuable social-networking skills.
>
> Allow me to build on this. Using modern methods of social networking, with their intended purpose of making our lives easier, oftentimes distract us from using efficient time management, even though they can increase our time efficiency many-fold; detract us from the personal connection that us human beings so desperately need and desire, creating the "lonely generation" and lead many of us down a destructive path of behaviors that would otherwise not materialize because we are hiding behind the disguise of an electronic device. Time wasting, inappropriate behavior, and changing attitudes of being self-centered instead of being others-centered has crept into our society in large part by our social networking methods, platforms, and devices. Being able to slow down socially here at Ford Mountain has given us an opportunity to recapture some of those skills we have seemed to have lost over the last fifteen to twenty years. These are skills that will help positive change as we make an effort to engage, socialize, employ team communication, and foster good will to each other. Thank you.

POST-JOURNAL
BOOK 7

Speeches & Poems

August 11, 2018

From This Day Forward

From this day forward, God gives me a second chance
The past is forgotten, the slate is clean

From this day forward, I go in a new direction
Walking a straight path, walking in the light

From this day forward, I make a new choice
A choice to do right, a choice to start afresh

From this day forward, I am not condemned
I am not judged, life given in my spirit

From this day forward, I begin to feel God's love
To learn to love myself, to learn to love others

From this day forward, I begin the process of healing
To forgive myself, receive God's forgiveness, and forgive others

Your Words O Lord

Your words are life, O Lord
Like springs of living water in my soul

Your words are love, O Lord
They bring wholeness to my heart

Your words are truth, O Lord
They show me the path to living

Your words are inspiring, O Lord
Full of color, beauty, and splendor

I love your words, O Lord
I love your words
They leave me in awe, just like you do

August 26, 2018

"Trash for Treasures"

I am trading my trash for treasures:
My sin – I trade it in for wholeness,
My pain – I trade it in for healing,
My suffering – I trade it in for peace,
My lies – I trade it in for truth.

I am trading my trash for treasures:
How I see myself – I trade it in for how I'm seen by you,
How I see others – I trade it in for how you see them,
My poverty – I trade it in for your abundance,
My rejection – I trade it in for your acceptance.

I am trading my trash for treasures:
My hate – I trade it in for love,
My anger – I trade it in for conciliation,
My bitterness – I trade it in for compassion,
My sadness – I trade it in for comfort.

I am trading my trash for treasures:
This is what You did on the cross.
You bought us with a great price.
You gave us an opportunity and a hope.
For you don't see us as trash, but as a great treasure.

September 8, 2018

A Fresh Look

In this season God is providing a fresh new look
A new look of who you are
Created in his image
An amazing work of art
Ready to be a trailblazer

God has a standard – a standard of holiness
He will bring you up to it
He will help you out
He will set you free
From the deep bondage of sin

God has a provision – his Son he provides
His blood shed on Calvary
Died, rose again, ascended to heaven
Jesus is his name
And his name is Most High

God has made a plan – a plan of salvation
He sees you as amazing
His standard – he will bring you up
He will set the captives free
By the power of his blood

This is the plan – the plan he has made
A fresh new look at redemption
Not judged, but lifted up
Not condemned, but told the truth
Not in bondage, but set free

September 15, 2018

Note: (names in bold are changed to protect the identities of the individuals)

This was written two days before leaving Ford Mountain; I was asked to write to the creator of 'B' Hut – the Mentoring Hut, sharing my gratitude for being an original participant. This version is just the draft, and an edited version was sent to the office.

Dear **Ms. Grandview,**

I just want to write and tell you that I personally appreciate your vision and effort you have put into the 'B' Hut, mentoring hut here in Ford Mountain. It is clear that in the initial development of the concept, care was taken to start with seven inmates so that with a small group, we could help define the scope and function of the hut, which was to my knowledge, never been tried before. The results in the three and a half months of my participation have been immense. First, the mentors and mentees have "bought in" to the hut concept, each learning different skill-sets from each other and developing positive outcomes, even from trying and/or adverse situations. Second, and because the hut has the opportunity to be influencers as to who may come and live in this environment, it has allowed us to foster a "family atmosphere," drawing the members to be closer in relationship to one another. Third, we are noticing positive change in the thinking, attitudes, and actions of those who have allowed themselves to be vulnerable and open to positive change because they have chosen to trust the relationships they have with their mentors, and the mentors have provided good and wise counsel to each mentee. Fourth, the social dynamic is helping with the hut's success. Not having a hut cleaner is at the forefront of this. We all, mentors and mentees, work together in teams to clean the hut daily. It not only helps teamwork skills, but it teaches to work with clearly defined roles. Another positive social aspect of this hut is holding fun tournaments (crib and rummy are what we have played most recently) that are only open to the hut membership. It has helped foster good sportsmanship, but more importantly, it has created social opportunities to members inside the hut to engage with each other in a fun, social atmosphere. In all, it is helping us all get to know each other better.

In conclusion, I feel the mentoring hut is a big success. I do encourage all FMCC staff to pre-qualify the mentees at the high standards that have been discovered and set and the mentors to the already higher standards to maintain its quality of living and successful mentorship, providing transformation in those who both need it and want it.

Ms. Grandview, congratulations. It is a risk in an environment like this to introduce something that could have de-railed early on. But instead, it has grown into this amazing opportunity, now with a strong foundation and just getting stronger each day. This is an example of true entrepreneurship at its finest. Thank you for allowing me to participate. All the best in the future.

Sincerely,
Mike Mahy
Mentor

Inspirations & Poems

At The Halfway House, Salvation Army, Victoria, BC Canada

September 18, 2018

The material world is only as useful as the impact provided by that of the Holy Spirit in the spirit world. Therefore, the material world in and of itself is not evil, but the evil stems from man's wicked ways and the evil desires in his heart.

The magnificence of God is with his children.

September 21, 2018

Attributes of a True Entrepreneur

A true entrepreneur knows how to think big and start small.

A true entrepreneur has a vision of the end-product and knows how to work backwards from it.

A true entrepreneur knows the risks involved and takes them anyways.

A true entrepreneur is never afraid of failure.

A true entrepreneur knows when to relinquish control to those who are more capable than himself/herself and empowers them to do so, therefore breeding loyalty to the company vision, mission, and direction.

A true entrepreneur does not micro-manage a business but allows managers to oversee the operation.

A true entrepreneur uses the power of duplication to have the business multiply and creates systems to achieve that goal.

A true entrepreneur is never afraid of a challenge, uses disaster, failures, and catastrophes as opportunities, especially financial ones.

September 23, 2018

If God shows you that he is entrusting you with material possessions, then show yourself to be a good steward to him that you're capable of managing it.

In order to manage material possessions – money, wealth, businesses, property, and other things that fall into the material world, we are to follow the Scriptures very clearly – that we are to put them to Christ first and then for our personal pleasures thereafter so that our love for God is higher than the possessions themselves.

Possessions are deceiving in the manner of they give us false hope, a false security, and we tend to lust after them. They give us the appearance of power and authority, influence, and command. They, in the end, are supposed to be an expression of God's love for us as he wants us to enjoy life, but we, ever so often, blow it out of proportion, take it out of context, and use it for our personal gain first rather than surrendering them back to God for the purposes of the Kingdom.

September 24, 2018

Words have no value until they are accompanied by actions.

\- Mike Mahy

September 30, 2018

Freedom

- Mike Mahy

First level of freedom – freedom to worship God in Jesus Christ and follow his ways in our will, actions, thoughts, and attitudes. Nobody, not even Satan, can take that away from us. God is always with us, so we are never physically, emotionally, mentally, or spiritually away from him.

Second level of freedom – freedom to love our families, friends, etc. We can be physically taken away from them, but we can still choose to love and pray for them no matter our circumstances, geographical location, or situation.

Third level of freedom – freedom to do right. We can choose to make the right choices, even if under duress and against all odds, such as persecution, torture, or even death. Just see the late John McCain's story of being a POW in Vietnam; there he did the right thing to stand up for the protection of his country even though he was tortured and interrogated; he withstood all of that, and in the later years of his life, became a United States Senator for Arizona.

Fourth level of freedom – our constitutional freedoms. Today in the United States and Canada, we have some of the greatest constitutional freedoms in the world. But we must recognize this freedom as not freedom, but privileges. They can be taken away from us, and according to the Bible, in the days of the tribulation, they will, to some degree, be taken from us if they have not been completely taken away from us before then.

Let us not take our constitutional freedoms for granted and recognize what our true freedoms are as believers of Jesus Christ. We mistake freedom for what has been given to us by our countries rather than what has been given to us by the kingdom of heaven. I suggest we read Galatians 5:1, understand it and apply it to our lives. Then we will walk in true freedom, hope, and love!

October 14, 2018

Three things that keep us from making a good decision when we see an opportunity:

1) I do not recognize that this is a good opportunity. I believe the opportunity is false, overrated, or too good to be true.

2) My intellect gets in the way of making a decision to *go for it.*

3) My pride gets in the way of making a good decision to go ahead with a good opportunity I see.

Now which one of these three are you? Or are you the one that is going to jump at the opportunity and make it work because it is so simple, profound, and it makes sense to participate.

Believe in who you are and what you can become with this opportunity. It is your time to be a *difference maker* and a *game-changer*! Make a difference and jump on board.

October 28, 2018

Help me understand that my actions do not define the value of who I am, nor that I should be dependent on that.

Rather, it is how you see me that defines my value, O Lord, and that I am solely dependent on you and you alone.

November 3, 2018

Steward of Surrender

Be a steward of surrender,
A student, the lesson of life

It gives you freedom
To trust him, to let go

You will know the voice of God
And his direction

He will lead you to do great things
He will bring you up in his glory

Life In Balance

Know who you are,
But know what you need.

Know who you are,
But know who he is.

Know that you are a child of the King,
But know that you are saved by grace.

Know that you have authority from the kingdom,
But know that you must walk in absolute humility.

Know that you can receive revelation from the Holy Spirit,
But know to walk in absolute surrender.

Know that you are a child of God,
But know you have been covered by the blood.

Know that you can do all things in him,
But know that he is more powerful.

Know that you know a lot about the kingdom and its application,
But know that he still knows more.

Know that you can be used in divine appointments,
But know that he is everywhere at the same time.

Know who you are in the kingdom,
But know who he is, your giver of life.

www.ingramcontent.com/pod-product-compliance
Lightning Source LLC
Chambersburg PA
CBHW071702120626
46550CB00001B/71